ECONOMICS IN DISEQUILIBRIUM

ECONOMICS IN DISEQUILIBRIUM

John D. Hey

Martin Robertson · Oxford

First published in 1981 by Martin Robertson & Company Ltd.,
108 Cowley Road, Oxford OX4 1JF.

British Library Cataloguing in Publication Data

Hey, John D.
    Economics in disequilibrium.
    1. Equilibrium (Economics)
    I. Title
    330'.01   HB145
    ISBN 0-85520-399-4

Typeset by Unicus Graphics Ltd., Horsham.
Printed and bound in Great Britain by
The Camelot Press, Southampton

CONTENTS

To Elizabeth, Marlene and Clare

PREFACE

This book is a natural sequel to my *Uncertainty in Microeconomics*; whereas the earlier book was essentially a survey of the literature on microeconomic behaviour under uncertainty, this present book is essentially a comprehensive survey of the analytical tools and techniques used in uncertainty economics together with a set of important illustrations of possible applications. Armed with this book, the reader should be in a position to undertake his or her own research into various aspects of economic behaviour under uncertainty.

The book not only examines microeconomic applications but also explores the macroeconomic implications of these theories. In particular, the book describes the recently developed 'new' macroeconomics and shows how it has a consistent and intellectually appealing microeconomic foundation.

Combined with my earlier book, this present book makes a most satisfying pair from my point of view; I hope the reader shares my opinion. I am very grateful to the various editors who have encouraged me to complete the pair: to David Martin for trusting me in the first instance, to Edward Elgar for so generously extending the trust, and finally to Michael Hay for doing all he could to ease the final pains.

As with the first of the pair, this book has been speeded elegantly to the printers with incredible efficiency by Mrs Jo Hall, who deserves special thanks for never once complaining about my handwriting. I owe a particular debt of thanks to my wife, Marlene, for devotion beyond the call of marital duty in reading through the entire manuscript and improving my stilted prose.

This book is dedicated to three marvellous ladies: my mother, without whom this book could not have been started; my wife, without whom this book could not have been finished; and our daughter, despite (or do I mean because of?) whom the book was finished.

John D. Hey
York, January 1981

PART I

ECONOMICS IN DISEQUILIBRIUM

1 INTRODUCTION

The title of this book is deliberately ambiguous. Two possible interpretations spring to mind: first, that the book is an account of economics as a discipline in a state of flux; secondly, that the book is about the treatment of disequilibrium within economics. Both interpretations are correct.

The past 15 years or so have witnessed many crucially important developments in economic theory, the cumulative effect constituting virtually a revolution in the prevailing paradigm – particularly in macroeconomics. At the very least, there has been a revolution in the understanding by economists of the nature of the problems that they are attempting to analyse.

A significant stimulus for this near-revolution was the 'reappraisal of Keynesian economics' which began during the 1960s. The main focus of this reappraisal was the mounting dissatisfaction with the conventional macroeconomic treatment of apparently disequilibrium phenomena such as unemployment and inflation. Consequently, much of the subsequent reformulation has been addressed to the problem of correctly modelling disequilibrium in economic theory.

In the literature that developed in response to this problem, two broad strands can be discerned; initially, they remained quite distinct, but the recent past has seen a gradual merging as their common roots have become increasingly apparent. The first strand started from the premiss that the fundamental lack in conventional (*IS–LM* type) macrotheory was the omission of uncertainty; accordingly, this strand spawned an exponentially growing body of literature[1] devoted to the incorporation of uncertainty into the various parts of microtheory. The second strand started from the premiss that the fatal flaw in conventional macrotheory was the inadequate treatment of quantity constraints (one obvious manifestation of disequilibrium) in the general equilibrium theory underpinning macroeconomics; accordingly, this strand has led to a similarly impressive, though rather smaller, body of literature on temporary general equilibrium in one form or another.

Initially, as we have already noted, neither strand took too much notice of the other: the 'uncertainty' strand did not worry too much about general equilibrium considerations whilst formulating descriptions of the behaviour of individual economic agents; likewise, the 'general equilibrium' strand did not pay overt attention to uncertainty whilst constructing models of sequential economies. In the very recent past, however, both have become increasingly aware of the existence and importance of the other: 'uncertainty' models are increasingly constructed with general equilibrium considerations in mind; 'general equilibrium' theorists are increasingly realising that only in the presence of uncertainty do their new models really make sense.

It would clearly be wrong for us to suggest that this reformulation is nearing completion, and that the final form of the new macroeconomics, based on and integrating the two strands of literature mentioned above, is about to emerge in the next few years. Many problems remain to be resolved. Indeed, much of the recent 'progress' has simply consisted of unearthing (or recognising) problems that were not even thought to exist a few years ago. Nevertheless, identifying the true problems is a crucial pre-requisite for finding the correct answers.

At the present time, although the 'final' form of the reformulated economics is not yet apparent, the problems that remain to be tackled are reasonably well identified. Moreover, the tools that are available to tackle these problems have become increasingly refined in the past few years: economists are currently much more aware of what their various tools and techniques of analysis can and cannot do. Thus the present time appears an appropriate moment for presenting a review of the present 'state of the art'; this book, therefore, is concerned with discussing the problems involved with the correct modelling of disequilibrium in economics, and with describing the techniques of analysis that are available to investigate these problems.

We begin in Part II, the central core of this book, with an extensive general discussion of the various tools available to the theorist for the analysis of disequilibrium and uncertainty. Using a single consistent notation, Part II brings together a large number of important devices and results that are frequently used in the theoretical analysis of economic behaviour under uncertainty. To the best of our knowledge, such a consistent collection is not yet available elsewhere in published form. Part III, devoted to microeconomic themes and theories, shows how the tools and techniques described in Part II are used in exploring particular aspects of microeconomic behaviour; this Part examines the behaviour of households, of firms and of other economic agents, as well as investigating the simultaneous interaction of such agents in (single) markets. The market theme is taken up and extended in Part IV which is concerned with the macroeconomic implications of the earlier material; it starts by examining theories of general equilibrium under various forms of uncertainty, and concludes with an exploration of the implications of these new temporary general equilibrium models for macrotheory. This leads us naturally to the reformulated macroeconomics mentioned earlier. Finally, Part V offers some summarising comments, and indicates the path of possible developments in the future. A more detailed overview of the contents of the book is given in Chapter 2.

Before concluding this introductory chapter, we must confess that the book displays a certain vagueness about the meaning of one of the words in its title. Although the reader might be tempted into thinking that this remark relates to the word 'Economics', we are in fact referring to the word 'Disequilibrium'. Our vagueness reflects a similar vagueness displayed by the economics profession as a whole. To a physicist, the term 'equilibrium' would suggest that the system under study showed no tendency to change its behaviour; thus, 'disequilibrium' would suggest a tendency to change. To identify which states were equilibrium states and which were disequilibrium states, the physicist would require a dynamic theory of the system under study. The economist typically tends to be much less precise in his use of these terms: an important example (which we will encounter frequently in Parts III and IV of this book) is that of market equilibrium and disequilibrium. Usually, an economist will speak of the market being in equilibrium if demand and supply are equal, and of the market being in disequilibrium if demand and supply are not equal. (For example, many people will refer to unemployment as a disequilibrium phenomenon.) But note carefully that the economist does not use an underlying dynamic theory of behaviour when making this distinction: indeed, the basic construct – of supply and demand – is essentially static in nature. In speaking of a non-market-clearing situation as a disequilibrium state, the economist usually has, at the back of his mind, an informally derived, and *ad hoc*ly appended, dynamic theory. We are all familiar with this kind of argument: 'if the market does not clear, there will be a tendency (for prices) to change since some of the agents in the market are unable to achieve their desired objective . . .'. While this is an intuitively acceptable procedure, it is, in logical terms, strictly illegitimate: it violates the assumptions under which the supply and demand curves were constructed in the first place. Indeed, paradoxically, these curves were derived under the assumption[2] that the resulting price would be the equilibrium one!

We will return to this important point later in the book; suffice it to say at the moment that, although strictly one should have a dynamic theory before one can distinguish between equilibrium and disequilibrium states, we may sometimes lapse into the economist's usual vagueness, and use the term disequilibrium to refer to a non-market-clearing situation. This will not become a real problem until Chapters 10, 11 and 12; that is, until market models are analysed. During Chapters 3–9 inclusive, we can safely and simply treat disequilibrium, as far as individual agents are concerned, as synonymous with uncertainty.

We hope that the reader finds this book useful for its systematic collection of analytical tools and techniques for the investigation of behaviour under uncertainty, and for the illustrations of the applications of such techniques. More importantly, we hope that the reader will be sufficiently excited by the material of the book to help in the important task of finding solutions to the economic problems left unsolved.

2 PREVIEW

2.1 INTRODUCTION

As its title indicates, this chapter previews the material that is to come. Section 2.2 previews Part II Analytical Tools and Techniques; Section 2.3 previews Part III Microeconomic Themes and Theories; Section 2.4 previews Part IV Macroeconomic Implications; and Section 2.5 previews Part V Review and Appraisal.

2.2 PART II

As already remarked in Chapter 1, Part II of the book constitutes its core; it contains a consistent, and notationally coherent, collection of tools and techniques that will be used throughout the remainder of the book.

The vast majority of the analysis contained in this book is based on Neumann–Morgenstern utility theory; this accurately reflects the balance of recent theorising in economics, and emphasises the prominence that this approach to decision-making under uncertainty has currently attained in economic theory. (This is not to imply that we, and the profession at large, are content with Neumann–Morgenstern utility theory as a description of behaviour under uncertainty. On the contrary, we are well aware of its deficiencies – which are briefly discussed in Chapter 9, but, in the absence of a concrete alternative, the choice is between using Neumann–Morgenstern utility theory and virtually ignoring uncertainty altogether. Needless to say, we prefer to do the former.)

Since numerous axiomatic derivations of Neumann–Morgenstern utility theory already exist elsewhere (for example, Hey 1979a), we decided that further repetition was unnecessary. Accordingly, Chapter 3 (which is entitled Utility Theory) simply begins with a statement of the conclusions of the theory. For our purposes, the important result is that, if an individual obeys the axioms of the theory, then a utility function for that individual can be constructed; this function encapsulates the preferences of the individual when faced with risky choices. More importantly, this utility function can then be used to predict the choice of the individual in risky situations – the key indicator of the preference of the individual being the expected value of utility. Hence the alternative name for the theory; expected utility theory.

The utility function will vary from individual to individual: the shape of the function indicates the *attitude to risk* of the individual. The precise connection between the functional shape and the risk attitude is explored in Section 3.3; there it is shown how concavity indicates risk aversion, convexity indicates risk loving and linearity risk neutrality. Moreover, the degree of concavity (as captured by the Arrow–Pratt risk-aversion indexes) indicates the degree of aversion. The 'conjugate' problem, that of measuring the amount of risk inherent in some risky prospect, is examined in Section 3.4. Various methods of measuring 'increasing risk' are explored, including the Rothschild–Stiglitz method which is currently the most popular. The concluding section of Chapter 3 (Section 3.5) contains a summary of the more important results of the chapter.

The remaining three chapters of Part II are all devoted to exploring, in general terms, various possible applications of Neumann–Morgenstern utility theory. The division of the material between the three chapters is determined by the 'rules of the game' of the application under consideration. We distinguish three different situations: these we term *passive*, *active* and *adaptive* situations; these are the concern of Chapters 4, 5 and 6 respectively. A brief account of what we mean by these terms is given below, but a full explanation must await the appropriate chapters.

It should go without saying that the common theme of all three chapters is that they all analyse the behaviour of individuals when faced with decision-making problems under uncertainty. For most of the problems under consideration, uncertainty is characterised by the existence of one or more random variables, whose realised value affects the utility of the individual directly or indirectly. Optimisation in *passive* situations is the concern of Chapter 4. A passive situation exists when two conditions are satisfied: first, the agent has no control over the number of realisations of the relevant random variables; secondly, the agent has no opportunity for learning anything about the iikely realised values (other than what he knew initially). Thus, the individual must simply react passively – no active or adaptive response is possible.

The simplest form of such a problem is when there is one random variable, X, and one decision variable, Y, with both entering into the utility function U. In a passive situation the number of realisations of X is outwith the control of the individual – without loss of generality, we can suppose that it is just one; moreover, no learning about the distribution of X is possible. The problem of the individual is thus to choose the value of Y which maximises $E[U(X, Y)]$ where the expectation is taken with respect to the (given known initial) distribution of X. In such problems, the economist is interested in how the optimal value of Y varies in response to changes in the various parameters of the model. Such considerations are explored in Sections 4.2 and 4.3; the former treating the general case, and the latter treating the special case where X and Y enter the utility function in the form $U(Z)$ where $Z = Z(X, Y)$ is linear in X. Of particular interest are the comparative static effects of a mean-preserving introduction of risk and a mean-preserving increase in risk.

Whereas Sections 4.2 and 4.3 are devoted to essentially static problems, Section 4.4 looks at the dynamic counterpart of the simple model described in the paragraph above. Specifically, it considers a problem in which there is a sequence of time periods, in *each* of which the individual must choose the value of some control variable in the face of uncertainty about the value of some other variable. The problem becomes a truly dynamic one if decisions made in one period affect utility in another. As we shall see in Section 4.4, the method of backward induction is of vital importance in solving finite horizon dynamic problems. Infinite and random horizon problems are also investigated.

Optimisation in *active* situations is the concern of Chapter 5. In contrast with a passive situation, an active situation is characterised by the endogeneity of the number of realisations of the relevant variables. In other words, the individual can choose the number of realisations. Obviously there must be a cost incurred by this extra freedom; otherwise there would be no economic problem to discuss. The reader will probably be more familiar with this type of situation under the more common terminology of 'search models'. Such models have enjoyed a great deal of popularity in recent years, particularly with regard to the job-search and consumer-search problems. Section 5.2 presents the simplest possible formulation: one in which the individual can observe as many realisations of the random variable X as he wishes, at a constant cost per observation, the objective being to maximise the reward (the maximum of the observed values of X) net of the observation costs. Clearly, there is a trade-off problem: the decision to be made is when to stop (taking observations). As well as deriving the solution to this simple problem (which is characterised by a *reservation* rule), Section 5.2 derives some comparative static implications, and investigates a simple extension to the basic model.

Like Chapter 4, Chapter 5 then turns its attention to dynamic models: Section 5.3 is devoted to optimisation in such circumstances. As with its counterpart (Section 4.4) in Chapter 4, Section 5.3 finds the method of backward induction invaluable for the analysis of finite horizon models. In Section 5.4, there is some brief discussion of how the general search methodology, developed in the preceding two sections, can be extended to encompass multi-stage optimisation problems – those is which search may take place over several random variables whose distributions are dependent.

Optimisation in *adaptive* situations is the concern of Chapter 6, the final chapter of Part II. An adaptive situation is one in which the individual can (if he wishes) learn about the distributions of the relevant random variables. Naturally, the information which leads to the learning must be costly; otherwise there would be no economic problem to discuss. With Neumann–Morgenstern utility theory being used to describe behaviour under uncertainty, the obvious way of modelling learning is through *Bayes' theorem*. This is derived and discussed in Section 6.2; both the version for events and the version for continuous random variables are presented. In addition, this section contains an important illustration of the use of the continuous version.

This apparatus is then used to show how learning can be incorporated into the analysis of the preceding two chapters. Specifically, Section 6.3 looks at learning in an otherwise passive situation (and hence extends the material of Chapter 4), and Section 6.4 looks at learning in active situations (thus extending the material of Chapter 5). The first of these two sections examines the important question of the *value* of information; this, of course, determines whether learning is worthwhile or not. The second of these two sections looks at adaptive search models – that is, those in which the searcher must learn about the distribution from which he is sampling as search proceeds. As will become apparent, the solutions to such problems, although analytically straightforward, are often computationally rather complex. This implies that such models may be rather poor descriptions of actual behaviour.

An alternative theory of learning (which requires rather less computational effort, but implies less-than-optimal behaviour) is the brief concern of Section 6.5. Although relatively unused in economics, this alternative theory is popular amongst some psychologists, and may be a fruitful alternative to the Bayesian approach.

2.3 PART III

Part III of the book shows how the tools and techniques of Part II are applied in the analysis of microeconomic behaviour, and contains four chapters, Households, Firms, Other Economic Agents and Markets.

Chapter 7 looks at the behaviour of households operating under various forms of uncertainty; it has three substantive sections corresponding to Chapters 4–6 of Part II. Section 7.2 looks at household behaviour in passive situations; it thus draws heavily on the material of Chapter 4. Its main concern is the analysis of the consumption (and saving) decision of the household, though there is also some discussion of labour supply and other passive problems. The consumption problem is analysed in both a two-period and an infinite-horizon setting, and the effects of both income uncertainty and rate of interest uncertainty are explored.

Section 7.3 is mainly devoted to the consumer-search and job-search problems; it thus draws heavily on the material of Chapter 5. The section begins with the problem of 'searching for the lowest price' of some consumer good: first in a very simple form and then in a series of more complex (and realistic) forms. Brief mention is made of the joint quality/price search problem: here the multi-stage optimisation techniques of Section 5.4 prove to be of value. The job-search problem is then analysed. Both with this and the consumer-search problem, important comparative-statics results are derived. As with all the chapters in this Part of the book, however, we are more concerned with demonstrating the general principles involved with the analysis of such problems rather than producing a comprehensive catalogue of results.

Chapter 7 concludes with two relatively brief sections: Section 7.4 looks at quality, learning and other adaptive problems, while Section 7.5 offers some comments in conclusion.

A similar pattern is adopted in Chapter 8 which investigates the behaviour of firms operating under uncertainty: the three major sections (8.2, 8.3 and 8.4) are devoted to passive, active and adaptive situations respectively. Most of the material in this chapter is concerned with the price-taking firm, though brief mention is made of other market situations. Section 8.2, which looks at the price-taking firm in passive situations, begins with a simple static (one-period) model. This kind of model achieves its simplicity by assuming that inventories never exist (either because the product is perishable or for some other reason). If inventories do exist, however, then a dynamic model is necessary; such a model is discussed in the second half of Section 8.2.

Section 8.3, which is relatively brief (mainly because of the limited interest shown by economists in active problems of the type discussed here) is concerned with productivity screening. Section 8.4 looks at the incorporation of learning into the decision problem of the firm. In addition to the price-taking firm, brief mention is made of learning in duopoly situations.

Chapter 9 examines the behaviour of 'other' economic agents. Since the preceding two chapters were devoted to firms and households who obey the axioms of Neumann–Morgenstern utility theory, the set of 'other' economic agents contains those who are either not firms or households or disobey Neumann–Morgenstern utility theory. The material in the chapter is arranged sequentially, beginning with agents who *do* obey the axioms (of *NM* utility theory) in Section 9.2, proceeding with agents who might be considered as conforming with the axioms in Section 9.3, and concluding with agents whose behaviour is inconsistent with the axioms. In a sense, this chapter represents something of a digression on the main theme of the book.

Section 9.2 looks at a residual category of Neumann–Morgenstern utility maximisers, and provides further important illustrations of the material of Part II. The section begins with an example of optimisation in a passive situation – the optimal invoicing strategy of an exporter facing exchange-rate uncertainty. There follows an example of optimisation in an active situation – this leads to a model of liquidity preference. The section concludes with a brief discussion of auction and bidding models – a recent growth area.

In Section 9.3, three alternative approaches to decision-making under uncertainty are discussed. Two of these three could be regarded, under certain circumstances, as being consistent with Neumann–Morgenstern utility theory: these are *mean-variance* analysis, and the *safety-first* approach. Interestingly, both of these are popular techniques for the analysis of financial problems. The third approach discussed in this section, 'ordinal certainty equivalence', can be considered as a natural extension of *NM* theory.

Section 9.4 discusses four alternative approaches which are actually antithetical to Neumann–Morgenstern utility theory. The first is *Prospect Theory*, a recent innovation which still relies heavily on probability as an essential component. The same is true of the robustness/flexibility approach, which has some attractive ideas but is largely undeveloped. The behavioural approach is also discussed in this section, which concludes with a brief mention of Professor Shackle's approach; this is one in which probability as conventionally understood plays a very minor rôle.

Part III concludes with Chapter 10 on market models. In this chapter, attention is restricted to single markets; the analysis of the simultaneous interaction of several markets is the concern of Part IV. There are two main sections in Chapter 10: Sections 10.2 and 10.3 which examine, respectively, markets without and with quality uncertainty. The main interest of Section 10.2 is the investigation of possible equilibrium price distributions in atomistic markets (these markets display all the characteristics of perfectly competitive markets except in so far as individual agents on one side of the market are price-setters rather than price-takers). This section combines the search models of Chapter 7 with the models of the firm of Chapter 8 to produce models of markets in which the question of the degeneracy or otherwise of the equilibrium price distribution is of particular concern.

While fixed quality but possibly varying prices are the features of Section 10.2, Section 10.3 explores markets in which prices are fixed but quality varies. More importantly, perceptions of quality vary. Thus, for example, buyers and sellers have differing information about the quality of the good being traded. As is shown in this section, this existence of asymmetrical information may lead to the breakdown of the market – in that poor quality products drive out the good quality products. Familiar examples include used-car markets and insurance markets. Chapter 10 concludes with a brief section on other market models.

2.4 PART IV

The simultaneous interaction of several (exhaustive) markets is the concern of Part IV of the book, investigating the macroeconomic implications of the preceding material. It is divided into two chapters, the first on General Equilibrium and Disequilibrium and the second on Macroeconomics.

Chapter 11 is concerned with general equilibrium under uncertainty. It begins with a brief overview of the conventional general equilibrium theory under certainty, and an account of how that basic apparatus can be extended to cover an uncertain world with complete contingent markets. The first substantive section (11.2) examines what happens if the set of markets is not complete; as we show, this necessitates a sequential model in which the backward induction method of analysis plays a prominent rôle. This temporary general equilibrium theory of Section 11.2 is considerably simplified by the use of the assumption that all markets clear each period. The more realistic situation, particularly in the presence of uncertainty, is that markets do not clear; under such circumstances agents will experience *quantity constraints*. The analysis of general equilibrium with quantity rationing is the concern of Section 11.3; as will become apparent in Chapter 12, this forms the basis for the 'reformulated' macro theory referred to in Chapter 1.

Sections 11.4 and 11.5 are relatively brief: the former looks at stochastic general equilibrium models while the latter discusses the problem of modelling general *dis*equilibrium.

In some ways the macroeconomics of Chapter 12 is simply a highly aggregated version of the general equilibrium theory of Chapter 11: whilst the latter allows for an arbitrary number of markets, the former is restricted to models with just two markets (goods and labour). The focus of interest in the two chapters is quite different, however. In particular, Chapter 12 is considerably more interested in the phenomenon of unemployment, and in the effect of various comparative statics exercises. In view of the preoccupation of this chapter with unemployment, the methods of Section 11.2 (dealing with quantity constraints) are uniquely relevant.

The bulk of the material of Chapter 12 is contained in Section 12.2, which describes in some detail the basic structure of the 're-formulated' macro theory: this consists of a fixed-price model with deterministic quantity rationing. Rationing is, of course, an essential component of any fixed-price model (in which the prevailing price vector is not the market-clearing vector); the various possible rationing schemes, and the implications of them, are discussed in some detail. Stochastic (or random) rationing schemes are singled out for discussion in Section 12.3. Some other models are appraised in Section 12.4. The final substantive section (12.5), which completes Chapter 12 and Part IV, is similar to the corresponding section of Chapter 11; it looks at the question of adjustment processes in disequilibrium.

2.5   PART V

Part V is relatively brief, providing a review and appraisal of the book as a whole; it consists of two chapters. Chapter 13, looking to the past and the present, is an overview of the book; in many ways it is similar to this chapter, though looking at the material from the perspective of hindsight. Chapter 14 looks to the future, and appraises the possible and probable future developments in the subject.

PART II

ANALYTICAL TOOLS AND TECHNIQUES

3 UTILITY THEORY

3.1 INTRODUCTION

Utility theory is the cornerstone of virtually all present-day theories of economic behaviour under uncertainty. Accordingly, this chapter constitutes an important foundation for the material in the remainder of the book. The chapter begins with a summary and description of Neumann–Morgenstern utility theory. For an individual whose behaviour is consistent with the axioms of this theory, a utility function exists which describes (and thus can be used to predict) the behaviour of that individual when faced with uncertainty. After showing (in Section 3.2), in broad outline, how this utility function may be used to predict behaviour, the following section (3.3) examines in more detail the actual shape of the function itself. The shape, as we shall see, reveals information about the attitude to risk of the individual – that is, whether or not he or she is averse to risk. Section 3.3 discusses a number of summary measures of such risk attitudes, and examines how comparative attitudes to risk of individuals can be investigated using such measures.

While attitudes to risk of individuals represent one side of the problem of decision-making under uncertainty, the other side relates to the uncertain prospects themselves. Just as it is useful to be able to say whether one individual is more risk-averse than another, it is also useful to be able to say whether one prospect is riskier than another. Accordingly, in Section 3.4, ways of measuring the riskiness of different prospects are investigated. As is shown, the two problems – measuring risk aversion and measuring risk – are very closely related: in a sense, they are 'conjugate' problems. The chapter concludes, in Section 3.5, with an overview of the chapter and a summary of the most important results.

3.2 UTILITY THEORY

Although the title of this section suggests otherwise, we do not intend to provide a proof of Neumann–Morgenstern utility theory here. A number of excellent (for example, Luce and Raiffa (1957)), and not-so-excellent (for example, Hey (1979a)) proofs already exist – further repetition would be superfluous. Readers who wish to acquaint themselves with, or refresh their memories about, the axioms underlying, and the proof of, this theory are recommended the references above. For completeness, we ought to provide references also to material challenging the Neumann–Morgenstern approach: in this category, significant contributions include those of Kahneman and Tversky (1979) and of Allais and Hagen (1979); further important references can be found in both these works.

Throughout virtually the whole of this book, we will be assuming that the economic agents under discussion obey the axioms of Neumann–Morgenstern utility theory. This theory is concerned with the choice of individuals among risky alternatives. In its simplest form, this choice problem can be described as follows (see Hey (1979a) for a fuller treatment): there is a finite set $A_i (i = 1, \ldots, I)$ of basic certain outcomes; the individual is faced with a set of risky choices involving the A_i as final outcomes – a particular choice C being denoted by

$$C = [(p_i, A_i), \quad i = 1, \ldots, I]$$

where

$$\sum_{i=1}^{I} p_i = 1 \quad \text{and} \quad p_i \geqslant 0, \quad i = 1, \ldots, I.$$

$$\left.\begin{array}{r}\\\\\\\\\\\end{array}\right\} \quad (3.1)$$

Thus p_i denotes the probability that, under choice C, the individual will eventually end up experiencing basic outcome $A_i (i = 1, \ldots, I)$; the restrictions placed on the p_i imply that choosing C will eventually lead to *one and only one* of the basic outcomes being presented to the individual.

Now assume that the individual obeys the axioms of Neumann–Morgenstern utility theory. (In Hey (1979a, pp. 27–8) they are: 'ordering of basic outcomes', 'transitivity among choices', 'continuity', 'substitutability', 'applicability of probability rule' and 'monotonicity'; however, more sophisticated proofs, using considerably fewer axioms, exist – see, for example, p. 194 of Borch's paper in Allais and Hagen (1979).) Then it can be shown that there exists a utility function $U(.)$, defined over the A_i, and unique up to a linear transformation such that the individual's ordinal preference of the individual for the choice C is determined by the magnitude of the expression

$$\sum_{i=1}^{I} p_i U(A_i), \qquad (3.2)$$

which is termed, quite naturally, the *expected utility* of the choice C. Thus, once the utility function of the individual is known, future choice between pairs of risky prospects of the form

$$[(p_i, A_i), \quad i = 1, \ldots, I] \qquad \text{and} \qquad [(q_i, A_i), \quad i = 1, \ldots, I]$$

can be predicted simply by determining which is the greater of

$$\sum_{i=1}^{I} p_i U(A_i) \qquad \text{and} \qquad \sum_{i=1}^{I} q_i U(A_i);$$

no further information is required.

Although the above discussion assumes a finite number of basic outcomes, the theory can be extended to cover an infinite number. Moreover, the A_i can be anything – they do not necessarily have to be quantifiable entities, all that matters is that they are known with certainty by the individual. In many (if not all) of the applications discussed in this book however, the A_i can be described by a vector (or a scalar) variable. For the remainder of this chapter we will confine ourselves to such cases.

Consider, therefore, choice among random prospects whose final outcomes can be described in terms of the value of the variable **X**. (Following conventional usage, we will use **bold**-face letters to denote **vectors** and the usual *italic* letters to denote *scalars*.) A particular risky choice can very simply be characterised by a particular *probability distribution* for the random variable **X**. We will describe probability distributions by means of their (cumulative) distribution functions, and will generally use the letter F (and sometimes G) for this purpose. Thus, by the statement that "**X** has the distribution F" we mean

$$F(\mathbf{x}) \equiv \text{Prob} \{\mathbf{X} \leqslant \mathbf{x}\},$$

that is, $F(x)$ measures the probability that the variable takes a value less than or equal to x. (Note that we are following convention in using capital letters to denote the *name* of some variable, and lower-case letters to denote a *particular value* of that variable.) It is useful to describe probability distributions in terms of their distribution functions, as it enables one common notation to serve for both discrete and continuous distributions (and, indeed, for mixed distributions). Thus, if **X** has a discrete distribution taking values $x_j (j = 1, \ldots, J)$, then the function $F(.)$ has discrete 'jumps' at the points x_j, and is 'horizontal' at values in between; if **X** is a continuous distribution, then $F(.)$ is differentiable everywhere, with derivative (denoted by $f(.)$) equal to the joint probability density function of **X**. Of course, whatever the distribution, $F(x) \epsilon [0, 1]$ for all x and $F(x)$ is non-decreasing in x; we shall assume such properties always hold.

If a (Neumann–Morgenstern) individual with utility function $U(.)$, defined over all values x, is faced with a random prospect **X** with distribution $F(.)$, then the previous result (cf. equation (3.2)) enables us to express the expected utility of the individual as follows:

$$EU_F = \int U(x)\, dF(x) \qquad (3.3)$$

where the (Riemann-Stieltjes) integration is carried out over all values of x. (For brevity, and clarity of expression, we omit the range of integration in such obvious cases.) To predict the choice of the individual when faced with a pair of distributions, F and G, a calculation as to which of EU_F and EU_G is the higher is all that is required. This general proposition is the core of the economics of uncertainty.

3.3   MEASURING RISK AVERSION

Different individuals, in general, have differently shaped utility functions. The differences in shape provide information about their differing attitudes to risk. This section explores how such differences may be encapsulated in a set of summary measures. For ease of exposition, we initially confine attention to risky prospects describable in terms of a scalar random variable X (though later we discuss possible multivariate extensions). For simplicity of analysis we assume that all utility functions (defined over all values of x) are twice differentiable everywhere.

We begin by defining a *risk-averter*. Following intuition, we define a (global) risk-averter to be someone who, when faced with a choice between a certain prospect and a random prospect with the same expected value, never prefers the random prospect. Formally

U is (globally) risk-averse if and only if $EU_F \leqslant U(E_F)$ for all F

(3.4)

where E_F denotes the expected value of a random variable with distribution F. Moreover, we describe the individual as being *strictly* risk-averse everywhere if the inequality in (3.4) is strict everywhere (except for degenerate distributions, that is those of the form $F(x) = 0$, $x < x_0$, $F(x) = 1$, $x \geqslant x_0$).

Likewise, a risk-lover is an individual who, when confronted with such pairs, never prefers the certainty. Finally, a risk-neutral individual is one who is always indifferent between the certainty and the random prospect. Formally,

U is (globally) risk neutral if and only if $EU_F = U(E_F)$ for all F

U is (globally) risk loving if and only if $EU_F \geqslant U(E_F)$ for all F. (3.5)

Consider a (global) risk-averter as defined in (3.4). Jensen's famous inequality can be used to show that such an individual must have a *concave* utility function — that is U'' is non-positive. Alternatively, this can be shown quite simply as follows. Consider random prospects of a particularly simple form: those that yield one of two outcomes $(a-b)$ and $(a+b)$ each with probability one-half (where $b > 0$). (Thus $F(x) = 0$, $x < a-b$; $F(x) = \frac{1}{2}$, $a-b \leqslant x < a+b$; and $F(x) = 1$, $x \geqslant a+b$.) The expected value of such a prospect is a. Condition (3.4) implies that the utility function of a risk-averter must satisfy

$$\tfrac{1}{2}U(a-b) + \tfrac{1}{2}U(a+b) \leqslant U(a) \qquad \text{for all } a, b.$$

Re-arranging this expression yields:

$$U(a) - U(a-b) \geqslant U(a+b) - U(a) \qquad \text{for all } a, b.$$

Now, if both sides of this are divided by b, it implies that the average slope of U over $[a-b, a]$ is no smaller than the average slope of U

over $[a, a+b]$; thus, over a higher range, the average slope is no larger. As this result must hold for all a and b it implies that the slope of U must be everywhere non-increasing. In other words $U''(x) \leqslant 0$ for all x. For an individual who is always risk neutral, then all the inequalities in the above expression become equalities (by virtue of (3.5)), and thus a risk-neutral individual has $U''(x) = 0$ for all x – that is, a linear utility function. Following a similar argument for a risk lover, we may summarise the discussion by the following result:

$$U \text{ is (globally) risk} \begin{Bmatrix} \text{averse} \\ \text{neutral} \\ \text{loving} \end{Bmatrix} \text{ if and only if } U''(x) \begin{Bmatrix} \leqslant \\ = \\ \geqslant \end{Bmatrix} 0 \text{ for all } x.$$

$$(3.6)$$

We note that there are strict forms of all these statements (and others that follow), but we shall omit them to avoid tedious repetition. We note also that a function is termed concave (convex) if its second derivative is everywhere non-positive (non-negative): thus (3.6) means that risk-averters have concave utility functions, risk-neutrals have linear utility functions, and risk-lovers have convex utility functions. This is a useful characterisation.

Clearly, a risk-averter is someone who generally dislikes risk, and who would therefore be willing to forego some part of the return in order to change a random prospect into a certain one. We can formalise this notion in terms of the *risk premium*, denoted by r_{UF}, and defined as follows:

$$EU_F = U(E_F - r_{UF}). \qquad (3.7)$$

This equation states that the individual is indifferent between the random prospect F (with expected value E_F) and the certain amount $E_F - r_{UF}$. In other words, r_{UF} is the maximum amount that the individual is willing to forego to exchange a risky prospect for a certain one with the same mean. We note that, in general, r_{UF} is a function of both F and U; though we omit subscripts (F and U) on r when there is no danger of ambiguity thereby resulting.

So far, we have said nothing about the sign of U' – that is, about whether more of x is preferred or not. If all individuals have the same preferences, it does not matter what we assume. For convenience, we shall assume $U'(x) > 0$ for all x; we will maintain this assumption throughout the remainder of the chapter. It now follows, if (3.7) is compared with (3.4), that $r \geqslant 0$ for a risk averter. Similarly (comparing (3.7) with (3.5)), $r = 0$ for a risk-neutral and $r \leqslant 0$ for a risk-lover. These results make perfect sense: a risk-averter will gladly pay to exchange risk for certainty, whereas a risk-lover would pay for the opposite exchange.

All of the above material relates to the question of the *absolute* risk attitude of an individual. What would also be of considerable use would be some indicator of the *relative* risk attitude of an individual – so that, for example, two individuals could be compared with respect to their attitude to risk. One obvious route is through the risk premium. Indeed, it seems reasonable to say that 'individual U' (shorthand for 'an individual with utility function U') is *more* risk averse than individual V if and only if

$$r_{UF} \geqslant r_{VF} \qquad \text{for all distributions } F. \qquad (3.8)$$

The only trouble with using the risk premium as such a measure is that it depends not only on U but also on F. Ideally, it would be better to have an indicator that depends only on U. Fortunately, a useful result is to hand. It can be shown that if (3.8) holds, then

$$U \text{ is a concave transformation of } V. \qquad (3.9)$$

(We do not intend to provide a proof of this result; the proof, and its converse, can be found in Pratt (1964). The result should agree with intuition, however, particularly in view of the previous result that showed that (absolute) concavity was an indicator of (absolute) risk aversion.)

The above discussion suggests that both the concavity (or otherwise) and the degree of concavity are important indicators of risk aversion. Clearly, as we have already seen, the *sign* of U'' provides useful information. Indeed, one is tempted to suggest the *magnitude* of U'' as an indicator of the *strength* of risk-aversion. This suggestion fails, however, when it is recalled that the Neumann–Morgenstern utility function is unique only up to a linear transformation – that is, U'' can be arbitrarily altered in magnitude by linear transformations of the utility function. This arbitrariness can be removed, however, if we 'correct' U'' in some way; the obvious candidate is to divide it by U'. Such reasoning leads to the following indicator of risk-aversion

$$R_A^U(x) = -U''(x)/U'(x). \qquad (3.10)$$

The minus sign is included so that it is an indicator of risk *aversion* – the greater the aversion the greater the indicator. Now, it can be shown (see Pratt (1964), though the intuition should be immediate) that if (3.9) holds then

$$R_A^U(x) \geqslant R_A^V(x) \qquad \text{for all } x. \qquad (3.11)$$

Indeed, Pratt (1964) proves the following important result:

$$(3.8) \Leftrightarrow (3.9) \Leftrightarrow (3.11), \qquad (3.12)$$

that is, all three approaches to comparing degrees of risk aversion (the risk premium, concavity, and the indicator R_A) are one and the same. This is an important result.

The indicator defined in (3.10) is known as the *Arrow–Pratt index of absolute risk aversion* after its (independent) originators. The suffix '*A*' refers to the word 'absolute', and is used to distinguish this index from an alternative one (the index of *relative* risk aversion) which we discuss below. The significance of the word 'absolute' can be seen as follows. Envisage some individual whose absolute risk-aversion index (as defined in (3.10)) is *constant* for all values of x; denote this constant value by R. Then from (3.10) we have[1]

$$U''(x)/U'(x) = -R.$$

Integrating this once, we get

$$\ln U'(x) = k_1 - Rx$$

where k_1 is a constant of integration. Thus

$$U'(x) = \exp(k_1 - Rx),$$

which integrates to give

$$U(x) = k_2 - R^{-1}\exp(k_1 - Rx)$$

where k_2 is another constant of integration.

Now, without any loss of generality, we may define two new constants a and b by:

$$a = k_2 \qquad \text{and} \qquad b = R^{-1}\exp(k_1).$$

Thus, we get

$$U(x) = a - b \exp(-Rx), \qquad (3.13)$$

and this is the general form of a *constant absolute risk-aversion utility function*. Now consider such an individual faced with risky prospects of the form

$$x_0 + x$$

where x_0 is fixed and x is a random variable with distribution F. The risk premium of our individual, r, for such a prospect is given by (cf. (3.7))

$$\int \{a - b \exp[-R(x_0 + x)]\} \, dF(x) = \{a - b \exp[-R(x_0 + E_F - r)]\}$$

where E_F is the mean of the distribution F. Since $\int dF(x) = 1$, the above equation reduces to

$$-b \int \exp[-R(x_0 + x)] \, dF(x) = -b [\exp - R(x_0 + E_F - r)].$$

Now, it is clear that both sides can be divided by $-b \exp(-Rx_0)$ leaving

$$\int \exp(-Rx) \, dF(x) = \exp[-R(E_F - r)],$$

from which it is seen that the *risk premium r does not depend upon the value of x_0*. In other words, our individual will pay exactly the same amount to exchange the risk for a certainty *irrespective of the absolute size* of the risky prospect. Clearly, it makes sense to say that this individual has an attitude to risk which is *constant* in *absolute* terms.

Similarly, it can be shown that if an individual becomes less averse to risk in absolute terms in that the risk premium declines as x_0 rises, then R_A is a decreasing function of x; this is likely to be the most realistic case in practice.

As noted above, an alternative indicator exists – namely, the *Arrow–Pratt index of relative risk aversion*. This is defined by

$$R_R^U(x) = -xU''(x)/U'(x). \qquad (3.14)$$

Since R_R is equal to xR_A its qualitative properties are similar to those of R_A for positive x. To interpret R_R, we follow a path similar to that above. Envisage an individual whose relative risk-aversion index is constant for all values of x; denote this constant value by R. Then from (3.14), by integrating twice, it can be shown that[2]

$$U(x) = a - bx^{-R+1};$$

this is the general form of a *constant relative risk aversion utility function*. By following a route similar to that above, it can be shown that such an individual will always pay the same *multiplicative* risk premium when faced with risky prospects of the form

$$x_0 x$$

where x_0 is fixed and x is a random variable with a given distribution, *irrespective of the value of x_0*. Since the multiplicative risk premium signifies the *proportion* of the expected return that the individual would be willing to forego to exchange the random prospect for a certain prospect with the same *geometric* mean, it clearly makes sense to call the attitude to risk of the individual *constant* in *relative* terms.

Similarly, it can be shown that if an individual becomes more averse to risk in relative rerms in that the multiplicative risk premium increases as x_0 rises, then R_R is an increasing function of x; this is likely to be the most realistic case in practice.

We may summarise the important results of this section as follows: the *shape* of the utility function of an individual contains information about the attitude to risk of that individual. Concavity implies risk aversion, linearity implies neutrality and convexity implies risk loving. (Of course, an individual may have some concave, some linear and some convex segments, and thus may display risk-averse behaviour in the face of some risks and risk-loving behaviour for other risks. But this is perfectly normal – do we not often witness individuals who simultaneously insure their possessions and take part in the football pools?) Moreover, the *degree* of concavity (or convexity) *indicates* the strength of the risk aversion (or risk loving); a useful measure of the degree of concavity is, as we have seen, the Arrow–Pratt index of absolute risk aversion (3.10). Furthermore, this measure facilitates the ordering of individuals in terms of their aversion to risk, and provides an ordering which agrees with that generated by a comparison of risk premiums. Of course, such an ordering is necessarily partial: in many pairwise comparisons of individuals, it will often be the case that one individual is more risk averse for some risks but less risk averse for others.

Further detail on the material provided above can be found in Arrow (1971) and in Pratt (1964). The reader is also recommended the excellent article by Yaari (1969) which provides some stimulating intuitive insight into the relationships between the various measures of risk aversion.

Finally, we re-iterate that the discussion of this section has been confined to cases where the random prospect is a scalar variable. The *basic ideas* can obviously be generalised to the multivariate case, but problems arise in that it becomes difficult to disentangle differences in attitudes towards risk and differences in taste (amongst the many variables in the utility function). Indeed, to get round this problem, one of the pioneer articles on the multivariate case (Kihlstrom and Mirman (1974)) restricted attention to individuals who all displayed the same tastes (ordinal preference). Some further work has been done on this problem (most notably that by Hanoch (1977) and Karni (1981)); however, most applications, and especially those discussed in this book, are restricted to the univariate case.

3.4 MEASURING RISK

As in the preceding section, we largely confine attention to the univariate case; some references to the multivariate extensions will be given in our closing remarks.

In this section, we turn our attention to the random prospects themselves, and ask the question: how do we measure the riskiness of a random prospect? More precisely, suppose we have two distributions, referred to by their distribution functions $F(.)$ and $G(.)$, can we say whether one is riskier than the other in some sense? Intuition suggests two things; first, that the question is meaningful only if the 'return' from the two distributions is the same (one intuitively thinks of riskiness *relative* to a given return); second, given that this condition is satisfied, then the answer must hinge around the relative variability, or spread, of the two distributions.

The 'natural' definition of return is the expected value (or arithmetical mean). Let us, therefore, begin our discussion by restricting attention to pairs of distributions which have the same mean. In terms of our earlier notation, $E_F = E_G$, or, equivalently,

$$\int x \, dF(x) = \int x \, dG(x). \tag{3.15}$$

The integrations are carried out over the range of the random variables; we shall follow the literature, and take this to be (without any significant loss of generality) the closed interval from 0 to 1. From (3.15), using integration by parts, we get

$$\int_0^1 [G(x) - F(x)]\,dx = 0, \qquad (3.16)$$

as an implication of the equality of means.

Greater variability, or spread, around the common mean might then be used as our criteria for greater risk; thus the distribution with 'more weight in the tails' might be deemed the more risky. 'More weight in the tails' could be the result of a transfer of density from the middle outwards (in such a way that the mean stayed constant). Such ideas have been pursued by Rothschild and Stiglitz (1970), who showed that an acceptable ordering by riskiness could be generated by such an approach.

Alternatively, one could approach the problem of measuring risk from an apparently entirely different stand-point – namely utility theory and the associated measures of risk aversion discussed above. Intuition suggests the eminently reasonable notion that 'risk is something that risk-averters shun'. More specifically, if F and G are two distributions with the same mean, then if *all* risk-averters prefer F to G it would seem reasonable to term F the less risky of the two distributions. Note that *unanimity* is important: if some risk-averters prefer F while others prefer G, we could not infer anything about the relative riskiness of the two distributions.

Can we translate the above intuitive notion into a precise mathematical condition? Consider individual U; he will prefer[3] distribution F to distribution G if and only if

$$EU_F \geqslant EU_G, \qquad (3.17)$$

that is, if and only if,

$$\int_0^1 U(x)\,dF(x) \geqslant \int_0^1 U(x)\,dG(x). \qquad (3.18)$$

Integrating both sides of (3.18) by parts, and re-arranging, we find that U prefers F to G if and only if

$$\int_0^1 [G(x) - F(x)]U'(x)\,dx \geqslant 0. \qquad (3.19)$$

Now, suppose that U is risk averse; thus $U'' \leqslant 0$ and so the function $U'(.)$ is non-increasing. Using the second mean value theorem of the integral calculus (see Apostol (1957, p. 217)), it follows that there exists some number $y \in [0, 1]$ such that

$$\int_0^1 \{G(x) - F(x)\}U'(x)\,dx = U'(0) \int_0^y [G(x) - F(x)]\,dx. \qquad (3.20)$$

If we continue to assume that $U' > 0$ everywhere (that is, more of x is preferred), then examination of (3.20) shows that a *sufficient* condition for U to prefer F to G is that

$$\int_0^y [G(x) - F(x)]\,dx \geqslant 0 \qquad \text{for } all \ y \in [0, 1]. \qquad (3.21)$$

(Note that (3.21) is true at $y = 1$ by virtue of (3.16), the equality-of-means condition.)

Moreover, it immediately follows that (3.21) is a *sufficient* condition not only for U to prefer F to G, but also for *any* risk-averter to prefer F to G. Thus, if (3.21) holds then all risk-averters prefer F to G. Furthermore, (3.16) and (3.21) together imply that

$$\int_y^1 [G(x) - F(x)]\,dx \leqslant 0 \qquad \text{for all } y \in [0, 1],$$

and by a repetition of the method used above, it can be shown that this implies that all risk-*lovers* prefer G to F. (Risk-neutral individuals are indifferent between F and G because F and G have the same mean.)

Summarising, we see that (combined with the equality-of-means condition (3.16)) (3.21) is *sufficient* for all risk averters to prefer F to G, and for all risk lovers to prefer G to F. Clearly, if (3.21) holds, it makes sense to talk of F being less risky than G.

Is (3.21) also *necessary*? Suppose all risk-averters prefer F to G. Consider, in particular, the individual with utility function

$$U(x) = \begin{cases} x & 0 \leqslant x \leqslant y \\ y & y \leqslant x \leqslant 1. \end{cases} \qquad (3.22)$$

This is clearly concave, so that the individual is risk averse. Also,

$$U'(x) = \begin{cases} 1 & 0 \leqslant x < y \\ 0 & y < x \leqslant 1 \end{cases}$$

(though U' does not exist at the point y).[4] Substituting this in (3.19), we find that

$$EU_F \geqslant EU_G \quad \text{if and only if} \quad \int_0^y [G(x) - F(x)]\, dx \geqslant 0.$$

Since the value of y in (3.22) was arbitrarily chosen it follows that (3.21) is also a *necessary* condition for all risk-averters to prefer F.

We have now proved that (3.21) (combined with the equality-of-means condition (3.16)) is both a necessary and a sufficient condition for F to be labelled less risky than G on our criterion of unanimity of preference of risk-averters. We thus have an intuitively satisfying way of ordering distributions by riskiness.

We note a number of important features of this ordering. First, it is a *partial* ordering, that is, not all pairs of distributions will satisfy (3.21) or its reverse – for such pairs, it is not possible to say which of the two distributions is the riskier. Secondly, it is the ordering proposed by Rothschild and Stiglitz (1970) in their famous paper; thus, hereafter, if (3.21) holds we will say that 'F is less risky than G according to Rothschild and Stiglitz' – or, in an obvious shorthand, $F \leqslant_{RS} G$. Thirdly, as Rothschild and Stiglitz (1970) showed, this ordering is precisely the same as that obtained by consideration of the 'more weight in the tails' argument which we discussed earlier in this section; to be specific G has more weight in the tails than F if and only if (3.21) holds. Fourthly, as Rothschild and Stiglitz (1970) also showed, this ordering is precisely the same as that obtained by consideration of a 'more risky means more noise' argument. Fifthly, and finally, if (3.21) holds, then it follows that the *variance* of G is greater than the *variance* of F; however, the converse is not true (for if it were, then the ordering would not be partial) – for

Neumann–Morgenstern utility maximisers increased variance *per se* is not a reason for diminished utility.

We emphasise that the equality-of-means condition (3.16) is an important pre-requisite of the Rothschild and Stiglitz ordering; both (3.16) *and* (3.21) must hold for F to be less risky than G according to Rothschild and Stiglitz. As we have seen, these conditions jointly imply that all risk-averters prefer F, all risk-neutrals are indifferent, and all risk-lovers prefer G – there is a partition by preference. If the means are *not* equal, but (3.21) holds, then F is said to *stochastically dominate G to the second degree*; in such a case, all risk-averters prefer F to G, but nothing can be said about the preferences of non-risk-averters.

Although the Rothschild and Stiglitz ordering is a partial ordering, there are some economic applications in which its restrictions are not sufficiently strong. In some of such cases, an alternative measure of increased riskiness, which is even more stringent in its requirements, has been found useful. This was proposed by Sandmo (1971) and is defined as follows. Let X be some random variable with mean EX; define a new random variable Y by

$$Y = \gamma(X - EX) + EX \qquad (3.23)$$

where $\gamma \geqslant 0$. Clearly $EY = EX$ for all γ. The variable Y, which has constant mean, becomes more risky, according to Sandmo, as γ increases. A 'Sandmo increase in risk' therefore represents a stretching of the probability density function (without a change in its shape) around a constant mean. As should be apparent, if G is riskier than F according to Sandmo, then G is also riskier than F according to Rothschild and Stiglitz; the converse, however, is not true. Thus, the Sandmo condition is stricter, and so the Sandmo ordering is even more partial.

The fact that the Rothschild and Stiglitz ordering is partial, and thus cannot order all pairs of distributions, has led several authors to investigate alternative orderings. Most notable amongst these alternatives is one proposed by Diamond and Stiglitz (1974); we discuss their proposal as generalised and clarified by Lambert and Hey (1979). In essence, the Diamond and Stiglitz proposal focused initial attention on the 'return' that was being held constant. Recalling our earlier discussion, we reiterate that the 'natural' definition of return appears to be the expected value, and it is the constancy of this that underlies the Rothschild and Stiglitz ordering. Suppose, however, something else is being held constant; to be specific, let us follow

Diamond and Stiglitz in supposing that the *expected utility of some reference individual U* is being held constant. Thus, suppose $EU_F = EU_G$, or using (3.19) that

$$\int_0^1 [G(x) - F(x)]U'(x)\,dx = 0. \qquad (3.24)$$

This restriction is an *alternative* to (3.16), the equality-of-means condition. Given this condition, it now seems natural (following our earlier discussion) to say that if all individuals *more* risk averse than *U* prefer *F* to *G*, if all individuals *equally* as risk averse as *U* are indifferent between *F* and *G*, and if all individuals *less* risk averse than *U* prefer *G* to *F*, then *F* is in some sense less risky than *G*. Again we have a partition of preference by risk aversion, but now *relative to the reference individual U*.

The condition for such a partition is simply that

$$\int_0^y [G(x) - F(x)]U'(x)\,dx \geqslant 0 \qquad \text{for all } y \epsilon [0, 1], \qquad (3.25)$$

and if this holds (in addition to (3.24)) we say that '*F* is less risky than *G* according to Diamond and Stiglitz with respect to the reference individual *U*' – in an obvious shorthand $F \leqslant_{DS(U)} G$. The proof of the above condition, which is both necessary and sufficient, can be found in Lambert and Hey (1979).

We note three things about this family of Diamond and Stiglitz orderings (there is a member of the family corresponding to each possible reference individual). First, condition (3.24) is the counterpart of (3.16) for the Rothschild and Stiglitz ordering, and (3.25) is the counterpart of (3.21). Secondly, as a comparison of these counterparts will reveal, the Rothschild and Stiglitz ordering is a *special case* of the Diamond and Stiglitz ordering when the reference individual is risk neutral. The Rothschild and Stiglitz ordering, however – perhaps because it appears more directly to intuition – has experienced considerably greater usage. Thirdly, for a given reference individual, the Diamond and Stiglitz is still a partial ordering (though there are now an infinity of such partial orderings as there are an infinity of possible reference individuals); an attempt at a complete ordering was made by Meyer (1975) – this attempt was not a conspicuous success.

A stochastic dominance counterpart of this risk ordering (comprising condition (3.25) on its own) was investigated by Meyer

(1977). Further remarks upon the general questions of measuring risk and measuring risk aversion (and their conjugate relationship) can be found in Hey (1980).

This concludes our discussion of measures of risk for univariate distributions; virtually all the applications discussed in this book will be of a univariate form, and will use one of the measures discussed above (namely, those of Sandmo, of Rothschild and Stiglitz, and of Diamond and Stiglitz). For completeness, however, we ought to mention that a number of multivariate extensions of these ideas have appeared in the literature; in essence, they provide conjugate measures for the multivariate risk-aversion indicators referred to at the end of the preceding section. The most important papers are those of Levy (1973), Levy and Paroush (1974a, b), Levhari, Paroush and Peleg (1975), Huang, Kira and Vertinsky (1978), Huang, Vertinsky and Ziemba (1978) and Russell and Seo (1978).

Finally, we note a multivariate extension in a somewhat different vein. The recent article by Epstein and Tanny (1980) examines pairs of *bivariate* distributions, and poses the interesting question: when is one distribution *more correlated* than the other? To answer this question, they exploit the general methodology proposed by Rothschild and Stiglitz, and thereby derive a partial ordering (which, incidentally, implies, but is not implied by, increased *linear* correlation). As might be expected, equality of the (respective) marginal distributions is a critical pre-requisite (corresponding to the equality-of-means condition for the univariate increasing risk case), and the bivariate distribution which has 'more weight along the positive diagonal' is the one that displays higher correlation. The paper contains some interesting results which suggest that Epstein and Tanny may well become as important for the bivariate case as Rothschild and Stiglitz have for the univariate case.

3.5 CONCLUSIONS

This chapter has contained a number of important ideas and concepts which will be used repeatedly throughout the remainder of the book. Central to this chapter have been the related concepts of measuring risk aversion and measuring risk.

In essence, the material in Section 3.3 on measuring risk aversion was concerned with ways of *summarising* the information contained in the utility function of an individual. As with any summarising exercise, the smaller the number of summary measures the better –

since comparisons *between* individuals are thereby facilitated. Indeed, the 'ideal' situation would be to have just one number which tells us everything about the behaviour of that individual under uncertainty. As with any other summarising exercise, however, it proves impossible (except in certain rather trivial special cases) to reduce an infinite-dimensional object (the utility function) to a uni-dimensional object. Thus, inevitably, our summary measures end up providing only partial orderings of individuals.

Likewise, the material in Section 3.4 on measuring risk was concerned with ways of *summarising* the information contained in a probability distribution; again the problem was essentially one of reducing an infinite-dimensional object to a uni-dimensional object. Once again, only partial orderings can result.

Thus, in many cases we are simply unable to say whether one individual is more risk averse than another, or whether one distribution is more risky than another; in such cases, general propositions are of no use, and specific results have, of necessity, to be obtained. There are also many cases in which definite statements *can* be made, however, and for which general propositions *can* be invoked. We summarise the most important of them here.

1. If the utility function of an individual is everywhere concave (linear, convex), then that individual always displays risk-averse (-neutral, -loving) behaviour.
2. If one individual has a utility function which is a concave (linear, convex) transformation of the utility function of a second individual, then the first individual always displays more (equally, less) risk-averse behaviour than the second.
3. If two distributions F and G satisfy the Rothschild and Stiglitz integral conditions ((3.16) and (3.21)), then all risk-averters will prefer F, all risk-lovers will prefer G and all risk-neutrals will be indifferent.
4. If two distributions F and G satisfy the Diamond and Stiglitz integral condition ((3.24) and (3.25)), then all individuals more (less) risk averse than U will prefer F (G), while those equally risk averse as U will be indifferent.

Some important consequences flow from these results. Generally they give the economic theorist some indication as to how particular individuals will respond to particular changes in the environment facing them. The next chapter begins the investigation of such issues.

4 OPTIMISATION IN PASSIVE SITUATIONS

4.1 INTRODUCTION

As with the other chapters in this part, the purpose of this chapter is to provide some general procedures for the analysis of the behaviour of economic agents operating under uncertainty. In this chapter, we examine behaviour in what we term 'passive situations' – that is, situations in which a passive, rather than an active or adaptive, response is all that the economic agent can provide. To be more precise, we term a situation passive if the following conditions hold: first, there are no opportunities for learning present (thus, either all the relevant probability distributions are objectively known, or due to lack of relevant information, the subjective assessment of them remains unchanged); secondly, the *number* of realisations of any random variables is outwith the control of the agent.[1] The meaning of these conditions should become clearer as we proceed.

The chapter considers optimisation in passive situations of both a static and a dynamic nature. Static problems are the concern of Sections 4.2 and 4.3, while Section 4.4 examines dynamic problems. The simplest, non-trivial, static problem is one in which the agent faces some random occurrence, as characterised by a scalar random variable X, and has some control over the effect that this random variable has on his welfare through the manipulation of a control variable Y. His utility is a function of the realised value of X and the chosen value of Y, and we assume that the individual is a Neumann–Morgenstern expected utility maximiser. Thus, the problem of the individual is to choose Y so as to maximise

$$EU(X, Y). \tag{4.1}$$

We emphasise that the distribution of X is fixed – an assumption which encompasses both the no-learning and the no-control-over-number-of-realisations features characterising a passive situation. We also note that the formulation (4.1) is equally appropriate for a problem in which m random variables $X_1, \ldots, X_m$ are relevant to the utility of the individual, whether they enter in the form

$$EU[\max(X_1, \ldots, X_m), Y] \qquad (4.2)$$

or, more generally, in the form

$$EU[f(X_1, \ldots, X_m), Y] \qquad (4.3)$$

as long as m is outwith the control of the individual. (In which case, of course, both (4.2) and (4.3) reduce rather trivially to (4.1).) If $X_1, \ldots, X_m$ enter in the completely general form

$$EU(X_1, \ldots, X_m, Y),$$

then (4.1) is no longer a possible simplification, though the problem still remains one of passive optimisation as long as m remains exogenous. Furthermore, a problem in which there is one random variable and n control variables $Y_1, \ldots, Y_n$ can also be reduced to the form (4.1) by appropriate choice of Y.[2]

We begin the study of the simple problem (4.1) in Section 4.2. Specifically, this section solves the problem, and derives sufficient conditions under which the response of the agent to, (a) an increase in the mean of the probability distribution, and (b) a mean-preserving increase in the riskiness of the distribution, can be predicted unambiguously. Section 4.3 also examines this simple problem, and derives sufficient conditions under which the response of the agent to, (c) a mean-preserving change from certainty to uncertainty, and (d) a Sandmo increase in risk, can be predicted unambiguously.

In Section 4.4 we turn to the simplest dynamic problem of a passive nature. In essence, this is a generalisation of the basic static problem (4.1), and consists of T random variables $X_1, \ldots, X_T$ and T control variables $Y_1, \ldots, Y_T$ which jointly enter into the maximand:

$$EU(X_1, \ldots, X_T, Y_1, \ldots, Y_T). \qquad (4.4)$$

If the problem were such that all the Ys were to be chosen simultaneously (and before any of the Xs were observed), the problem would trivially collapse to that of the basic static problem (4.1). What makes the problem a dynamic one is the relative timing of the decisions and of the realisations of the random variable. The simplest dynamic model is one in which Y_1 is first chosen, and then X_1 observed (in 'period one'), and then Y_2 is chosen and X_2 observed (in 'period two'), and so on, until Y_T is chosen and X_T observed (in the 'final period'). It is this *sequential* nature which makes the problem a dynamic one.

Section 4.4 begins the study of such dynamic models. In this section, we examine both *finite horizon* models (in which T is fixed) and *infinite horizon* models (in which T is infinite); as we shall see, the method of *backward induction* is of crucial importance in solving the finite horizon problem, while (under certain simplifying assumptions) the stationary nature of the solution strategy facilitates the solution of the infinite horizon problem. This section will also examine briefly the *random horizon* case (in which T is a random variable). Finally, Section 4.5 summarises the main results of the chapter, and offers some comments in conclusion.

4.2 STATIC OPTIMISATION 1

The basic problem to be discussed in this section is the one outlined in the Introduction. The agent faces some random variable X and must choose a value for the control variable Y *before* X is observed. The utility of the agent is a known function of both X and Y; thus, the problem is to choose Y so as to maximise

$$EU(X, Y). \tag{4.5}$$

The expectation is taken with respect to the (subjective) distribution of X as represented by the distribution function $F(\,.\,)$. We emphasise that $F(\,.\,)$ remains fixed throughout the analysis as a consequence of our characterisation of a 'passive situation'.

Before proceeding to the solution of this uncertainty problem, we solve the associated certainty problem; as we shall see, this provides a useful base for comparison. In a certain world, the value of X is known; the maximand is therefore $U(X, Y)$, and the first- and second-order conditions for the maximisation are

$$U_Y(X, Y^*) = 0 \tag{4.6}$$

and

$$U_{YY}(X, Y^*) < 0, \tag{4.7}$$

where an asterisk superscript denotes the optimum, and where subscripts, as usual, denote partial derivatives. To facilitate the subsequent analysis, we assume that (4.7) holds everywhere. Thus (4.6) becomes both necessary and sufficient under certainty. The comparative static properties of this solution are found by totally differentiating (4.6); this yields

$$\mathrm{d}Y^*/\mathrm{d}X = -U_{XY}(X, Y^*)/U_{YY}(X, Y^*). \tag{4.8}$$

Thus (using (4.7))

$$\mathrm{d}Y^*/\mathrm{d}X \gtreqless 0 \qquad \text{according as } U_{XY}(X, Y^*) \gtreqless 0; \tag{4.9}$$

in a certain world, the agent responds to an increase in X by increasing (decreasing) Y^* if the cross-partial U_{XY} is everywhere positive (negative).

Returning now to an uncertain world, the first- and second-order conditions for the maximisation of (4.5) are (cf. (4.6) and (4.7)):

$$EU_Y(X, Y^*) \equiv \int U_Y(x, Y^*)\, \mathrm{d}F(x) = 0 \tag{4.10}$$

and

$$EU_{YY}(X, Y^*) \equiv \int U_{YY}(x, Y^*)\, \mathrm{d}F(x) < 0 \tag{4.11}$$

(where the integrations are performed over $-\infty$ to $+\infty$ – a fact which, from now on, we shall take as given).

Under our assumption that (4.7) holds everywhere, it follows immediately that the second-order condition (4.11) is automatically satisfied.[3] Thus (4.10) is both necessary and sufficient.

As far as comparative static exercises are concerned, a 'change in X' is no longer meaningful, since X is now a random variable. We can talk about changes in the *distribution* of X, however; indeed, two obvious candidates present themselves – first, an increase in the mean of X; secondly, a mean-preserving increase in the riskiness of X. We examine these in turn.

Actually, an 'increase in the mean of X' is not a sufficiently precise concept – we need to be more specific. Accordingly, we consider a *bodily rightward shift of the whole distribution*. Such a

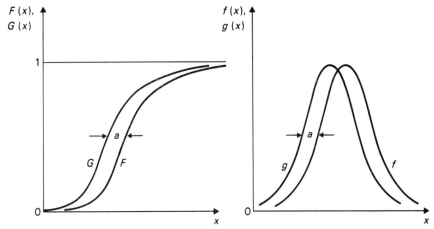

Figure 4.1   Illustration of a bodily rightward shift of a distribution

situation, which is portrayed in Figure 4.1, can be characterised by an *increase* in the parameter a in the distribution function $G(x - a)$. More precisely, if the distribution $F(.)$ is defined in terms of the distribution $G(.)$ by

$$F(x) \equiv G(x - a) \qquad \text{for all } x, \qquad (4.12)$$

then the distribution F is simply that of G *shifted to the right* by a distance a. (Alternatively, if F and F are *continuous* distributions, with respective p.d.f.s $f(.)$ and $g(.)$, then clearly

$$f(x) = dF(x)/dx = dG(x - a)/dx = g(x - a),$$

and so f is simply g shifted to the right by a distance a.) This is illustrated in Figure 4.1.

Take the distribution G as fixed, and use (4.12) to substitute for F in terms of G in the first-order condition (4.10); this yields

$$\int U_Y(x, Y^*)\, dG(x - a) = 0. \qquad (4.13)$$

Using the standard change of variable technique (and noting that the limits of integration remain $-\infty$ and ∞), (4.13) becomes

$$\int U_Y(x + a, Y^*)\, dG(x) = 0. \qquad (4.14)$$

We can now investigate how bodily rightward shifts of the distribution affect the optimal choice of Y. Totally differentiating (4.14) we get

$$\mathrm{d}a \left[\int U_{XY}(x+a, Y^*)\,\mathrm{d}G(x)\right] + \mathrm{d}Y^* \left[\int U_{YY}(x+a, Y^*)\,\mathrm{d}G(x)\right] = 0,$$

which, when rearranged and evaluated at $a = 0$, gives

$$(\mathrm{d}Y^*/\mathrm{d}a)|_{a=0} = -\left[\int U_{XY}(x, Y^*)\,\mathrm{d}G(x)\right] \Big/ \left[\int U_{YY}(x, Y^*)\,\mathrm{d}G(x)\right],$$

that is

$$(\mathrm{d}Y^*/\mathrm{d}a)|_{a=0} = -EU_{XY}(X, Y^*)/EU_{YY}(X, Y^*). \qquad (4.15)$$

In view of the second-order condition (4.11), it follows immediately from (4.15) that a *sufficient* condition for an unambiguous comparative static result is the following:

$(\mathrm{d}Y^*/\mathrm{d}a)|_{a=0}$ is positive (zero, negative) if U_{XY} is positive
(zero, negative) everywhere.   (4.16)

When examined in conjunction with the 'corresponding' result in a certain world (4.9), this is an eminently sensible conclusion.

We now turn to the second of our two comparative static exercises – namely, a Rothschild–Stiglitz increase in risk. As we discussed in Chapter 3, the crucial feature of such an increase in risk is that a risk-averter does not like it. Put another way, a Rothschild–Stiglitz increase in risk leads to a reduction in the expected utility of a risk-averter. Or, since a risk-averter has a concave utility function, a Rothschild–Stiglitz increase in risk leads to a reduction in the expected value of a concave function (of the random variable in question, of course). Now consider our first-order condition (4.10):

$$EU_Y(X, Y^*) = 0.$$

If the function U_Y is concave in X, it follows from our discussion above that if Y^* remains unchanged while the distribution of X experiences a Rothschild–Stiglitz increase in risk, then the expected value of U_Y will fall. Being zero to begin with, it must become negative. Now examine Figure 4.2.

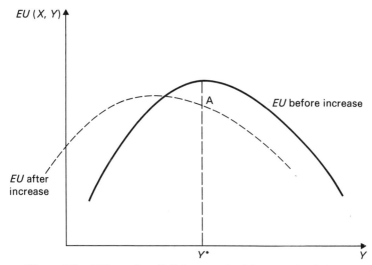

Figure 4.2   Effect of an *R–S* increase in risk on optimal choice

Since, by definition of Y^*, the expected utility function *before* the increase is horizontal at Y^*, it follows from the above discussion that, if U_Y is concave in X, then the expected utility function *after* the increase must have a negative slope at the old Y^* value (at the point A). Since we are assuming U_{YY}, and hence EU_{YY}, is always negative, it follows that the maximum of the *new* expected utility function must lie to the *left* of the old Y^*. Given that precisely parallel arguments hold if U_Y is convex or linear, we may summarise our findings as follows:[4]

> If U_Y is concave (linear, convex) in X then a Rothschild–Stiglitz increase in risk leads to a reduction (no change, an increase) in the optimal choice of Y. $\left.\begin{array}{}\\\\\\\end{array}\right\}$ (4.17)

This result is stated in Rothschild and Stiglitz (1971, p. 67; but note the misprint) and in Diamond and Stiglitz (1974, p. 340, Theorem 1). It yields a simple sufficient condition: if U_{XXY} always has the same sign (or is always zero), then the effect of an *R–S* increase in risk on the optimal choice of Y of the individual can be determined unambiguously. For example, if U is bilinear ($U(X, Y) = a + bX + cY$

$+ dXY$), then the optimal choice of Y of the individual is unaffected by the riskiness of the distribution.

We will find this result useful in subsequent chapters (several examples of its use are presented in Rothschild and Stiglitz (1971)). Also useful is its natural generalisation – to a Diamond–Stiglitz increase in risk. This generalisation is explored in Diamond and Stiglitz (1974) to which the reader is referred for formal proofs of the following statements. Here we rely on intuition.

Recall from Section 3.4 that a Diamond–Stiglitz increase in risk results from a mean-*utility* preserving spread. All individuals more (less) risk averse than the reference individual dislike (like) such an increase in risk. Given that an individual who is more (less) risk averse than individual U has a utility function which is a concave (convex) transformation of U, then a repetition of the arguments used above with respect to an R–S increase in risk leads immediately to the following result:[4]

> If U_Y is concave (linear, convex) in U then a Diamond–Stiglitz increase in risk (with respect to the reference individual U) leads to a reduction (no change, an increase) in the optimal choice of Y.   (4.18)

Elementary differentiation shows that U_Y is concave (linear, convex) in U according as

$$(U_X U_{XXY} - U_{XY} U_{XX})/U_X > (=, <) 0. \qquad (4.19)$$

This is probably the easier condition to examine.

As the reader can easily verify, the expression in (4.19) is zero if, and only if, the utility function is of the form

$$U(x, Y) = a(Y) - b(Y) e^{-Rx} \qquad (4.20)$$

where $a(.)$ and $b(.)$ are arbitrary functions. The reader should recognise this, from Section 3.3, as being a constant absolute risk aversion utility function (with respect to the random variable X, of course). In view of our remarks in Section 3.3 about the behaviour of an individual with such a utility function, result (4.18) makes perfectly good sense: such an individual will not alter his choice of Y in the face of a spread which preserves *his* expected utility.

Several examples illustrating the power of (4.18) are given in Diamond and Stiglitz (1974). Also presented is an important theorem which examines the effect of an increase in risk aversion on the optimal choice of Y. In essence, it states that if the graph of U_Y when plotted against X has a single crossing of the X axis, then an increase in risk aversion leads to an increase (decrease) in the optimal choice of Y if the crossing is from above (below). The proof is in Theorem 4 of Diamond and Stiglitz (1974, p. 349). The intuition should be reasonably straightforward: suppose U_Y is positive (negative) to the left of the crossing and negative (positive) to the right; at an optimal the weighted average of the negatives and positives must balance out to zero; now, an 'increase in risk aversion' can be considered intuitively as putting more weight on low x values and less on high x values; if Y were kept unchanged the weighted average of the U_Y would increase (decrease); the new optimum must therefore lie to the right (left) of the old.

This section has derived and stated a number of important sufficient conditions for obtaining unambiguous comparative static results relating to economic behaviour in static passive situations. These conditions will be employed in subsequent chapters. It should be noted, however, that some of the conditions are very strong. Accordingly, the next section investigates weaker conditions under which weaker conclusions may be obtained.

4.3   STATIC OPTIMISATION 2

This section is concerned with two relatively simple comparative static exercises: first, a mean-preserving *introduction* in risk; secondly, a *Sandmo* increase in risk (see Section 3.4). Both of these are simpler than the exercises considered in Section 4.2.[5] We consider these effects in relation to a problem of a slightly different form to that examined above.

As before, let X be a random variable, Y a control variable and $U(.)$ the utility function of the individual. But now suppose that the argument of the utility function is some intermediate variable Z, which is related to X and Y by

$$Z = Z(X, Y). \tag{4.21}$$

The problem of the agent is to choose Y so as to maximise

$$EU[Z(X, Y)]. \tag{4.22}$$

Mathematically, there is essentially no difference between this formulation and that discussed in Section 4.2. Economically, however, there is a significant difference, in that in (4.22) utility is a *scalar* function of Z, whilst in (4.5) utility is a *vector* function of X and Y.

From (4.17) a *sufficient* condition for unambiguously signing the effect of a Rothschild–Stiglitz increase in risk in the optimal choice of Y is that U_{XXY} is unambiguously signed. Now, it can easily be shown that

$$U_{XXY} = U'Z_{XXY} + 2U''Z_{XY}Z_X + Z_Y(U''Z_{XX} + U'''Z_X^2)$$

from which it follows that *if Z_Y changes sign* then the sign of U_{XXY} is in general ambiguous (except in the rather trivial case when U is linear in Z). But, in any interesting problem Z_Y *must* change sign, since in a certain world $Z_Y = 0$ and $Z_{YY} < 0$ are the first- and second-order conditions for the optimal choice of Y (assuming $U' > 0$).

A particularly important example occurs when Z is a *linear* function of the random variable X; that is, when

$$Z = a(Y)X + b(Y) \tag{4.23}$$

where $a(.)$ and $b(.)$ are some functions. If utility is an increasing function of Z (that is, if $U' > 0$), then in a *certain world*, the first- and second-order conditions for utility maximisation are

$$Z_Y = a'(Y^*)X + b'(Y^*) = 0$$

and

$$\left.\begin{array}{l} \\ \\ \\ \end{array}\right\} \tag{4.24}$$

$$Z_{YY} = a''(Y^*)X + b''(Y^*) < 0.$$

Clearly Z_Y changes sign, and ambiguity as to the sign of U_{XXY} (and hence as to the effect of a Rothschild–Stiglitz increase in risk) is likely to prevail. The effect of a mean-preserving *introduction* in risk is not ambiguous, however; consider the following argument. From (4.24), in a certain world the effect on Y^* of changes in X is given by

$$dY^*/dX = -a'(Y^*)/[a''(Y^*)X + b''(Y^*)].$$

Suppose $a' > 0$ everywhere, so that $dY^*/dX > 0$ everywhere (a parallel argument holds if $a' < 0$ everywhere). Now, consider the first- and second-order conditions for the optimal choice of Y in an uncertain world:

$$dEU[Z(X, Y)]/dY \equiv E[U'(Z)(a'(Y^*)X + b'(Y^*))] = 0 \quad (4.25)$$

and

$$D \equiv E[U''(Z)(a'(Y^*)X + b'(Y^*))^2 + U'(Z)(a''(Y^*)X + b''(Y^*))] < 0$$
$$(4.26)$$

where Z is given by (4.23).

The first-order condition can be written

$$E[U'(Z)(X - EX)]a'(Y^*) + E[U'(Z)][a'(Y^*)EX + b'(Y^*)] = 0.$$
$$(4.27)$$

The first of the two terms in (4.27) is simply $a'(Y^*)$ times the co-variance between X and $U'(Z)$. If $a(Y) > 0$ everywhere, then an increase in X always leads to an increase in Z, which will lead to a decrease in $U'(Z)$ if the individual is risk averse, to no change in $U'(Z)$ if the individual is risk neutral, and to an increase in $U'(Z)$ if the individual is risk loving. Thus,

$$\text{cov}(X, U'(Z)) \lesseqgtr 0 \qquad \text{according as the individual is risk} \begin{cases} \text{averse} \\ \text{neutral} \\ \text{loving.} \end{cases}$$

Using this in (4.27), in conjunction with the assumption that $U' > 0$, implies that

$$a'(Y^*)EX + b'(Y^*) \lesseqgtr 0 \qquad \text{according as the individual is risk} \begin{cases} \text{averse} \\ \text{neutral} \\ \text{loving.} \end{cases}$$

Comparing this with the certainty conditions (4.24), and using our result that $dY^*/dX > 0$ in a certain world, we get the following important result:

$$\left. \begin{array}{l} \text{a mean-preserving introduction in risk leads to a decrease} \\ \text{(no change, an increase) in the optimal choice of } Y \text{ if} \\ \text{the individual is risk averse (neutral, loving).} \end{array} \right\} (4.28)$$

Thus ambiguous comparative static results *are* obtainable.

In order to obtain these results we examined a particular functional form: namely the linear form of (4.23). A more general treatment can be found in Kraus (1979), and a further discussion of the kinds of results that this approach may yield is in Hey (1980).

The linear form (4.23) arises in a number of important economic applications, and so we continue to use it in our final exercise – the effect of a Sandmo increase in risk on optimal behaviour. Recall from equation (3.23) that such an increase in risk is defined by an increase in γ (from an initial value of 1) in the expression

$$\gamma(X - EX) + EX$$

defining the random variable of interest. If this expression is substituted for X in the first-order condition (4.25), and if the resulting equation is then differentiated with respect to γ, and then evaluated at $\gamma = 1$, the following result can be obtained:

$$dY^*/d\gamma|_{\gamma=1} = (-1/D)E\{U'(Z)(X-EX)a'(Y^*) + U''(Z)a(Y)$$
$$\times (X-EX)[a'(Y^*)X + b'(Y^*)]\} \qquad (4.29)$$

where D is given in (4.26). Now suppose the individual is *risk-averse*; then, as we have shown above, the first term in curly brackets in this expression has a negative expectation. It therefore remains to find the sign of the second term. Simple algebra shows that

$$E\{U''(Z)(X-EX)[a'(Y^*)X + b'(Y^*)]\,a'(Y^*)\}$$
$$= E\{U''(Z)[a'(Y^*)X + b'(Y^*)]^2\} - [a'(Y^*)EX + b'(Y^*)]$$
$$\times E\{U''(Z)[a'(Y^*)X + b'(Y^*)]\} \qquad (4.30)$$

As we shall show shortly, $E\{U''(Z)[a'(Y^*)X + b'(Y^*)]\} > 0$ *if the individual displays decreasing absolute risk aversion.* Thus, as we have already shown that $a'(Y^*)EX + b'(Y^*)$ is positive for a risk-averter, the right hand side of (4.30) is negative. Thus, the right hand side of (4.29) is also negative (since $D < 0$ by (4.26)). Hence a Sandmo increase in risk leads to a decrease in Y^* if the individual is risk averse and displays decreasing absolute risk aversion.

It remains to prove the assertion in the paragraph above. Denote by $\bar{Z}$ the value of Z when $a'(Y^*)X + b'(Y^*) = 0$, and denote by $\bar{R}$ the value of the index of absolute risk aversion when $Z = \bar{Z}$. Thus $\bar{R} = -U''(\bar{Z})/U'(\bar{Z})$. Now, if absolute risk aversion is decreasing in

Z, then

$$-U''(Z)/U'(Z) \gtreqqless \bar{R} \qquad \text{according as } a'(Y^*)X + b'(Y^*) \lesseqqgtr 0$$

(since we are assuming $a' > 0$). Hence

$$U''(Z)[a'(Y^*)X + b'(Y^*)] > -\bar{R}U'(Z)[a'(Y^*)X + b'(Y^*)].$$

Taking expectations, and using the first-order condition (4.25) to show that the expected value of the right hand side is zero, the result follows.

To summarise. If Z is a linear function of X, and if $dY^*/dX > 0$ in a certain world, then (a) a mean-preserving introduction in risk leads to a decrease (no change, an increase) in Y^* if the individual is risk averse (neutral, loving); (b) a Sandmo increase in risk leads to a decrease in Y^* if the individual is risk averse and displays decreasing absolute risk aversion.[6]

One important application of these results is to the theory of the perfectly competitive firm under price uncertainty. The study of this problem (which we examine in Chapter 8) was pioneered by Sandmo (1971) and extended by Ishii (1977). In these two articles specific examples of the above results can be found; Sandmo's paper also contains a number of further results which rely essentially on the linearity of the basic problem for their validity. The astute reader should be able to generalise them to the general linear form examined in this section.

4.4 DYNAMIC OPTIMISATION

As outlined in the Introduction, the crucial feature of a dynamic optimisation problem is that decision-making is *sequential*, with decisions and realisations of random variables interwoven. The simplest dynamic problem is that described earlier – in which in each time period the economic agent must decide the value of some control variable, while in each period there is a realisation of some random variable; 'lifetime' utility is some function of control variables and random variables. Since different applications will differ in their detailed specifications of the 'rules of the game' (and, in particular, with respect to the relative timing of decision and realisation), a general formulation appears impossible. Instead, we present a specific formulation which, we feel, has widespread applicability.

Consider first a *finite horizon* problem; that is, one in which the number of periods T is finite.[7] Suppose further that 'lifetime' utility can be expressed in the particularly simple form:

$$\sum_{t=1}^{T} \rho^{t-1} U_t(Y_t). \tag{4.31}$$

Thus, $U_t(.)$ is the utility function relevant to period t (we assume that $U_t' > 0$) and future utilities are discounted at the constant rate $\rho \, (0 < \rho < 1)$. Moreover, utility is *directly* obtainable only from the control Y_t, and not from the random variable X_t. The latter enters *indirectly* into utility through the following constraints, however:

$$\left. \begin{array}{l} Y_t \leqslant Z_t \\[2mm] Z_{t+1} = h(X_t, Y_t, Z_t). \end{array} \quad t = 1, \ldots, T \right\} \tag{4.32}$$

These constraints *link together* the various periods, and thus make the problem a genuinely dynamic one. For reasons of expositional simplicity, we assume here that the function h is constant; in some applications it may be time-dependent, but this would not alter the thrust of the argument that follows. In any economically sensible application, the following restrictions on the function h will hold:

$$h_Y < 0 \quad \text{and} \quad h_Z > 0. \tag{4.33}$$

The problem of the individual is to choose sequentially optimal values of $Y_1, \ldots, Y_T$, taking into account the fact that when he comes to choose Y_t the values of $X_1, \ldots, X_{t-1}$ and $Y_1, \ldots, Y_{t-1}$ will all be known to him (though the values of $X_t, \ldots, X_T$ will remain uncertain).

The method of solution is known as *backward induction*. As this name suggests, the individual works backwards: first, deciding his optimal strategy in period T (the final period); then, in the light of this, deciding his optimal strategy in period $T-1$; and so on, until he arrives at period 1. Let us look at this process in more detail.

Suppose the individual has arrived at period T. By then, utility in all previous periods has been decided, and all that remains is to choose Y_T so as to maximise final period (expected) utility $U_T(Y_T)$. The value of Z_T (which forms the upper bound on Y_T – see (4.32)) is also predetermined. Since we have assumed that $U_T' > 0$, the problem is trivial: the optimal choice of Y_T is simply given by

$$Y_T^* = Z_T. \tag{4.34}$$

This equation defines the optimal strategy in the final period conditional on the value of Z_T 'inherited' from earlier periods. Clearly the maximal value of final period utility is $U_T(Z_T)$; for reasons which should become apparent, we introduce a new function $V_T(\,.\,)$, which measures this maximal utility. Thus

$$V_T(Z_T) \equiv U_T(Z_T). \tag{4.35}$$

Note $V_T' = U_T' > 0$.

Now move back to period $(T-1)$. The problem is now slightly more complicated: the individual must choose Y_{T-1} (subject to an upper bound of Z_{T-1} which is a predetermined number) in such a way as to maximise total expected utility over periods $T-1$ and T. The higher Y_{T-1}, the higher will be utility in period $T-1$, but the lower will be expected utility in period T (since an increase in Y_{T-1} will lead to a decrease in Z_T – because $h_Y < 0$ – and hence to a decrease in $V_T(Z_T)$). A trade-off problem exists. Formally, the problem is to choose Y_{T-1} so as to maximise

where

$$\left. \begin{array}{c} U_{T-1}(Y_{T-1}) + \rho E V_T(Z_T) \\[2mm] Z_T = h(X_{T-1}, Y_{T-1}, Z_{T-1}) \end{array} \right\} \tag{4.36}$$

and where the expectation (E) is taken with respect to the known distribution of X_{T-1}. If an interior solution to this problem exists, it is given by

$$U_{T-1}'(Y_{T-1}^*) + \rho E[V_T'(Z_T)h_Y(X_{T-1}, Y_{T-1}^*, Z_{T-1})] = 0. \tag{4.37}$$

As should be apparent the value of Y_{T-1}^* that satisfies this will depend on Z_{T-1}; that is

$$Y_{T-1}^* = Y_{T-1}^*(Z_{T-1}). \tag{4.38}$$

Similarly, the maximal level of expected utility over the final two periods will depend upon Z_{T-1}; if we denote this maximal level by V_{T-1}, we have

$$V_{T-1}(Z_{T-1}) = U_{T-1}(Y_{T-1}^*) + \rho E\{V_T[h(X_{T-1}, Y_{T-1}^*, Z_{T-1})]\}$$

(4.39)

where, again, the expectation is taken with respect to the known distribution of X_{T-1}. It can be shown that $V_{T-1}' > 0$, a result which makes good sense.

Now move back to period $(T-2)$. By exactly the same argument as that used above, it follows that the problem of the individual is to choose Y_{T-2} so as to maximise

$$\left.\begin{array}{c} U_{T-2}(Y_{T-2}) + \rho E V_{T-1}(Z_{T-1}) \\[2em] Z_{T-1} = h(X_{T-2}, Y_{T-2}, Z_{T-2}) \end{array}\right\}$$

where   (4.40)

and where the expectation is taken with respect to the known distribution of X_{T-2}. Equation (4.40) should be compared with (4.36) to show that the structure of the problem is essentially the same. Thus the optimal choice of Y_{T-2} is given by an equation analogous to (4.37) – with T replaced by $T-1$, and $T-1$ by $T-2$, everywhere.

As should now be apparent the individual can continue to work back through the periods, thereby determining his optimal strategy in each and every period. Indeed, the overall optimal strategy is determined recursively by the following equations:

$$\left.\begin{array}{l} Y_t^* = Y_t^*(Z_t) \qquad (t = 1, \ldots, T-1) \text{ is the solution to} \\[1em] U_t'(Y_t^*) + \rho E\{V_{t+1}'[h(X_t, Y_t^*, Z_t)]h_Y(X_t, Y_t^*, Z_t)\} = 0 \end{array}\right\}$$
(4.41)

where

$$V_t(Z_t) = U_t(Y_t^*) + \rho E\{V_{t+1}[h(X_t, Y_t^*, Z_t)]\} \qquad \text{for } t = 1, \ldots, T-1.$$

(4.42)

For $t = T$ the relevant equations are (4.34) and (4.35). Note that (4.38) and (4.37) represent a special case of (4.41), while (4.39) is the corresponding special case of (4.42).

In principle, the solution is now complete: equations (4.41) and (4.42) determine the optimal choice of Y_t conditional on the value of Z_t inherited from the past. The economic interest is contained in the form of the functions $Y_t^*(\,.\,)$, and in how these functions shift in response to changes in the parameters of the problem. As a glance at (4.41) and (4.42) will make clear, however, such issues depend crucially on the form of the function $h(\,.\,,\,.\,,\,.\,)$. Rather than attempt to present some general results here, we will await some specific applications before proceeding further. One important application, which will be discussed in Chapter 7, is the problem of choosing an optimal consumption path when there is income uncertainty. In this application, the 'linking' variable Z has a natural economic interpretation as wealth, and the function $h(\,.\,,\,.\,,\,.\,)$ takes the specific form:

$$Z_{t+1} = r(X_t - Y_t + Z_t)$$

where X is income, Y is consumption and r is one plus the (certain) rate of return on savings.

Before leaving the finite horizon problem, we note that, although we have illustrated the method of backward induction with respect to a simplified decision problem, the general method can obviously be used for more complicated problems. In particular, the method can cope with a considerably more general utility function than that described by (4.31).

We now turn to *infinite horizon* problems. In these, by definition, the number of periods T is infinite. This feature, of course, renders the method of backward induction inapplicable – there is no fixed point from which to work back. Thus an alternative solution method must be sought.

An immense simplification can be achieved if the problem is made *time-independent*; by this latter term, we mean a situation in which the actual 'date' (the number of the time period) is *irrelevant* to the optimal strategy. In other words, the problem is time-independent if the optimal decision (conditional, of course, on the current values of any relevant variables) is the same whether the decision is being made in period 1, or period 10, or period 152, or . . . . An obvious example which has the property of time-independence is one in which the utility function is the same in every period, and in which the random variables $X_1, X_2, \ldots$ are all identically and independently distributed.

Suppose, therefore, that the utility function takes the form

$$\sum_{t=1}^{\infty} \rho^{t-1} U(Y_t). \tag{4.43}$$

((4.43) should be compared with (4.31); (4.43) has no time subscript on U.) If $X_1, X_2, \ldots$ are all identically and independently distributed (i.i.d.), then if the individual enters some period with a particular value of Z (the 'inheritance from the past'), the individual's optimal strategy *is the same regardless of whether the period in question is period 1, or period 10, or period 152, or . . . .* This property (which can be formally proved) is a consequence of the fact that, given a particular value of Z the future always looks the same irrespective of from where it is viewed; moreover, except for the inherited value of Z, the past is irrelevant – bygones are bygones.

We can now introduce the following notation. Denote by

$$Y^* = Y^*(Z) \tag{4.44}$$

the optimal choice of decision variable Y in a period in which Z is the value of Z inherited from the past. Furthermore, denote by $V(Z)$ the *maximised* total expected discounted lifetime utility as viewed from a period in which Z is the value of Z inherited from the past. Note crucially that neither $Y^*(.)$ nor $V(.)$ have time-subscripts, because of our argument above. But note also that they are the analogues of the $Y_t^*(.)$ and V_t functions used in the finite horizon problem; in particular they have exactly the same interpretation.

In the finite horizon problem these functions were defined recursively by (4.41) and (4.42). As we have already argued, this procedure does not work in the infinite horizon case; however, the time-independence property of our present formulation allows us to proceed as follows. First, by definition of $V(.)$:

$$V(Z) = \max_{Y \leqslant Z} \{U(Y) + \rho EV[h(X, Y, Z)]\}, \tag{4.45}$$

where the expectation is taken with respect to the (constant) distribution of X. A few words of explanation may help. Consider the individual arriving at some period with Z inherited from the past. The first term in curly brackets is utility gained this period, and the second term is the discounted expected maximum utility achievable in all future time periods given that a Z value $h(X, Y, Z)$ is 'bequeathed' to the next period. By definition $V(Z)$ is the maximised value of this sum. Moreover, Y^* is the value of Y that achieves this maximum. Thus, $Y^* = Y^*(Z)$ is given by[8]

$$U'(Y^*) + \rho E\{V'[h(X, Y^*, Z)]h_Y(X, Y^*, Z)\} = 0 \qquad (4.46)$$

and definitionally (from (4.45))

$$V(Z) = U(Y^*) + \rho E\{V[h(X, Y^*, Z)]\}. \qquad (4.47)$$

This completes the solution: equations (4.46) and (4.47) solve jointly for the functions $Y^*(.)$ and $V(.)$ in terms of the various parameters of the problem. Unlike their finite horizon counterparts (equations (4.41) and (4.42)), which are solved recursively, these equations are solved simultaneously. The economic interest remains in the form of the function $Y^*(.)$ and how it shifts in response to changes in the parameters of the problem; again these issues depend crucially on the form of the function $h(., ., .)$. Again, we leave further investigation to a specific application.

As should be apparent, the time-independent infinite horizon problem is simpler to deal with than the finite horizon problem: only 2, rather than $2T$, functions need to be investigated. As far as modelling the actual situation of an individual human being is concerned, however, both leave something to be desired: clearly, individuals do not live infinitely long, but neither do they live a known and certain finite number of years. In practice, the date of death is usually uncertain.

This fact can be incorporated into the finite horizon model by postulating a probability distribution relating to date of death (and making T sufficiently large so that the probability of dying before T periods has elapsed is unity). This would simply have the effect[9] of prefacing the expectation term in both (4.41) and (4.42) by a number equal to the probability of surviving to period $(t + 1)$ given that the individual was alive at the beginning of period t. Such probabilities could easily be found from actuarial life tables. Thus the incorporation of a random (but finite) horizon would not alter the basic structure of the finite horizon model.

In an infinite-horizon model, to preserve the time independence, the probability distribution of date of death would have to be such that the probability of dying at the end of a period, given that the individual was alive at the beginning of the period, was some constant, say $(1 - \theta)$. In practice, actuarial tables suggest that this property is not valid at all ages, though it is a reasonable approximation during large parts of the lifetime of most people. If this property holds, then the only modification necessary to our solution is the prefacing of the expectation term in both (4.46) and (4.47) by θ. As the reader will quickly verify, this is precisely the same as replacing the discount rate ρ by $\rho\theta$. Thus, an individual with a low θ will act as if he is discounting the future more heavily than an individual with a high θ. This is an eminently sensible result, especially when taken in conjunction with the fact that life expectancy (under our assumed probability distribution) is $1/(1 - \theta)$.

4.5   SUMMARY AND CONCLUSIONS

This chapter has been concerned with optimisation in passive situations of both a static and a dynamic nature. Static problems were characterised by a random variable X, a decision variable Y and a Neumann–Morgenstern utility function defined over X and Y. Dynamic problems were characterised by a sequence of random variable Z (that is, utility = $U[Z(X, Y)]$). In the first form, assuming $Y_1, \ldots, Y_T$, and a utility function defined over the Xs and the Ys; T could be finite, infinite or random.

Two forms of static problems were considered: the first in which X and Y entered directly into the utility function $U(X, Y)$; the second in which X and Y entered indirectly through an intermediate variable Z (that is, utility, $= U[Z(X, Y)]$). In the first form, assuming that $U_{YY} < 0$, we found that unambiguity of sign of U_{XY} was sufficient to determine the effect on Y^*, the optimal choice of Y, of a bodily shift of the X distribution. Moreover, unambiguity of sign of U_{XXY} was sufficient to determine the effect on Y^* of a Rothschild–Stiglitz increase in risk of the X distribution. Other comparative static effects were also investigated. In the second form, we found that linearity of Z in terms of X was sufficient to determine the comparative static effects of a mean-preserving introduction in risk, and a Sandmo increase in risk, for a large set of Neumann–Morgenstern utility maximisers.

Three forms of dynamic problems were considered; namely, T finite, T infinite and T random. In contradistinction to the approach adopted with respect to the static problems, we simply outlined the general problems and sketched their solutions; no attempt at deriving comparative statics results was made. For the finite horizon problem, we described the method of backward induction and showed how it led in principle to the solution. For the infinite horizon problem, we introduced the idea of time-independence, and illustrated how this simplified the solution enormously. Finally, we discussed how random lifetimes could be incorporated into our analyses.

All of the above methods will be utilised in later chapters to describe the optimal behaviour of economic agents operating in passive situations.

5 OPTIMISATION IN ACTIVE SITUATIONS

5.1 INTRODUCTION

This chapter is concerned with optimisation in situations in which the decision-maker takes an active role in determining the number of realisations of the relevant random variables. Thus, in contrast with the situation envisaged in the previous chapter (where the economic agent was forced to accept an exogenously determined number of realisations), the agent in this chapter is actively involved in deciding which realisations to accept (and how many to observe). Naturally there is a cost incurred by this extra freedom; otherwise there would be no economic problem to discuss.

The class of problems discussed in this chapter have enjoyed immense popularity in economics in recent years under the more familiar nomenclature[1] of 'search models'. The most obvious applications of the material of this chapter are to the 'consumer search problem' (the search for the lowest price of a consumer good) and to the 'job search problem' (the search for the highest wage), though there are numerous other examples. We will examine such applications in subsequent chapters.

We begin, in Section 5.2, with the simplest problem: one in which the decision-maker can observe as many realisations of some random variable X as he wishes at a constant cost c (>0) per observation; all observations are from a known constant distribution function $F(.)$, and the reward is the maximum value of X observed. We derive the optimal strategy, and draw attention to the various important properties it possesses. Section 5.2 also examines a simple extension of this basic problem – an extension in which the reward is the maximum value of some function of X. Subsequent sections then go on to consider more complicated versions of the search problem. Section 5.3 looks at dynamic problems of both a finite and infinite horizon form; issues such as 'recall' are also discussed in this section.

Multi-stage problems (in which search takes place sequentially from multivariate distributions) are examined in Section 5.4, while Section 5.5 qualifies the material of the chapter and offers some comments in conclusion.

5.2 THE BASIC PROBLEM AND A SIMPLE EXTENSION

As outlined in the Introduction, the simplest active optimisation (or search) problem has the following form. The searcher can observe sequentially any number of realisations of a random variable X which has a known (and constant) distribution function $F(.)$. Each observation costs a constant amount c (>0), and this amount is independent of the way that the observations are generated. This latter assumption rules out the possibility that anything but a *sequential* strategy would be optimal.[2] The reward of the searcher is the maximum value of X observed, and the problem of the searcher is to determine a strategy which maximises the reward net of all search costs incurred (thus the searcher is assumed to be risk-neutral). The key issue, of course, is when to stop sampling; the optimal strategy thus involves deciding on an *optimal stopping rule*, or, equivalently on an *optimal acceptance set* (of stopping values of X).

We will examine several different methods of determining the optimum strategy. The first such method proceeds along the following lines. Suppose that at some stage in the search process, the maximum value of X that the searcher has so far observed is z, and the searcher is wondering whether it is likely to be worthwhile taking another observation. If he does *not* take another observation his reward will be z (ignoring any previously incurred search costs, which are lost irrespective of what he does now). If he does take another observation *and then stops*, his net reward will be either z or the new observation (whichever is the greater) less the search cost incurred. Thus, the expected gain (which we denote by $G(z)$) from searching once more before stopping is given by

$$G(z) = [zF(z) + \int_z^\infty x \, dF(x) - c] - z. \qquad (5.1)$$

A few words of explanation may help. The term in square brackets is the expected net reward after searching once more. The extra observation (which costs an amount c) is either less than or equal to

z or is greater than z; if the former, which happens with probability $F(z)$, z remains the maximum value – hence the first term in square brackets; the second term is the expected value of the extra observation given that it is greater than z multiplied by the probability that it is greater than z.

Using integration by parts to simplify (5.1), we find:

$$G(z) = \int_z^\infty [1 - F(x)]\, dx - c. \qquad (5.2)$$

From this it follows that

$$G'(z) = -[1 - F(z)] \lessgtr 0 \qquad \text{according as } z \lessgtr \min\{x; F(x) = 1\},$$

and

$$G(\infty) = -c < 0.$$

Now suppose that $G(-\infty) > 0$ (which is simply a condition that implies that some search is preferable to none); then it follows from the properties of $G(\,.\,)$ derived above that there exists a unique value at which $G(\,.\,)$ attains the value zero. Denote this value by x^*; thus

$$G(x^*) = \int_{x^*}^\infty [1 - F(x)]\, dx - c = 0 \qquad (5.3)$$

and clearly

$$G(z) \gtreqless 0 \qquad \text{according as } z \lesseqgtr x^*. \qquad (5.4)$$

In words, (5.4) states that if the maximum value of X obtained so far is less than x^* then the expected gain from searching once more is positive, but if the maximum observed value of X exceeds x^* then the expected gain from searching once more is negative. It follows immediately that the optimal strategy[3] is the following:

Keep on searching until a value of X greater than or equal to x^* is observed (where x^* is given by (5.3)); then stop searching and take the reward.

The critical value x^* is called the optimal *reservation value* of X. The optimal strategy is simply to keep on searching until a value of X greater than this optimal reservation value has been observed.

Before we investigate the properties of the optimal strategy, it will be instructive to derive it by an alternative method. This alternative method uses as its basis the fact that, given the structure of the problem, the optimal strategy must be of a 'reservation value' form. (By this, we simply mean a strategy which involves stopping as soon as an observation greater than some reservation value has been obtained.) Moreover, because of the *stationary* structure of the problem, this reservation value must be constant. (The stationarity property arises because of the unchanging nature of the problem of the searcher.[4]) Therefore, let us suppose that the searcher decides to employ a reservation value strategy, but that an *arbitrary* reservation value x is chosen. If the searcher follows this strategy, what is his expected net reward? If we denote it by V_x (this notation emphasising its dependence upon the arbitrarily chosen reservation value x), then the following equation holds:

$$V_x = -c + \int_x^\infty t \, dF(t) + V_x F(x). \qquad (5.5)$$

Again a few words of explanation may help. On the right hand side of (5.5) the first term is simply the cost of an observation; the second term is the expected reward if the observation is greater than x (in which case search stops) multiplied by the probability that the observation is greater than x; the third term is the expected net reward if the observation is less than, or equal to x (in which case search continues) multiplied by the probability that the observation is less than, or equal to x. Crucial to this equation is the fact that if the observation is less than x then the expected net reward *from then* is still V_x: the searcher is 'back to square one'.

If (5.5) is solved for V_x we get:[5]

$$V_x = \left[-c + \int_x^\infty t \, dF(t) \right] \Big/ [1 - F(x)], \qquad (5.6)$$

or, using integration by parts:

$$V_x = \{ -c + x[1 - F(x)] + \int_x^\infty [1 - F(t)] \, dt \} / [1 - F(x)]. \quad (5.7)$$

Now, by definition, the *optimal* reservation value x^* is the value of x that maximises the net reward V_x. Denoting the maximum value by V, we have

$$V = V_{x^*} \text{ and } V \geqslant V_x \text{ for all } x.$$

The first-order condition is given, as usual, by $dV_x/dx = 0$; or, from (5.7) by

$$dV_x/dx = f(x^*)\left\{-c + \int_{x^*}^{\infty} [1 - F(t)]\, dt\right\}\Big/[1 - F(x^*)]^2 = 0 \quad (5.8)$$

where $f(.)$ is the p.d.f. of X. Examination of the second-order condition shows that the relevant solution of (5.8) is found when the term in curly brackets is zero; thus

$$\int_{x^*}^{\infty} [1 - F(t)]\, dt - c = 0. \quad (5.9)$$

But this is precisely the same as (5.3); as, of course, should have been anticipated. Moreover, using (5.9) in (5.7) we find

$$V \equiv V_{x^*} = x^*, \quad (5.10)$$

which is a vitally important and significant result. This result states that the *expected net reward following the optimal strategy is exactly equal to the optimal reservation value*. An alternative way of viewing this result (and a view we shall frequently adopt in other search applications) is in terms of the *indifference property* of the reservation value itself. Equation (5.10) (and, indeed (5.4)) states that if the searcher gets an observation equal to x^* then he is *indifferent* between stopping and continuing. Furthermore, if the observation is strictly greater than x^* then stopping is preferred, but if the observation is strictly less than x^* then continuing is preferred.

Before concluding our study of the basic search problem, we examine some of the properties of the solution. The optimal reservation value x^* is given by (5.3) (or (5.9)); from this it follows that[6]

$$dx^*/dc = -[1 - F(x^*)] < 0. \quad (5.11)$$

Thus, the individual becomes less choosy (and so search intensity declines) if the search cost increases. Additionally, if $F(x^*) > 0$ (that is, the optimal strategy is *not* to stop after the first observation irrespective of its value), then $dx^*/dc > -1$: the reservation value falls by a smaller amount than the search cost rises.

A rightward shift of the X distribution can be investigated using the technique described in Section 4.2; replace $F(x)$ in (5.3) by $G(x - a)$ to get

$$\int_{x^*}^{\infty} [1 - G(x - a)]\, dx = c$$

Now use the standard change of variable technique to get

$$\int_{x^* - a}^{\infty} [1 - G(x)]\, dx = c$$

Without further ado, it is obvious from this that $dx^*/da = 1$: an increase of a by a certain amount requires an increase of x^* by exactly the same amount.

Let us now consider an increase in the riskiness of the X distribution. Suppose G is riskier than F according to Rothschild and Stiglitz; then (see Section 3.4, and especially equation (3.21))

$$\int_{0}^{y} [G(x) - F(x)]\, dx \geqslant 0 \qquad \text{for all } y, \text{ with equality at } \infty.$$

From this it follows that

$$\int_{y}^{\infty} [G(x) - F(x)]\, dx \leqslant 0 \qquad \text{for all } y.$$

In particular, if x_F^* and x_G^* denote the optimal reservation values under F and G respectively, then

$$\int_{x_F^*}^{\infty} [G(x) - F(x)]\, dx \leqslant 0. \tag{5.12}$$

Now consider the identity:

$$\int_{x_F^*}^{\infty} [1 - G(x)] \, dx \equiv \int_{x_F^*}^{\infty} [1 - F(x)] \, dx - \int_{x_F^*}^{\infty} [G(x) - F(x)] \, dx.$$

$$(5.13)$$

Since the first term on the right hand side of (5.13) is equal to c by virtue of (5.3), it follows using (5.12) that

$$\int_{x_F^*}^{\infty} [1 - G(x)] \, dx \geq c.$$

But x_G^* is defined by

$$\int_{x_G^*}^{\infty} [1 - G(x)] \, dx = c.$$

Thus $x_G^* \geq x_F^*$. Actually, in general there will be a strict inequality in this expression. Thus, increased risk leads to an increased reservation value (the searcher becomes more choosy); moreover, from (5.10), it follows that increased risk leads to an increased expected net reward: the searcher prefers to sample from a riskier distribution. This is an important result.

Penultimately, we derive an expression for the expected number of observations when following the optimal strategy. Let the random variable N denote the number of observations taken before stopping. We have

$$P(N = n) = [F(x^*)]^{n-1}[1 - F(x^*)] \qquad n = 1, 2, \ldots \quad (5.14)$$

since the first $(n - 1)$ observations must have been less than x^* and the nth must have been greater than or equal to x^*. The distribution described by (5.14) is known as the *geometric* distribution. From standard texts (for example, Degroot (1970, p. 36)), or directly from (5.14), we get

$$EN = 1/[1 - F(x^*)]. \qquad (5.15)$$

Thus the higher is x^*, the larger is the expected number of observations.

Finally, Figure 5.1 illustrates the determination of the optimal reservation value (using (5.3)).

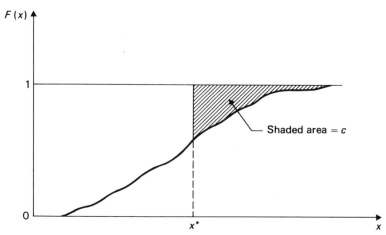

Figure 5.1   The determination of the optimal reservation value

One immediate extension of this basic model should be noted. Suppose that the reward on stopping is not the maximum value of X, but rather the maximum value of some function $U(.)$ of X. (U *may* be a utility function, as the notation suggests, but this is not necessary for the material that follows. Indeed it is probably best to consider U as some arbitrary function.) If U is a *monotonic* function, then the solution straightforwardly follows from the material above. Suppose that U is monotonically *increasing*, and define the variable Y by

$$Y = U(X). \qquad (5.16)$$

Then $G(.)$, the distribution function of the random variable Y, is given by

$$G(y) = P(Y \leqslant y) = P[U(X) \leqslant y] = P[X \leqslant U^{-1}(y)] = F[U^{-1}(y)].$$
$$(5.17)$$

If y^* denotes the optimal reservation value for Y, it follows from

(5.3) or (5.9) that $y*$ is given by

$$\int_{y*}^{\infty} [1 - G(y)] \, dy = c.$$ (5.18)

Using (5.17) this becomes

$$\int_{y*}^{\infty} \{1 - F[U^{-1}(y)]\} \, dy = c,$$

which can be simplified, by using the change of variable $y = U(x)$, to

$$\int_{x*}^{\infty} [1 - F(x)] \, dU(x) = c,$$ (5.19)

where $x*$ is defined by $y* = U(x*)$.

If U is differentiable (5.19) reduces to

$$\int_{x*}^{\infty} [1 - F(x)] \, U'(x) \, dx = c.$$ (5.20)

The optimal strategy is to keep on searching until a value of Y greater than or equal to $y*$ (where $y*$ is given by (5.18)), or equivalently, until a value of X greater than or equal to $x*$ (where $x*$ is given by (5.19) or (5.20)), is found. If U is monotonically *decreasing*, the reservation rule in terms of Y (and its value as given by (5.18)) still holds, but the reservation rule in terms of X is now different; as the reader can quickly verify, the optimal strategy is now to keep on searching until a value of X *less than*, or equal to $x*$ is found, where $x*$ is given by

$$-\int_{-\infty}^{x*} F(x) \, dU(x) = c.$$ (5.21)

For example, suppose $U(X) = -X$, so that lower values of X are preferred to higher values. Then, it follows from (5.21) that the optimal strategy is to keep on sampling until an observation less than or equal to $x*$ is found, where $x*$ is given by

$$\int_{-\infty}^{x*} F(x) \, dx = c.$$ (5.22)

This is a familiar expression from the consumer search literature (in which the agent is searching over price).

An alternative method of obtaining these results exploits the indifference properties of the reservation value(s). Let V denote the *maximum* value of expected net rewards; that is, V denotes the expected net reward following the optimal strategy. Using the indifference properties, it follows that, if the searcher has just observed a value x, then:

1. if $U(x) > V$, the searcher strictly prefers to stop searching;
2. if $U(x) = V$, the searcher is indifferent between stopping and continuing;
3. if $U(x) < V$, the searcher strictly prefers to continue searching.

Clearly, V provides a *reservation value for the variable* $U(X)$. In the particular cases when U is monotonic, this can be translated into a reservation value for X itself. To be specific, if U is monotonic *increasing*, then a *lower* reservation value for X is given by $U^{-1}(V)$, while if U is monotonic *decreasing* then an *upper* reservation value for X is given by $U^{-1}(V)$.

U need not be monotonic, however. In the general case, the optimal acceptance set[7] is given by:

$$A^* = \{x; \ U(x) \geqslant V\}. \tag{5.23}$$

An example is portrayed in Figure 5.2. As should be apparent from this example, the optimal acceptance set may consist of various segments; in other words, it need not be a connected set.

All that remains is to calculate V. Using an argument which should now be familiar, we have

$$V = -c + \int_{A^*} U(x) \, dF(x) + \left[1 - \int_{A^*} dF(x)\right] V,$$

and so

$$V = \left[-c + \int_{A^*} U(x) \, dF(x)\right] \Big/ \int_{A^*} dF(x). \tag{5.24}$$

This completes the solution:[8] (5.23) and (5.24) together determine the optimal acceptance set and the maximum expected net reward.

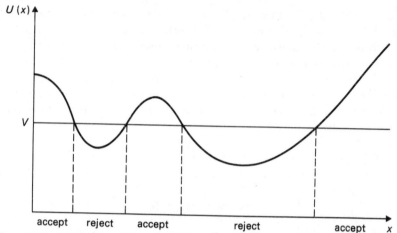

Figure 5.2   The optimal acceptance set for a non-monotonic reward function

Note that in the special case considered earlier (that is, when $U(x) = x$), (5.23) and (5.24) reduce respectively to (5.9) and (5.10).

5.3   DYNAMIC OPTIMISATION

The basic principles of search theory are all contained in the section above. One principle is of particular importance (indeed it assumes the same stature in the economics of uncertainty as the famous 'marginal equalisation' principle in certainty economics). This principle is the 'indifference condition' defining the boundary of the optimal acceptance (or stopping) set. Clearly, if this condition did not hold, then the acceptance set in use would not be the optimal one.

The material in Section 5.2 was timeless; however, depending upon the specifications of the particular application, it could form the basis of either a static or a dynamic optimisation problem. It is with the latter of these two possibilities that this present section is concerned. We begin with an infinite horizon problem, after which we examine the complications introduced by the existence of a finite horizon.

Suppose then that the searcher is sequentially taking observations from some distribution with known distribution function $F(.)$. To make the problem dynamic, assume that observation requires the passage of time: to be specific, define a 'period' as a length of time in which the searcher gets *at most* one observation. To add further interest to the problem, suppose that there may be some uncertainty as to whether a particular period yields an observation; denote by $1 - q$ the probability that no observation is obtained – so that q is the probability that an observation is obtained. We assume that q is *exogenous*; thus search *intensity* is fixed. As a slight variant on the theme of Section 5.2, we now assume that there is no *direct* cost of observation (though there is, as we shall see, an opportunity cost). The 'reward' of the searcher depends on whether he is still taking observations or whether search has terminated: to be specific, while still searching the searcher gets reward U_0 *per period*, and when search has terminated the reward, *per period* of the remainder of the infinite lifetime, is the maximum value of $U(X)$ over the observed values of X. To keep the subsequent exposition simple, we assume that U is strictly monotonically increasing everywhere (that is $U' > 0$ for all x), though the argument generalises to non-monotonic, or monotonically decreasing, functions. Finally, we assume that the objective of the searcher is to devise a strategy which maximises the expected total discounted lifetime reward, where future rewards are all discounted at the constant rate ρ per period ($0 < \rho < 1$).

In keeping with our previous notation, we let V denote the maximised value of this objective function (as viewed from a period in which search is actively continuing). We note the important fact that this value is *independent of time*; in the terminology of Section 4.4 the problem is a *stationary* dynamic optimisation problem. Using the material of Section 4.2, the optimal strategy is defined by the optimal acceptance set A^*, as given by[9] (cf. (5.23))

$$A^* = \{x; \, U(x)/(1 - \rho) \geqslant V\}. \tag{5.25}$$

Since, by assumption, U is strictly increasing everywhere, (5.25) can be written

$$A^* = \{x; \, x \geqslant x^*\}$$

where

$$x^* = U^{-1}[V(1 - \rho)] \text{ (or } U(x^*) = V(1 - \rho)) \tag{5.26}$$

where x^* denotes the unique optimal (lower) reservation value for X. The value of V is given by

$$V = U_0 + \rho \left\{ \left[(1 - q) + q \int_{-\infty}^{x^*} dF(x) \right] V + q \int_{x^*}^{\infty} \frac{U(x)}{1 - \rho} dF(x) \right\}. \tag{5.27}$$

This type of expression should, by now, be familiar: since the agent is actively involved in search, the reward in the current period is U_0; in the following period (hence the discount factor ρ), the agent either continues search (if he got no offer, or an unacceptable offer, in the current period), in which case his expected lifetime reward from then is still V, or he terminates search (if he gets an acceptable offer x) in which case he gets $U(x)$ *per period* thereafter. Equation (5.27) solves to give

$$V = \left\{ U_0 + [\rho q/(1-\rho)] \int_{x*}^{\infty} U(x) \, dF(x) \right\} \Big/ \{(1-\rho) + \rho q \, [1 - F(x*)]\}.$$

$$(5.28)$$

Alternatively, if U is differentiable, then integration by parts can be used to simplify (5.28), and using the fact that $U(x*)/(1-\rho) = V$ (from (5.26) it can be shown that:[10]

$$V(1-\rho) = U_0 + [\rho q/(1-\rho)] \int_{x*}^{\infty} U'(x) [1 - F(x)] \, dx. \quad (5.29)$$

The solution is now complete: it consists of (5.26) and either (5.28) or (5.29); jointly these two equations solve for $x*$ (the optimal reservation value) and V (the maximum expected lifetime reward) in terms of the parameters of the problem U_0, ρ, q and $F(\,.\,)$. We now examine the comparative static properties of this solution.

First, we note an extremely important property. From either (5.28) or (5.29), and using (5.26), it is a straightforward, though tedious, exercise to show that:

$$\partial V/\partial x* = 0. \qquad (5.30)$$

On reflection, this is a sensible result: indeed, it is simply an alternative way of expressing the fact that $x*$ is the *optimal* reservation value.

This result simplifies the analysis of the comparative statics effects enormously. Consider, for example, the effect of a change in q. From (5.26) we have

$$(dx*/dq) \, U'(x*) = (dV/dq) \, (1-\rho), \qquad (5.31)$$

and from (5.29)

$$(dV/dq)(1 - \rho) = [\rho/(1 - \rho)] \int_{x^*}^{\infty} U'(x)[1 - F(x)] \, dx$$

$$+ (\partial V/\partial x^*)(dx^*/dq).$$

But the second term on the right hand side of this is zero by (5.30), and so we get

$$(dV/dq)(1 - \rho) = [\rho/(1 - \rho)] \int_{x^*}^{\infty} U'(x)[1 - F(x)] \, dx. \quad (5.32)$$

Inspection of (5.31) and (5.32) shows immediately that, under our assumptions, it must follow that

$$dV/dq > 0 \quad \text{and} \quad dx^*/dq > 0; \quad (5.33)$$

thus the searcher gets better off, and hence becomes more 'choosy', as the probability of getting an observation increases.

Indeed it is clear from (5.31) that, with U' positive everywhere, V and x^* always move in the same direction; thus any parameter change which increases the maximum expected reward will also have the effect of increasing x^*, and thus making the searcher more 'choosy'. An obvious example of this is an increase in U_0, as is apparent from (5.29); such an increase reduces the opportunity cost of search. Another straightforward example is an increase in ρ: examination of the solution shows that this will lead to increases in $V(1 - \rho)$ and in x^*. Thus, an increased weight on future rewards leads to a greater investment in search activity. We leave the remaining comparative statics exercises to the reader.

Although the 'rules of the game' of the problem discussed in this section differ somewhat from those of the problem discussed in Section 5.2, the basic structure of the two problems is essentially the same. In particular, both problems exhibit a 'stationary' structure in that the reservation value remains constant. The 'stationary' structure of the dynamic model of this section results essentially from the infinite-horizon feature; as we shall now demonstrate, this property is not preserved in a finite-horizon problem.

Consider, therefore, a problem identical in all respects to that described at the beginning of this section, except in so far as the number of periods is finite. Let T denote this number. This finite horizon not only destroys the stationary structure of the problem, but also necessitates an alternative method of proof. As in Chapter 4, we now need to use the method of *backward induction*. Moreover, we need to add a time subscript to the decision variables. To be specific, let x_t^* denote the optimal reservation value in period t, and let z_{t-1} denote the *maximum* value of X observed in the first $t-1$ periods. Thus, the strategy is of the form:

if $z_{t-1} < x_t^*$ continue searching in period t;
if $z_{t-1} \geqslant x_t^*$ stop searching.

Now let $V_t(z_{t-1})$ denote the *maximum* total expected discounted reward over periods t to T inclusive where z_{t-1} has the meaning given above. For expositional clarity, we will find it helpful to introduce a further function, denoted by $W_t(z_{t-2})$, which represents the expected value of $V_t(z_{t-1})$ as viewed from the beginning of period $t-1$. (Thus z_{t-2}, rather than z_{t-1}, appears as the argument of W_t, since z_{t-1} is as yet unobserved.) By definition, we have:

$$W_t(z) = [(1-q) + qF(z)] \, V_t(z) + q \int_z^\infty V_t(x) \, dF(x). \quad (5.34)$$

Note that this equation is valid whether search takes place in period $t-1$ or not. If search does take place, two possibilities exist: either no observation is received or the new observation is less than z (the original maximum) – in which case z remains the maximum; or an observation greater than z is received – in which case it becomes the new maximum. If search does not take place, then rather trivially $z_{t-1} = z_{t-2}$ and so $V_t(z_{t-1})$ equals $V_t(z_{t-2})$ and hence is constant (and thus equal to $W_t(z_{t-2})$) as viewed from the beginning of period $t-1$.

Our notational preliminaries over, we now turn to the backward induction. We begin, as usual, in period T. In this period, the decision rule (and hence the determination of the reservation value) is straightforward. We must have

$$U(x_T^*) = U_0 \text{ or } x_T^* = U^{-1}(U_0) \quad (5.35)$$

and

$$V_T(z) = \max\{U(z), U_0\}, \quad (5.36)$$

since the optimal strategy is to take as reward the higher of U_0 and $U(z)$. We can now find $W_T(z)$ using (5.36) and (5.34) (with $t = T$).

Moving back to period $T - 1$, we employ the usual indifference condition to find the optimal reservation value (x^*_{T-1}) in that period. We have

$$U(x^*_{T-1}) (1 + \rho) = U_0 + \rho W_T(x^*_{T-1}), \qquad (5.37)$$

since the right hand side measures the total expected discounted reward (over periods $T - 1$ and T) from searching in period $T - 1$ and then behaving optimally in period T, while the left hand side measures the discounted reward (over periods $T - 1$ and T) from stopping searching. Moreover,

$$V_{T-1}(z) = \max\{U(z)(1 + \rho), U_0 + \rho W_T(z)\}. \qquad (5.38)$$

The induction can now continue. The general cases are as follows. First, the determination of the tth period reservation value:

$$U(x^*_t) \left(\sum_{i=0}^{T-t} \rho^i\right) = U_0 + \rho W_{t+1}(x^*_t). \qquad (5.39)$$

Second, the determination of $W_t(.)$, (5.34) repeated for convenience here:

$$W_t(z) = [(1 - q) + qF(z)] V_t(z) + q \int_z^\infty V_t(x) \, dF(x). \qquad (5.40)$$

Third, the determination of $V_t(.)$:

$$V_t(z) = \max \left\{U(z) \left(\sum_{i=0}^{T-t} \rho^i\right), U_0 + W_{t+1}(z)\right\}. \qquad (5.41)$$

Note that (5.35) and (5.37) are particular cases of (5.39), and that (5.36) and (5.38) are particular cases of (5.41) (if we adopt the obvious convention that $W_{T+1} \equiv 0$).

The solution (consisting of (5.39), (5.40) and (5.41)) is complete. We now investigate its properties. Intuition suggests two things: first, if the agent is still actively searching, then as the horizon approaches, he must be getting worse off; second and consequently, the searcher must get less 'choosy' as the horizon approaches. In order to verify our intuition, we use the method of proof known as *mathematical induction*. First, we introduce some new notation: let $v_t(z)$ denote the per period value of $V_t(z)$; that is

$$v_t(z) = V_t(z) \bigg/ \left(\sum_{i=0}^{T-t} \rho^i \right). \tag{5.42}$$

Thus, a stream of rewards of $v_t(z)$ per period in periods t to T inclusive has discounted value $V_t(z)$ in period t. Further, we let $w_t(z)$ denote the per period value of $W_t(z)$; that is

$$w_t(z) = W_t(z) \bigg/ \left(\sum_{i=0}^{T-t} \rho^i \right). \tag{5.43}$$

Note that w_t bears the same relation to v_t as W_t does to V_t (through (5.40)).

To begin our induction, suppose that

$$[U_0 + \rho W_{t+1}(z)] \bigg/ \left(\sum_{i=0}^{T-t} \rho^i \right) < [U_0 + \rho W_t(z)] \bigg/ \left(\sum_{i=0}^{T-t+1} \rho^i \right) \tag{5.44}$$

is true for some t. It then follows from (5.39) that

$$U(x_t^*) < U(x_{t-1}^*),$$

and hence (since U' is assumed strictly positive everywhere) that

$$x_t^* < x_{t-1}^*. \tag{5.45}$$

Moreover, if (5.44) is true for some t, then from (5.41), dividing both sides by $(\Sigma_{i=0}^{T-t} \rho^i)$, we have

$$v_t(z) \leqslant v_{t-1}(z) \tag{5.46}$$

with equality if, and only if $z \geqslant x_t^*$.

Now examine (5.40); if both sides of this are divided by $(\Sigma_{i=0}^{T-t} \rho^i)$, it follows from (5.46) that[11]

$$w_t(z) < w_{t-1}(z). \tag{5.47}$$

Finally, as the Appendix to this chapter shows, (5.47) implies that

$$[U_0 + \rho W_t(z)] \left/ \left(\sum_{i=0}^{T-t+1} \rho^i \right) \right. < [U_0 + \rho W_{t-1}(z)] \left/ \left(\sum_{i=0}^{T-t+2} \rho^i \right) \right. . \qquad (5.48)$$

Noting that (5.48) is simply (5.44) with t replaced by $t - 1$ everywhere, it follows that we have proved that, if (5.44) holds for some t, then it also holds for $t - 1$. But (5.44) does hold for $t = T$, since the left hand side is just U_0 and the right hand side is $[U_0 + \rho W_T(z)]/(1 + \rho)$ which, as inspection of (5.36) and (5.40) clearly shows, is larger than U_0. Thus (5.44) holds for all t.

Moreover, our proof shows that (5.45) holds for all t. In words, the reservation value declines as the horizon approaches, or the searcher gets less 'choosy' as time passes. Our intuition is confirmed. The solution is illustrated in Figure 5.3.

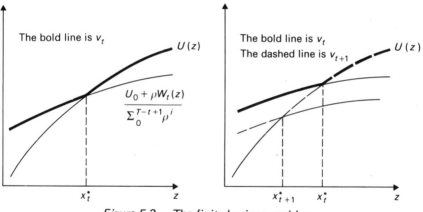

Figure 5.3   The finite horizon problem

A number of comparative statics exercises could be performed on the solution; most of them are straightforward, though tedious. For example, consider the effect of an increase in q. As is obvious from (5.36) this has no effect on $V_T(z)$; using (5.40) (with $t = T$) this implies that $W_T(z)$ increases for all z. Now, apply mathematical induction: suppose an increase in q causes an increase in $W_t(z)$ for some t; from (5.39) and (5.41) this causes an increase in x_{t-1}^* and in $V_{t-1}(z)$; hence from (5.40), $W_{t-1}(z)$ increases. Applying the standard argument, it follows that an increase in q makes the searcher better off (in that $V_t(z)$ and $W_t(z)$ both increase), and consequently the searcher becomes more choosy in all time periods (in that each x_t^* increases). We leave other inferences to the reader.

The finite-horizon model we have just discussed approaches the infinite-horizon model discussed earlier when T approaches infinity. The actual proof is rather tedious, so we omit it here; however, the following outline may aid readers interested in deriving the proof for themselves. If T is infinite we can, as we have seen, drop the time-subscripts on x^*, V and W. Thus (5.39) becomes

$$U(x^*)/(1 - \rho) = V \qquad\qquad (5.49)$$

where (using (5.40))

$V = U_0 + \rho W$

$$= U_0 + \rho \left\{ [(1 - q) + qF(x^*)] \, V + q \int_{x^*}^{\infty} U(x)/(1 - \rho) \, dF(x) \right\} \quad (5.50)$$

since, from (5.41)

$$V(z) = \begin{cases} U(z)/(1 - \rho) & \text{for } z \geqslant x^* \\ V & \text{for } z < x^*. \end{cases} \qquad (5.51)$$

Now note that (5.49) is the same as (5.26) whilst (5.50) is the same as (5.27). In terms of the diagrammatic representation of Figure 5.3, $v(.)$ is horizontal to the left of x^* and coincides with $U(.)$ to the right of x^*.

Throughout the whole of the above discussion, it has been assumed that observations can be *collected*; or, in more conventional terminology, that the searcher can *recall* earlier observations. In some important economic applications, however, recall is not possible; in such cases, the searcher must decide, immediately upon observing a particular x value, whether to accept it or not. How does this affect our analysis?

Clearly in the infinite-horizon model, the question of recall is of no consequence, since the reservation value is constant; an unacceptable observation is always unacceptable. In the finite-horizon model, however, this is not the case, since the reservation value falls as the horizon approaches. Thus the question of recall is crucial. Let us briefly investigate a finite-horizon model in which recall is *not* permitted; in all other respects our model remains the same as that discussed above. Since recall is not permitted, z_t now denotes the value of X observed in period t. $V_t(.)$ retains the same meaning as before, but now W_t no longer has an argument (since observations cannot be carried forward). Indeed, W_t is now given by (cf. (5.40)):

$$W_t = (1 - q) [U_0 + \rho W_{t+1}] + q \int_{-\infty}^{\infty} V_t(x) \, dF(x). \qquad (5.52)$$

(The first term on the right hand side of this results from the fact that if one does not receive an observation in a given period, then one is forced to take the 'reward' U_0 in that period, and continue searching in the following period.)

As far as period T is concerned, (5.35) and (5.36) remain valid. The expression for x_t^* (cf (5.39)) becomes

$$U(x_t^*) \left(\sum_{i=0}^{T-t} \rho^i \right) = U_0 + \rho W_{t+1}, \qquad (5.53)$$

and V_t is given by (cf. (5.41)):

$$V_t(z) = \max \left\{ U(z) \left(\sum_{i=0}^{T-t} \rho^i \right), \ U_0 + \rho W_{t+1} \right\}. \qquad (5.54)$$

It is clear from the structure of these equations that the qualitative properties of the 'no-recall' model are similar to those of the 'recall' model. In particular, x_t^* falls as the horizon approches. Moreover, since the facility of recall clearly makes the searcher better off, the reservation values in the 'no-recall' model are *all* (except in the final period) lower than their counterparts in the 'recall' model. This result should be obvious from a comparison of (5.39) and (5.53).

We leave further exploration of these results until the relevant applications in Parts III and IV of this book. Before concluding, however, we ought to mention one or two extensions to these basic univariate search models. First, the issue of recall: above, we have discussed the polar cases of total recall and zero recall; in between these cases is the intermediate case of *partial recall*. This case (which can be characterised in several different ways) is partially examined by Landsberger and Peled (1977) and by Karni and Schwartz (1977); further work remains to be done, however.

Another important extension is to a situation in which observations can be taken from several different distributions: in such a situation, the *order* in which distributions are sampled is important. An initial investigation into this problem was carried out by Salop (1973); a complete and highly elegant solution was obtained by Weitzman (1979). In essence, Weitzman's solution is as follows. For each distribution there exists a specific reservation value, and there may be some limit to the number of observations taken from one distribution. The optimal strategy of the searcher is to take the next observation from the distribution with the highest reservation value, and to keep on taking observations until the maximum observed value is larger than the reservation values of all the distributions from which observations can still be taken. For details of this beautifully simple result the reader is referred to Weitzman (1979). A more general class of problems, with a similar structure and solution, is examined by Gittins (1979).

5.4   MULTI-STAGE OPTIMISATION

All of the material above has related to univariate distributions. There are, however, a number of important economic applications in which sampling takes place from multivariate distributions. Of course, if all dimensions of the multivariate distribution were revealed simultaneously, then the added dimensions would add nothing but notational complexity to our analysis. There is an important class of economic problems, however, in which dimensions are revealed *sequentially*.

Let us give a concrete example. Suppose there are two dimensions of interest to the searcher, and let these be represented by the random variables X and Y. Further, let us denote the joint distribution of X and Y by the bivariate distribution function $F(x,y)$. Moreover, suppose the reward conditional on stopping taking observations is some function $U(X, Y)$ of X and Y. The general kind of problem we have in mind is one in which the searcher obtains (possibly at a cost) observations on just the x dimension of the pair (X, Y); at some stage the searcher hits on an acceptable x. At this stage, the searcher obtains (possibly at a further cost) one or more observations on the y dimension conditional on the x value 'accepted' earlier. At some stage, the searcher either hits on an acceptable y or decides that the available y values are not acceptable and so returns to observing the X-dimension. When search terminates, the reward is the value of $U(x, y)$ for the finally accepted (x, y) pair.

Clearly there are numerous possible versions of this story. Here we consider just one. To be specific, suppose any number of observations on the X-dimension are available at cost c per observation. (In a sense, we are returning to the model of Section 5.2). Moreover, suppose that, for any observed x, *just one* observation on Y (from the conditional distribution of Y given the observed x) can be obtained at cost x. Finally, let the reward from accepting a particular (x, y) pair be simply y.

Let V (as usual) denote the *maximum* expected reward, as viewed from a position before an acceptable value of x has been observed. Using our familiar indifference argument, there exists a reservation value for Y, denoted by y^*, given simply by

$$y^* = V. \tag{5.55}$$

The optimal strategy, once a particular y value has been observed, is to accept it (and thus gain reward y) if it is greater than or equal to y^*, and to reject it (and thus return to observing the X-dimension) if it is less than y^*. Suppose now that a particular x value has just been observed; should the searcher ask for the y dimension to be revealed (at cost x as previously specified)? Well, the net reward from so doing is

$$\begin{cases} y - x & \text{if } y \geqslant y^* \\ V - x & \text{if } y < y^*. \end{cases}$$

Clearly the expected value of this net reward depends upon x; to emphasise this fact, let us denote it by $U(x)$. We have

$$U(x) = (V - x)\, G(y^* \,|\, x) + \int_{y^*}^{\infty} (y - x)\, \mathrm{d}G(y \,|\, x) \tag{5.56}$$

where $G(y \,|\, x)$ denotes the distribution function of Y *conditional* on the given value of x. As is well known $G(y \,|\, x)$ is given by

$$G(y \,|\, x) = F(x, y)/F(x, \infty), \tag{5.57}$$

since $F(x, \infty)$ is the marginal distribution function of x.

To find the set of acceptable x, recall the material of Section 5.2. If A^* denotes this set, it is given by (cf. (5.23))

$$A^* = \{x;\ U(x) \geqslant V\}. \tag{5.58}$$

If U is monotonic, this leads to a unique (upper or lower) reservation value for X itself. As a glance at (5.56) will show, however, there is no particular reason why U should be monotonic. Of course, if X and Y were *independent* random variables, then $U'(x)$ would simply equal -1 everywhere, so there would exist a unique upper reservation value for X. But independence removes interest. In the general case, when X and Y are dependent, the function $U(.)$ could exhibit a variety of different forms.

The value of V (which is needed to find the acceptance sets at both stages) is given by (5.24); the material at the end of Section 5.2 is precisely relevant to the problem in hand.

Although the particular multi-stage example discussed above was very simple, it contained sufficient interest and complexity to demonstrate that the methods of this chapter remain relevant. In particular, the indifference condition (defining the optimal acceptance set(s)), combined with the method of backward induction, are jointly sufficient to determine the solution. Moreover, our example has demonstrated that the method can extend indefinitely to cover as many dimensions as are required. The search solution methods developed in this chapter are clearly very powerful.

5.5 QUALIFICATIONS AND CONCLUSIONS

We have examined in some detail a variety of active optimisation (or search) problems of a general nature, though there is a limit to how far one can fruitfully go without a specific economic application in mind. These applications are contained in subsequent chapters, and we leave further development of the methods until then.

The most obvious qualification to the material of this chapter is the observation that, throughout we have assumed that all probability distributions are known, or at least their subjective perceptions remain unchanged. No learning was allowed. The obvious next step is to incorporate learning; this we do in the next chapter.

Finally, we draw attention to some similarities between the material of this chapter and that of the preceding one. Obviously some methods bear the same names and share the same approaches (for example, backward induction, and the 'stationary structure' of infinite-horizon problems). We have tried to emphasise the connections by deliberate and careful choice of notation. For example, the letter z is used in both chapters to describe the 'inheritance from the past'. We commend to the reader a study of these connections; we feel that such a study would amply pay dividends in the form of increased understanding and insight.

5.6   APPENDIX

To prove (5.47) implies (5.48). (5.58) is true if and only if

$$\left[U_0 + \rho w_t(z) \left(\sum_{i=0}^{T-t} \rho^i \right) \right] \Big/ \left(\sum_{i=0}^{T-t+1} \rho^i \right)$$

$$< \left[U_0 + \rho w_{t-1}(z) \left(\sum_{i=0}^{T-t+1} \rho^i \right) \right] \Big/ \left(\sum_{i=0}^{T-t+2} \rho^i \right).$$

Now denote $a = \rho + \ldots + \rho^{T-t+1}$ and $b = \rho + \ldots + \rho^{T-t+2}$; clearly $a < b$. From the above (5.48) is true if and only if

$$[U_0 + a w_t(z)] \, (1 + b) < [U_0 + b w_{t-1}(z)] \, (1 + a),$$

that is, if and only if

$$b(1 + a) [w_t(z) - w_{t-1}(z)] + [U_0 - w_t(z)] \, (b - a) < 0,$$

which is true, by virtue of (5.47) and the obvious fact that $w_t(z) > U_0$ for all z and t. Q.E.D.

6 OPTIMISATION IN ADAPTIVE SITUATIONS

6.1 INTRODUCTION

So far, we have ignored the possibility of learning. Indeed, in the preceding two chapters, we have assumed that the economic agent knows with certainty the relevant probability distributions, or alternatively that his subjective assessment of the distributions remains fixed throughout the decision-making process. Clearly, in many important economic applications, such assumptions are unrealistic.

This chapter attempts to remedy this deficiency by showing how information and learning are incorporated into the decision-making process. Since information is knowledge, and since knowledge reduces uncertainty, we would expect that the incorporation of learning would be of potential value to the economic agent operating under uncertainty.

This chapter, then, is concerned with the process of learning about the probability distributions which affect the decisions of the individual and hence his welfare. In particular, we examine three questions: first, how information affects the subjective assessment of the probability distributions; secondly, how information thereby affects the decisions made by the individual; thirdly, in the light of the answers to these questions, whether the information is of potential value to the individual, and thus, accordingly, whether he should obtain it.[1]

Of the several alternative approaches to the modelling of learning processes, the one most obviously compatible with the underlying philosophy of this book is that motivated by Bayes' theorem. Accordingly, the first substantive section (6.2) of this chapter derives and discusses Bayes' theorem. Subsequent sections then go on to examine how Bayes' theorem helps in answering the three questions posed above: to be specific, Section 6.3 looks at learning in situations which (apart from the learning itself) would otherwise be described as passive, while Section 6.4 looks at learning in active situations. Thus, Section 6.3 incorporates learning into the material of Chapter 4, while Section 6.4 does the same for Chapter 5. Although Bayes' theorem will be used almost exclusively to model learning processes throughout the remainder of the book, Section 6.5 briefly examines an alternative approach; in addition, in Section 6.6 we discuss situations in which Bayesian learning appears to break down, or, at least, is inapplicable. This final section also offers some comments in conclusion.

6.2 BAYES' THEOREM

Bayes' theorem, as presented in modern statistics texts, is a simple implication of the well-known multiplication rule of probability (though the reader of the original Bayes (1763) essay could be forgiven for failing to recognise it as such). If A and B denote any two events, then the joint probability that A and B happen simultaneously can be written in two alternative ways; thus

$$P(A \text{ and } B) = \begin{cases} P(B|A)P(A) \\ P(A|B)P(B) \end{cases}, \tag{6.1}$$

where $P(A|B)$ denotes the conditional probability that A happens given that B happens. If the two right hand sides of (6.1) are equated, and then re-arranged, the following expression immediately results:

$$P(A|B) = P(B|A)P(A)/P(B). \tag{6.2}$$

In essence, this is Bayes' theorem.

To interpret it, and to apply it to a learning problem, consider A as being some random event in whose occurrence one is interested, and consider B as being some other random event whose occurrence or otherwise potentially sheds light on the question of whether or not A is going to occur. In equation (6.2), $P(A)$ denotes the probability that A will happen as viewed from *before* information as to whether or not B has occurred is received; in conventional terminology this is termed the *prior* probability of A. On the other hand, $P(A|B)$ is the probability that A will happen as viewed from *after* the information that B has occurred is received; this is termed the *posterior* probability of A. In (6.2) the posterior is linked to the prior probability through the term $P(B|A)$, which represents the probability of receiving the information that B has occurred conditional on the event that A is to happen; this is termed the *likelihood* of the information.

Another way of viewing (6.2) is in terms of an *updating* of the probability of event A in the light of information. Of course, one might receive the information that B has *not* happened; if we denote this event by $\bar{B}$, the appropriate updating formula in this case would be:

$$P(A|\bar{B}) = P(\bar{B}|A)P(A)/P(\bar{B}). \tag{6.3}$$

Let us now ask an obvious question: as viewed from *before* knowing whether B or $\bar{B}$ has occurred, what is the expected posterior probability of A? In words, this probability is simply the posterior probability given B times the probability that B occurs plus the posterior probability given $\bar{B}$ times the probability that $\bar{B}$ occurs; in symbols it is

$$P(A|B)P(B) + P(A|\bar{B})P(\bar{B}),$$

or using (6.2) and (6.3)

$$P(B|A)P(A) + P(\bar{B}|A)P(A) = [P(B|A) + P(\bar{B}|A)]P(A) = P(A).$$

This is hardly a surprising result; indeed if the *expected* posterior probability were anything other than the prior probability, we would suspect some bias in the learning process. One other reassuring feature of the updating, or learning, process represented by (6.2) is the fact (easily verified by the reader) that

$$P(A|B) + P(\bar{A}|B) = 1. \tag{6.4}$$

and so posterior probabilities add up to unity (which, of course, is a necessary requirement of any probabilities).

An alternative, and more conventional, way of expressing (6.2) is found by making use of the obvious result that:

$$P(B) = P(B|A)P(A) + P(B|\bar{A})P(\bar{A}).$$

Thus (6.2) becomes

$$P(A|B) = P(B|A)P(A)/[P(B|A)P(A) + P(B|\bar{A})P(\bar{A})]. \tag{6.5}$$

Alternatively, if there is a set of I mutually exclusive and exhaustive events A_i of interest $(i = 1, \ldots, I)$, then (6.5) straightforwardly generalises to the most familiar form of *Bayes' theorem*:

$$P(A_i|B) = \frac{P(B|A_i)P(A_i)}{\sum\limits_{i=1}^{I} P(B|A_i)P(A_i)} \qquad i = 1, \ldots, I. \qquad (6.6)$$

The crucial point remains the fact that the posterior probability is proportional to the product of the likelihood and the prior probability. Note that the denominator of (6.6) does not depend upon i; indeed, the denominator is simply a scaling factor which ensures that the posterior probabilities sum to unity.

Throughout the above discussion, we have used the word 'information' – and have thus tacitly assumed that knowledge of the occurrence of B or $\bar{B}$ is actually informative. Under what circumstances would this *not* be the case? Clearly, if the posterior probability of A is the same whether B or $\bar{B}$ has occurred then knowledge of the occurrence of B is valueless. Formally, the 'information' is uninformative if

$$P(A|B) = P(A|\bar{B}). \qquad (6.7)$$

That is, using (6.2) and (6.3) if

$$P(B|A)P(A)/P(B) = P(\bar{B}|A)P(A)/P(\bar{B}).$$

Or, simplifying and using the facts that $P(\bar{B})$ equals $1 - P(B)$ and $P(\bar{B}|A)$ equals $1 - P(B|A)$, if

$$P(B|A)/P(B) = [1 - P(B|A)]/[1 - P(B)].$$

Or, simplifying, if

$$P(B|A) = P(B).$$

Clearly if this holds, then it also follows that

$$P(B|A) = P(B|\bar{A}) = P(B). \qquad (6.8)$$

We therefore arrive at the intuitively satisfying conclusion: 'information' is uninformative if the probability of its occurrence is independent of the event in whose occurrence one is interested. Moreover, note that (6.7) immediately implies that all posteriors are equal to the corresponding prior.

So far we have discussed Bayes' theorem in terms of probability statements about *events*. As most of the economic applications that we will be examining will be phrased in terms of random *variables* (rather than random events), it will prove useful to express Bayes' theorem in the form appropriate for random variables. There are, of course, forms appropriate for both univariate and multivariate distributions of both discrete and continuous random variables (as well as variables that are partly discrete and partly continuous). Here, we will concentrate on the form appropriate for univariate continuous random variables, as this form will prove to be of most use in subsequent chapters.[2]

For reasons that should soon become apparent, we can no longer rely totally on the *distribution function* as a description of the distribution of the random variable; instead, we have to make use of the *probability density function* (pdf). We also need some new notation to indicate marginal and conditional pdfs. Suppose W and X are the random variables of interest: with W representing the information and X the variable whose distribution is being updated in the light of the information. Let $g(w, x)$ denote the joint pdf of W and X; note, of course, that the joint distribution function $G(.,.)$ is related to $g(.,.)$ by

$$G(w, x) = \int_{s = -\infty}^{w} \int_{t = -\infty}^{x} g(s, t)\, ds\, dt. \qquad (6.9)$$

Let $e(w)$ and $f(x)$ denote the marginal pdfs of W and X respectively; thus

$$e(w) = \int_{x = -\infty}^{\infty} g(w, x)\, dx \qquad \text{and} \qquad f(x) = \int_{w = -\infty}^{\infty} g(w, x)\, dw. \qquad (6.10)$$

Also, let $e(w|x)$ and $f(x|w)$ denote the conditional pdfs of W given x and of X given w respectively; thus

$$e(w|x) = g(w, x)/f(x) \qquad \text{and} \qquad f(x|w) = g(w, x)/e(w). \qquad (6.11)$$

Note that $e(w)$, the marginal pdf of W, is, in general, different from $e(w|x)$, the conditional pdf of W given x, though the use of the common symbol e emphasises that both are distributions of W; likewise, $f(x)$ is, in general, different from $f(x|w)$.

We can now express Bayes' theorem in terms of W and X; from (6.6) or (6.1) the appropriate expression is seen to be:

$$f(x|w) = \frac{e(w|x)f(x)}{\int_{x=-\infty}^{\infty} e(w|x)f(x)\,\mathrm{d}x} \tag{6.12}$$

As before, the denominator[3] of this expression is simply a scaling factor (it is independent of x) which ensures that the area under $f(.|w)$ equals unity. We can make use of this fact (and also save space) by writing (6.12) in the far simpler form:

$$f(x|w) \propto e(w|x)f(x), \tag{6.13}$$

where '$\propto$' means 'proportional to'. Equation (6.13) expresses the now familiar result that the posterior probability is proportional to the product of the likelihood and the prior probability.

Let us give a simple illustration of the use of this result. Suppose that the decision-maker knows that the random variable W is normally distributed; suppose further that the variance of W is known but that its mean is unknown. For reasons which will become apparent, we denote the variance of W by $1/r$; thus r denotes the *reciprocal of the variance*, termed the *precision* by Bayesian statisticians. The mean of W, which is unknown, we denote by X; the subjective assessment of the decision-maker of X is encapsulated in a prior pdf of X, denoted by $f(x)$. Suppose that this prior pdf is, in fact, a normal distribution with mean m and precision p (and thus variance $1/p$).

Clearly in this example the distribution of W depends upon the true value of X; thus, observations on W are potentially informative. Let us apply Bayes' theorem to find the posterior distribution of X after receiving one observation on W. We have[4]

$$f(x) \propto \exp\{-p(x-m)^2/2\}$$

and

$$e(w|x) \propto \exp\{-r(w-x)^2/2\}.$$

Hence, using (6.13)

$$f(x|w) \propto \exp\{-\tfrac{1}{2}[p(x-m)^2 + r(w-x)^2]\}. \qquad (6.14)$$

Now, note that the term in square brackets in (6.14) can be simplified to

$$p(x-m)^2 + r(w-x)^2 = (p+r)\left[x - \frac{pm+rw}{p+r}\right]^2 + \frac{pr(m-w)^2}{p+r}.$$

From this it follows that (6.14) can be written (ignoring all the terms which do not involve x):

$$f(x|w) \propto \exp\left\{-(p+r)\left[x - \frac{pm+rw}{p+r}\right]^2 \Big/ 2\right\}. \qquad (6.15)$$

Thus the posterior distribution of X given the observation w is normal with mean $(pm+rw)/(p+r)$ and precision $(p+r)$. Three things should be noted about this result. First, the posterior mean: this is simply a weighted average of the prior mean m and the observation w, with the weights being the prior precision and the precision of W respectively; thus the greater the prior precision the more weight is given to the prior mean, while the greater the precision of the observation the more weight is given to the observation. Clearly this is sensible. Secondly, the posterior precision: this is simply the sum of the prior precision and the precision of the observation; in particular, therefore, the posterior precision is larger than the prior precision – or, in other words, the posterior variance is smaller than the prior variance.

Thirdly, the posterior distribution itself: it is a normal distribution just like the prior distribution; in other words, the prior and posterior distributions are of the same form. Obviously, this is unlikely to happen in all applications of Bayes' theorem: it clearly depends upon the form taken by the likelihood function. When it *does* happen, the sampling distribution (which gives rise to the likelihood function) is said to have come from a family of distributions *conjugate* to the family used to model the prior and posterior distributions. In our illustrative example above, the normal distribution was shown to be conjugate to itself (a rare phenomenon). We do not have space here to go into further details or to give more examples; the reader interested in pursuing these issues is referred to Degroot (1970), particularly Chapter 9.

One final point about our example above: it can be straight-forwardly extended to the case of several observations. If we denote the observations by $w_1, \ldots, w_n$, and if the prior distribution of X is normal with mean m and precision p, then, as we have seen above, the posterior distribution of X after w_1 has been observed is normal with mean $(pm + rw_1)/(p + r)$ and precision $(p + r)$. Before w_2 is observed this posterior becomes the new prior; using again the result derived above, it follows that the new posterior after w_2 has been observed is normal with mean

$$\{(p + r)[(pm + rw_1)/(p + r)] + rw_2\}/[(p + r) + r]$$

and precision $(p + r) + r$. Or, simplifying, the posterior distribution after w_2 has been observed is normal with mean

$$(pm + 2r\bar{w}_2)/(p + 2r)$$

and precision $p + 2r$, where $\bar{w}_2 = (w_1 + w_2)/2$. Extending this argument, it follows immediately that after n observations $w_1, \ldots, w_n$, the posterior distribution of X is normal with mean

$$(pm + nr\bar{w}_n)/(p + nr)$$

and precision $p + nr$, where $\bar{w}_n = (w_1 + \ldots + w_n)/n$. Moreover, it clearly does not matter in what order the observations occur, nor the way that the posterior distribution is calculated. (That is, whether the information is considered as the *block* of data $(w_1, \ldots, w_n)$, or whether, as above, the information is considered as the *sequence* of observations $w_1, \ldots, w_n$.)

6.3 LEARNING IN AN OTHERWISE PASSIVE SITUATION

In this section, we examine how learning is incorporated into situations which, in all other respects, are of the passive type. That is, we return to the material of Chapter 4, and investigate the role of learning in such problems. Of particular interest is the value of information in the decision-making process. For reasons of expositional simplicity, we confine attention to static problems, though the basic ideas generalise straightforwardly to dynamic problems.

Analytical Tools and Techniques

Consider, therefore, a problem in which the decision-maker must decide on the value of a control variable Y in order to maximise expected utility, which is a function of both Y and X, a random variable outwith the control of the decision-maker. We now suppose, however, that the decision-maker has the option, prior to choosing Y and observing X, of obtaining some information which may be of value in predicting X. Naturally, we assume that the information is costly, so that the potential benefit of the information is not without its cost. We investigate two questions: first, how should the information, if obtained, be optimally used? Second, in the light of the answer to this question, is the information likely to be of (net) value?

In Hey (1979a), we considered a particular example of this type of problem: one in which *perfect* information was available (at a cost). Perfect information is information which specifies exactly which value of X is going to occur; given such perfect information the decision-maker can always make the best (*ex post*) decision. It may be useful to begin with this example, so that we have a reference point for our subsequent discussion on the value of less-than-perfect information.

We continue to work with continuous distributions, so that the version of Bayes' theorem given in (6.13) remains relevant. We continue to denote the prior pdf of X by $f(x)$; this is the pdf which describes the subjective assessment of the decision-maker of the distribution of X *before* the information becomes available. In the absence of information, the optimal choice of Y is the value which maximises

$$EU(X, Y) = \int U(x, Y)f(x)\, dx \qquad (6.16)$$

(where the integration is from $-\infty$ to $+\infty$).

The optimal value, denoted by y^*, satisfies (cf. Section 4.2)

$$EU_Y(X, y^*) = \int U_Y(x, y^*)f(x)\, dx = 0. \qquad (6.17)$$

(As in Chapter 4 we assume that $U_{YY} < 0$ everywhere, so the second-order condition is satisfied.)

If perfect information (to the effect that the variable X *will* take the value x) is available, then the decision-maker would simply choose the value of Y which maximises $U(x, Y)$ in a certain world; denoting this value by y_x^*, we have

$$U_Y(x, y_x^*) = 0, \qquad (6.18)$$

with the second-order condition being satisfied by assumption. The maximum level of utility is then $U(x, y_x^*)$. Now, consider the position as viewed from *before* the perfect information is available; since the distribution of X is given by its pdf $f(x)$, it follows that the expected value of the maximum level of utility is:

$$\int U(x, y_x^*) f(x)\,dx. \qquad (6.19)$$

Hence, the expected value of perfect information is the difference between (6.19) and the value of (6.16) with Y put equal to y^*; that is, the expected increase in utility is

$$\int [U(x, y_x^*) - U(x, y^*)] f(x)\,dx \qquad (6.20)$$

Since by definition of y_x^*, $U(x, y_x^*) \geqslant U(x, y)$ for all y (with, except in certain trivial cases, a strict inequality for some y), it follows that (6.20) is strictly positive. If the cost of perfect information is a constant deduction from utility, then the decision whether to acquire it hinges on whether the cost is less than the expression in (6.20). Clearly this depends upon the particular case in hand.

Consider now the case of less-than-perfect information. To be specific, suppose the decision-maker has the option of observing the variable W, whose value depends stochastically rather than deterministically on the value of X. The variable W can be either a scalar (a single observation) or a vector (several observations); here we consider the scalar case, though the vector case is a straightforward generalisation. After $W = w$ has been observed, the posterior distribution of X is $f(x|w)$. The optimal choice of Y, following this information, is denoted by y_w^*, and is the value which maximises

$$E[U(X, Y)|w] = \int U(x, Y) f(x|w)\,dx. \qquad (6.21)$$

Thus, y_w^* is given by

$$E[U_Y(X, y_w^*)|w] = \int U_Y(x, y_w^*)f(x|w)\,dx = 0 \qquad (6.22)$$

(and the second-order condition remains satisfied by assumption). The maximum expected utility given w is $E[U(X, y_w^*)|w]$; as viewed from *before* W is observed, this has expectation

$$\int E[U(X, y_w^*)|w]\,e(w)\,dw, \qquad (6.23)$$

where, as in Section 6.2, we denote the pdf of W by $e(w)$. Combining (6.21) with (6.23), we find that as viewed from *before* W is observed, the expected maximum expected utility is given by

$$\int_{w=-\infty}^{\infty} \int_{x=-\infty}^{\infty} U(x, y_w^*)f(x|w)\,e(w)\,dw\,dx,$$

or using Bayes' theorem (6.12) by

$$\int_{w=-\infty}^{\infty} \int_{x=-\infty}^{\infty} U(x, y_w^*)\,e(w|x)\,f(x)\,dw\,dx.$$

Hence the expected gain in utility from observing W is

$$\int_{x=-\infty}^{\infty} \left\{ \int_{w=-\infty}^{\infty} [U(x, y_w^*) - U(x, y^*)]\,e(w|x)\,dw \right\} f(x)\,dx. \qquad (6.24)$$

This must be non-negative, though this property is not immediately obvious.

Clearly, the value of (6.24) and thus whether the benefit of the information outweighs its cost depends crucially on the particular problem in hand. At this level of generality, concrete results are difficult to obtain. Let us instead look at a specific example.

Suppose that the utility function is given by

$$U(X, Y) = a - b\,\exp(-RXY),$$

which is (see Section 3.3) a constant absolute risk aversion utility function. Further, suppose that prior to observing any information X is normal with mean m and precision p. Using standard results,[5] expected utility is given by

$$EU(X, Y) = a - b \exp [-RYm + \tfrac{1}{2}R^2Y^2/p];$$

this is maximised when the contents of the square bracket are minimised. Thus y^* is given by

$$y^* = pm/R, \qquad (6.25)$$

and so

$$EU(X, y^*) = a - b \exp (-m^2p/2). \qquad (6.26)$$

Now, suppose as in Section 6.2 that observations on a random variable W are available, and that W is normal with mean X and precision r. If just one observation is taken, then the posterior distribution of X is normal with mean $(pm + rw)/(p + r)$ and precision $(p + r)$. In the light of the information, the optimal value of Y, denoted by y_w^*, is given by:

$$y_w^* = (pm + rw)/R. \qquad (6.27)$$

Note that (6.27) is simply (6.25) with m and p 'updated' to $(pm + rw)/(p + r)$ and $(p + r)$ respectively. Hence, the maximum expected utility after observing w is

$$EU(X, y_w^*) = a - b \exp [-(pm + rw)^2/2(p + r)]. \qquad (6.28)$$

Again note that (6.28) is simply (6.26) with m and p 'updated'. It remains to calculate the expected value of (6.28) as viewed from before W is observed. We know that the marginal distribution of W is normal with mean m and precision[6] $pr/(p + r)$. Using standard results[7] it therefore follows that

$$E[EU(X, y_w^*)|w] = a - b\sqrt{p/(p + r)} \exp (-m^2p/2) \qquad (6.29)$$

where the first expectation is with respect to W and the second with respect to X (conditional on W). The expected value of information is thus

$$b \exp\left(- m^2 p/2\right)[1 - \sqrt{p/(p + r)}]. \qquad (6.30)$$

From this it follows that the information is of greater value, the higher is b, the smaller is m, the smaller is the prior precision p and the higher is the ratio r/p (the precision of the information relative to the precision of the prior); all these accord with intuition.

The expression in (6.30) relates to the expected value of a single observation. By applying the argument at the end of Section 6.2 it follows that the expected value of n observations is given by

$$b \exp\left(- m^2 p/2\right)[1 - \sqrt{p/(p + nr)}]. \qquad (6.31)$$

As inspection of this shows, there are diminishing returns to information. In practice, if the cost per observation was independent of the way in which observations were collected, a sequential procedure should be followed: in a sequential procedure the value of m in (6.30) would vary after each observation depending upon the value of the observation.

Before concluding this section, we note the obvious point that perfect information is of greater value than less-than-perfect information: this is apparent from (6.20) and (6.24). If the perfect information also costs more, however, it remains an open question as to which is the 'better buy'.

6.4   LEARNING IN ACTIVE SITUATIONS

This section investigates learning in search models; it therefore incorporates adaptive behaviour into the type of active problem discussed in Chapter 5. In that chapter it was assumed that the distribution (or distributions) from which the searcher was taking observations was either objectively known or its subjective assessment remained fixed throughout the search process. We now investigate problems in which the distribution is unknown; thus there is scope for learning about the distribution as the search procedure continues.

For simplicity we confine our attention to the simplest type of search problem, though our methods generalise to more complicated types. We begin our discussion with the infinite horizon model as discussed in Section 5.3. The reader will recall that in that model the searcher obtains at most one observation (with probability q) in any one period from the distribution $F(.)$ of the random variable X. Whilst searching, the reward is U_0 per period; when search is terminated the reward per period thereafter is the maximum value of $U(X)$ observed during the search process. It is assumed that U is strictly increasing everywhere, and that the searcher wishes to maximise total expected discounted rewards, where future rewards are discounted at the constant rate ρ. In keeping with the rest of the material in this chapter, we assume that X is a continuous random variable, so that its distribution can be represented either by $F(.)$ or by its pdf $f(.)$. If this distribution is unknown, there are two possible sources of information about it: first, observations on some external (scalar or vector) variable W; second, observations on X itself. The analysis of the first type of information follows exactly the same line of argument as that used in Section 6.3; further discussion is unnecessary. This section, therefore, concentrates on the second source – observations on X itself. Of course, such observations are generated during the search process itself: indeed, these observations fulfil a dual role – they are both of potential direct value in themselves and of indirect value in providing information about the distribution from which they come.

It will be recalled from Section 5.3 that the optimal strategy when $f(.)$ is known is to keep on searching until a value of X greater than or equal to x^* is found where $x^* = U^{-1}[V(1 - \rho)]$, and where V is the total expected discounted reward starting from a position in which the maximum value of X is less than x^*. Alternatively, if $V(z)$ denotes the *maximum* total expected discounted reward as viewed from a position in which the maximum value of X equals z, then

$$V(z) = \begin{cases} U(z)/(1 - \rho) & z \geqslant x^* \\ V & z < x^*. \end{cases} \qquad (6.32)$$

Now x^* is given by $U(x^*)/(1 - \rho) = V$. Using the value of V from (5.50), we can write this condition as

$$U(x^*)/(1 - \rho) = U_0 + \rho W(z) \qquad (6.33)$$

where

$$W(z) = [(1 - q) + qF(z)]V(z) + \int_z^\infty V(x) f(x) \, dx. \qquad (6.34)$$

Equation (6.33) is our familiar indifference condition: the left hand side is the lifetime reward from stopping; the right hand side is the expected reward from searching once more and then behaving optimally – note that $W(z)$ is simply the expected value of $V(.)$ as viewed from before the extra search is carried out.

We note that in this no-learning case $W(z)$ has a particularly simple form: combining (6.32) and (6.34) we find that, in fact, $W(z)$ has a constant value, independent of z, given by

$$W = [(1 - q) + qF(x^*)]V + \int_{x^*}^{\infty} [U(x)/(1 - \rho)] \, f(x) \, dx.$$

Notwithstanding this feature we emphasise that the crucial result is that $V(z)$ is the maximum of $U(z)/(1 - \rho)$ and $U_0 + \rho W(z)$, and that the optimal strategy is to stop if the first is larger, and to continue if the second is larger. We shall exploit this feature in the learning case.

In the no-learning case, the current value of z (the maximum value of X so far obtained) is the only variable that the searcher needs to monitor, the optimal strategy depends solely and simply upon z. No other information is necessary. This is because the only thing that changes *is z*; given a particular value of z the future always looks the same whatever date it is – nothing else changes. This is because we have assumed an infinite horizon world with constant discounting and with a *known distribution*. In our learning case, however, something does change – namely, the assessment by the individual of the distribution. Thus, in addition to z, the optimal strategy in the learning case depends upon the current assessment of the probability distribution.

Let us be more specific. Suppose that the subjective assessments of the distributions are all from the same family; the assessment at any one time thus depends upon the current values of the *parameters* of the distribution. (For example, the searcher may know that the distribution is normal, and describes his assessment by the mean and variance as currently estimated.) Using our terminology of Section 6.2, the observations on the variable are from a distribution *conjugate* to the family of distributions used to model the subjective assessment.

Let the parameters describing the subjective assessment be denoted by the vector **a**. As observations are generated, the value of **a** will change. Let $\mathbf{a}(x)$ denote the posterior values of the parameters given observation x, conditional on the prior values being **a**. The precise connection between $a(x)$ and a will, of course, depend upon the family of distributions under consideration, and can be found using Bayes' theorem; we will give an example in due course. We now extend the notation used for our no-learning case as follows. Let $V(z; a)$ denote the *maximum* total expected discounted reward as viewed from a position in which the maximum value of X equals z, and in which the current parameters are a. Furthermore, let $W(z; a)$ denote the expected value of this as viewed from before the final search is carried out; we have (cf. (6.34)):

$$W(z; a) = (1 - q) V(z; a) + q \int_{-\infty}^{z} V[z; a(x)] \, f(x \,|\, a) \, dx$$

$$+ q \int_{z}^{\infty} V[x; a(x)] \, f(x \,|\, a) \, dx. \tag{6.35}$$

On the right hand side of this, the first term represents the case of no observation (in which case z remains the maximum, and a the current assessment), the second term represents an observation less than z and the third term an observation greater than z (in the former z remains the maximum, in the latter the new x becomes z, in both $a(x)$ becomes the current assessment). Of course, $f(x \,|\, a)$ denotes the current assessment of the pdf of X.

Furthermore, $V(z; a)$ is the maximum value of $U(z)/(1 - \rho)$ and $U_0 + \rho W(z; a)$ and the optimal strategy is to stop if the first is larger, and to continue if the second is larger. *If* there is a unique solution to the equation

$$U[x^*(a)]/(1 - \rho) = U_0 + \rho W[x^*(a); a], \tag{6.36}$$

then the value $x^*(a)$ will be the unique reservation value; we emphasise that this will be a function of a by our choice of notation. In principle, therefore, the problem is solved. The searcher simply needs to calculate the functions $W(z; a)$ and $V(z; a)$ (as described above) for all values of z and a. In practice, however, this might be rather tedious!

Let us give a concrete example. This will be based on the illustration of Bayes' theorem given earlier in Section 6.2. Despite the risk of confusion, however, we will interchange the names of the variables so as to be consistent with the notation of this section. Suppose, therefore, that the searcher knows that the distribution of

X is normal with precision r, and with unknown mean W. The searcher's view of W is also normal with mean m and precision p; these parameters changing as more evidence accumulates. The combination of these conditions implies a *marginal* distribution of X which is normal with mean m and precision $pr/(p + r)$; again these parameters will change as evidence accumulates. Indeed, exploiting our previous results of Section 6.2, and using the notation of this section, it follows that if

$$\mathbf{a} = \{m, pr/(p + r)\}$$

then

$$\mathbf{a}(x) = \{(pm + rx)/(p + r),\ (p + r)r/(p + 2r)\}.$$

$$\left.\begin{array}{c}\\ \\ \\ \\ \end{array}\right\} \quad (6.37)$$

Thus $W(\,.\,;\,.\,)$ and $V(\,.\,;\,.\,)$ are given by (from (6.35))

$$W(z; \mathbf{a}) = (1 - q)V(z; \mathbf{a}) + q\,\frac{pr}{\sqrt{2\pi}(p + r)}\int_{-\infty}^{\infty} \max_{x,z} V[\,.\,; \mathbf{a}(x)]$$

$$\times \exp\left[-\frac{pr(x - m)^2}{2(p + r)}\right]\mathrm{d}x \qquad (6.38)$$

and

$$V(z; \mathbf{a}) = \max\{U(z)/(1 - \rho);\ U_0 + \rho W(z; \mathbf{a})\}. \qquad (6.39)$$

In principle the solution is now complete; all that remains is to solve (6.37), (6.38) and (6.39) for $W(\,.\,;\,.\,)$ and $V(\,.\,;\,.\,)$. We leave this rather gruesome task to the interested reader! It should be noted, however, that some straightforward comparative statics implications are obtainable.

Although the discussion above has been confined to the infinite horizon problem, it should be clear that the basic method is applicable to finite horizon problems (with or without recall). In essence, the only complication introduced by the learning process is the incorporation of the current value of the parameter vector into the V and W functions; these functions, it should be remembered, not only describe the expected lifetime reward of the searcher, but also dictate his optimal strategy. We have therefore demonstrated the rather obvious point that the current assessment of the individual of the relevant distributions affects his optimal strategy. Perhaps not so obvious is the fact that the learning opportunity itself affects the optimal strategy. The reader interested in pursuing this point further should consult Kohn and Shavell (1974) who derive some interesting propositions about the comparative intensity of search in adaptive and non-adaptive situations.

6.5 AN ALTERNATIVE THEORY OF LEARNING

Although Bayes' theorem represents an intellectually satisfying way of describing learning processes and the incorporation of information into subjective assessments of uncertain phenomena, there is some evidence to suggest that it is not particularly satisfying as a description of how people actually behave. Consequently, a number of psychologists, and indeed some economists, have proposed alternative theories of learning which are claimed to be better descriptors of actual behaviour. We will examine just one of these alternatives here – one that has found some popularity in economic theories of behaviour under uncertainty.

Rather than give a general treatment, we simply illustrate this alternative approach by means of a simple example. In this example, the decision-maker is told that in each of a succession of time-periods, either an event A happens, or it does not. (The event could be a light turning on, or food given or an electric shock administered, or employment offered, or whatever.) The decision-maker is also told that A happens a certain proportion (π) of the time, and $\bar{A}$ the remainder, though he is *not* informed of the actual value of π. Also events in different time-periods are independent. The task of the decision-maker is to *predict* in each time-period whether A will happen or not. The reward for a correct prediction (predicting A when A happens, or $\bar{A}$ when $\bar{A}$ happens) is one unit of money; the reward for an incorrect prediction (predicting A when $\bar{A}$ happens, or $\bar{A}$ when A happens) is zero. The objective is to choose a strategy which maximises the total expected reward (discounted or not as appropriate).

To a Bayesian, the problem is trivial – particularly since the choice of prediction does not affect the amount of information the decision-maker receives. This property implies that each prediction can be considered in isolation; that is, the optimal prediction in any time period is that which maximises the expected reward in *that period*. To find this, consider the alternatives: if he predicts A, his expected reward will be $1(E\pi) + 0(1 - E\pi) = E\pi$; if he predicts $\bar{A}$

his expected reward will be $0(E\pi) + 1(1 - E\pi) = 1 - E\pi$; where $E\pi$ denotes his current expectation as to the true (but unknown) value of π. Now $E\pi \gtreqqless 1 - E\pi$ according as $E\pi \gtreqqless \frac{1}{2}$; thus his optimal strategy is simply to predict the event which he currently regards as the most likely. Moreover, since samples from the Bernoulli distribution (which is what, in effect, he is observing) are conjugate to the Beta family of probability distributions, the Beta distribution is the obvious way to characterise the beliefs of the decision-maker about π. Two parameters, α and β, characterise the Beta distribution; they are updated to $(\alpha + 1)$ and β if A occurs, and to α and $(\beta + 1)$ if $\bar{A}$ occurs.[8] At any stage, the expected value of π is given by $\alpha/(\alpha + \beta)$. Clearly, using the law of large numbers, if this updating scheme is used the ratio $\alpha/(\alpha + \beta)$ will eventually converge to the true value of π. Thus, the Bayesian decision-maker will eventually end up predicting all the time the event that happens most of the time; he will therefore be actually obtaining the maximum reward.

Apparently some people do not behave like this. Indeed, according to Bush and Mosteller (1955), Cross (1973), and others, actual behaviour is as follows. At time t, the decision-maker predicts A with probability p_t (and therefore predicts $\bar{A}$ with probability $1 - p_t$); this probability is updated through time by the scheme:

$$p_{t+1} = \begin{cases} p_t + \theta(1 - p_t) & \text{if } A \text{ occurred at time } t \\ (1 - \theta)p_t & \text{if } \bar{A} \text{ occurred at time } t \end{cases} \quad (6.40)$$

where θ is some number between zero and one.

In this case, the law of larger numbers implies that p_t will eventually equal π. Thus, the decision-maker ends up predicting A the same proportion of the time that A actually occurs. But, of course, the predictions do not match: indeed, the average number of correct predictions will converge to $\pi^2 + (1 - \pi)^2$ which is less than $\max(\pi, 1 - \pi)$, the average number of correct predictions using the Bayesian approach. Nevertheless, despite the clear sub-optimality of the scheme described in (6.40), it seems that it does describe some individuals' behaviour. The reader is encouraged to refer to the reference given above for further details.

6.6 CONCLUSIONS

There are two apparent problems with the Bayesian approach to learning. The first is that discussed in the section above; this relates to the question of whether people actually behave in a Bayesian fashion. If they do not, but if they nevertheless behave in a consistent fashion, then the theorist should be able to describe and predict their behaviour; possibly this is where research efforts should be currently concentrated. On the other hand, if people do not behave in a Bayesian fashion, and additionally behave in an inconsistent manner, it is not clear what role economic theory has to play.

The second problem with the Bayesian approach is more fundamental. In any specific example, the decision-maker must clearly distinguish between things he does know and things he does not (and is therefore going to learn about). Moreover, there must be some things in the former category. That is, there must be some aspects of the world that the decision-maker takes as given. The Bayesian approach requires some starting point – it cannot function with nothing being given. (For example, it could be taken as given that distributions are normal, or that all observations will lie in a given finite range.) The question then arises; how does the decision-maker know that what he takes as given is, in fact, true? Indeed, once we have entertained the idea that the 'given' may possibly turn out not to be true, then an even more worrying question arises: what happens if some evidence is generated which suggests that the 'given' is, in fact, not true? (For example, suppose having taken as given a normality assumption, a set of clearly non-normal observations are generated? Or worse, suppose having taken as given that observations will lie in the range 0 to 100, say, an observation equal to 2000 is obtained?) In other words, what happens if the decision-maker is *surprised*? It seems to us that the Bayesian approach rules out the possibility of surprise, and, therefore, that it has no advice to offer to the decision-maker if he does get surprised. This seems a rather alarming deficiency. Perhaps economists ought to take more heed of the works of Shackle.

PART III

MICROECONOMIC THEMES AND THEORIES

7 HOUSEHOLDS

7.1 INTRODUCTION

This chapter applies the general techniques developed in Part II of this book to the analysis of the behaviour of individuals or households (we shall use these terms interchangeably) when operating under conditions of uncertainty. In broad outline, the chapter is structured along the lines of the final three chapters of Part II: we begin by looking at problems that are of the passive type; then move on to problems of the active type; and (almost) finally examine problems of the adaptive type.

The examination of problems of the passive type is the concern of Section 7.2. One of the most important problems in this category is the choice of consumption, or savings, strategy of the household when there is uncertainty either about the income stream or about the rate of return on savings of the household. We also investigate the labour supply decision of the individual when faced with wage rate, or exogenous income, uncertainty. Other examples in this passive category include insurance, signalling, portfolio selection, the evaluation of human life, and the problem of optimal tax evasion: a mixed category indeed!

Section 7.3 explores problems of the active type. Naturally, these are mainly search problems of one form or another. The most important are job search models (where the individual is searching over wage offers) and consumer search models (where prices and qualities are the objects of search); however, other interesting problems fall into this category – not least the decision as to whether to submit an insurance claim when there is a 'no claims bonus' clause in the contract.

Adaptive behaviour is the concern of Section 7.4. Of particular importance in this section is the acquisition of information about quality. We also examine search behaviour when the distribution (of prices or wages or whatever) is initially unknown. Finally, Section 7.5 offers some brief comments in conclusion.

7.2   CONSUMPTION, LABOUR SUPPLY AND OTHER PASSIVE PROBLEMS

We begin our study of household problems of the passive type with an examination of the choice of the optimal savings strategy when faced with (exogenous) uncertainty about income or about the rate of return on savings. Depending upon the focus of interest, the problem can be formulated either in the static form described in Sections 4.2 and 4.3 or in the dynamic form described in Section 4.4. The former is appropriate if the problem of the household is expressed in a two-period (the present and the future) framework; the latter is relevant if a multi-period (finite, infinite or random horizon) framework is employed. We begin with the former.

Consider then a two-period model, in which the two periods (indexed by 1 and 2 respectively) together cover the lifetime of the household; for convenience they can be thought of as the present and the future. Let C_1 and C_2 denote consumption, and Y_1 and Y_2 income, in the two periods, and let r denote one plus the rate of return on savings between the two periods. Suppose that lifetime utility is a function solely of C_1 and C_2: denote it by $u(C_1, C_2)$, and suppose that it is strictly increasing in both arguments. In our first formulation we consider the case of *pure income risk*; in this case, there is (at the time that a decision on C_1 must be taken) uncertainty about the future value of Y_2; however, the values of Y_1 and r *are* known. Moreover, the household knows the pdf of Y_2, or alternatively it has a fixed subjective assessment of its pdf. Uncertainty about Y_2 is resolved before the decision on C_2 is taken. This last feature implies that the following condition will (optimally) hold:

$$C_2 = Y_2 + r(Y_1 - C_1). \qquad (7.1)$$

The only remaining decision for the household is the choice of C_1. As emphasised above, this is taken before the value of Y_2 is known. In terms of the material of Chapter 4, the problem is formally equivalent to that discussed in Sections 4.2 and 4.3: the random variable X of those sections in the Y_2 of this, and the control variable Y of those sections is the C_1 of this. We have

$$X \equiv Y_2$$
$$Y \equiv C_1$$

and

$$U(X, Y) \equiv u[Y, X + r(Y_1 - Y)] = u(C_1, C_2). \qquad (7.2)$$

Note the crucial differences between Y_1, Y_2 and Y, and between $U(.,.)$ and $u(.,.)$. The problem of the household is to choose Y so as to maximise the expected value of $U(X, Y)$ where the expectation is taken with respect to the distribution of X. In order to solve the problem we make use of the material of Sections 4.2 and 4.3. From (4.9) and (4.16) we see that under both certainty and uncertainty the sign of U_{XY} is crucial in determining the comparative static effect on Y of an 'increase in X' (strictly, a 'shift in the distribution of X' under uncertainty). Probably the most usual case under certainty is for an increase in future income (Y_2) to increase present consumption (C_1); in which case $U_{XY} > 0$ (see (4.9)). Let us assume this holds everywhere. Examination of (7.2) shows that this implies[1]

$$u_{12} - ru_{22} > 0 \qquad\qquad (7.3)$$

everywhere. It immediately follows that under this condition, the effect, in an uncertain world, of a rightward shift of the Y_2 (or X) distribution is to increase C_1 (or Y). This is equivalent to a result derived in Sandmo (1970) and discussed in Hey (1979a, pp. 72–4); the same condition guarantees that under certainty an increase in Y_1 leads to an increase in C_1.

The effect of a Rothschild–Stiglitz increase in risk on the optimal choice of Y depends (as was shown in Section 4.2) on whether U_Y is concave or convex in X, or alternatively on whether U_{XXY} is negative or positive everywhere. Now, from (7.2) we have that

$$U_{XXY} = u_{122} - ru_{222},$$

and hence a sufficient condition for a Rothschild–Stiglitz increase in risk to increase (decrease) first-period consumption, and thus to decrease (increase) intra-period saving is that

$$u_{122} > (<) ru_{222} \qquad\qquad (7.4)$$

everywhere. This simple condition facilitates the derivation of the comparative static effect for a variety of different utility functions. One obvious example is when the function u is separable in its two arguments; in this case u_{122} is zero, and thus the sign of u_{222} determines the effect. In general one would expect that u_{222} would be positive (for otherwise the Arrow–Pratt index of absolute risk aversion with respect to C_2 would be increasing in C_2); if so, the result above implies that a *Rothschild–Stiglitz increase in income risk will decrease first-period consumption and increase saving.* As the discussion above clearly indicates, however, the opposite effect cannot be ruled out. (It might be of interest to note that Sandmo (1970) derived the italicised result above with respect to a *Sandmo* increase in risk for a non-separable utility function for which the Arrow–Pratt index of absolute risk aversion with respect to C_2 was decreasing in C_2 and increasing in C_1.)

The above discussion was concerned with the case of pure income risk; let us now turn to the case of pure capital risk. Here Y_1 and Y_2 are known with certainty, but r is unknown at the time a decision on C_1 has to be made. In terms of our notation of Section 4.2, the random variable is now r and the control variable remains C_1; thus

$$\left. \begin{array}{c} X \equiv r \\[2mm] Y \equiv C_1 \\[6mm] \text{and} \\[4mm] U(X, Y) = u\,[Y, Y_2 + X(Y_1 - Y)] = u(C_1, C_2) \end{array} \right\} \tag{7.5}$$

We note that $U_{XY} = (Y_1 - Y)(u_{12} - Xu_{22})$. Thus, if (7.3) holds and if, in addition $Y_1 - Y > 0$, that is some first-period income is saved, then (a) under certainty an increase in X (r) leads to an increase in $Y\,(C_1)$, and (b) under uncertainty a rightward shift of the distribution of X (r) leads to an increase in Y (C_1); if, on the other hand $Y_1 - Y < 0$, that is, money is borrowed between the two periods, then the opposite comparative static effects hold. Moreover, since $U_{XXY} = (Y_1 - Y)^2(u_{122} - Xu_{222})$, then a sufficient condition for a Rothschild–Stiglitz increase in rate of return risk to increase (decrease) first-period consumption is that

$$u_{122} > (<) Xu_{222}$$

everywhere. Thus, once again, if utility is separable and absolute risk aversion (with respect to C_2) is non-increasing in C_2, then an increase in risk decreases consumption and increases savings. We leave other inferences to the reader; references to previous explorations of this problem are given in Hey (1979a, p. 75).

While the analysis of the two-period consumption problem is greatly facilitated by the general results of Section 4.2, the material in Section 4.4 sheds considerable light on the multi-period problem. We begin, for simplicity, with an infinite horizon problem and make the assumptions necessary for the solution to be stationary. Specifically, we suppose that the distributions of the relevant random variables are the same in every time period (and independent of each other). We consider, in turn, the two cases discussed above – pure-income risk and pure rate-of-return risk. In a pure income-risk model, the incomes in the various periods are uncertain; consumption decisions have to be taken in ignorance of future income values. The precise details of the relative timing of decision and resolution (of uncertainty) depend upon the particular application under consideration; here we give an example which enables us to exploit directly the material of Section 4.4. To be specific, we assume that consumption in any time period must be chosen *before* income in that time period is known. Moreover, to avoid confusion, we tie our notation here to that used in Section 4.4. Thus, X_t and Y_t denote respectively income and consumption in period t, and our 'linking variable' Z_t denotes wealth at the end of period t. Hence

$$Z_{t+1} = r(X_t - Y_t + Z_t) \qquad (7.6)$$

where r is one plus the (constant) rate of return on savings. Note that (7.6) is a specific form of the function h introduced in (4.32); that is,

$$h(X_t, Y_t, Z_t) = r(X_t - Y_t + Z_t). \qquad (7.7)$$

Further, we assume that the objective of the consumer is to devise a strategy which maximises expected discounted lifetime utility of consumption as given by (cf. (4.43)):

$$\sum_{t=1}^{\infty} \rho^{t-1} U(Y_t), \qquad (7.8)$$

where $U(\,.\,)$ is a time-independent utility function, and ρ is a constant discount rate.

The problem is now formulated in such a way that the material of Section 4.4 is directly applicable; we encourage the reader to refer back to that section for details. The optimal strategy in any period in which initial wealth is Z is to consume an amount Y^* given by $Y^* = Y^*(Z)$, where (from (4.46) and (4.47) using (7.7))

$$U'(Y^*) = r\rho E\{V'[r(X - Y^* + Z)]\} \qquad (7.9)$$

and

$$V(Z) = U(Y^*) + \rho E\{V[r(X - Y^* + Z)]\}. \qquad (7.10)$$

Now, if (7.10) is differentiated throughout with respect to Z, and if the resulting expression is simplified by using the optimality condition (7.9), we get

$$V'(Z) = r\rho E\{V'[r(X - Y^* + Z)]\} = U'(Y^*). \qquad (7.11)$$

The splendidly simple result has a familiar economic interpretation: the optimal strategy is such that the marginal utility of present consumption equals the marginal utility of wealth. Equations (7.9) and (7.11) can be combined to give a single equation for $Y^*(.)$:

$$U'[Y^*(Z)] = r\rho E[U'(Y^*\{r[X - Y^*(Z) + Z]\})]. \qquad (7.12)$$

A number of comparative statics results concerning the optimal strategy can be derived from this expression. Rather than investigate the general case (which is straightforward though tedious), however, we derive the specific form of $Y^*(.)$ for a particular case. Suppose that the utility function displays constant absolute risk aversion, that is, it is given by (see (3.13))

$$U(x) = a - b \exp(-Rx),$$

then it is a question of simple algebra to verify that the optimal strategy is given by

$$Y^*(Z) = \alpha + \beta Z \qquad (7.13)$$

where the parameters β and α are the solutions to

$$r(1 - \beta) = 1 \qquad (7.14)$$

and

$$r\rho E\{\exp[R(r - 1)(\alpha - X)]\} = 1. \qquad (7.15)$$

These results, which hold whatever the form of the distribution of X (as long as the expectation in (7.15) exists), have some interesting implications. For example, (7.14) implies that if the rate of interest is zero (that is, if r equals 1) then β should equal zero: hence the marginal propensity to consume out of wealth should be zero. Moreover, as r increases, then β also increases – in the limit, when r approaches infinity, β approaches unity. Thus, the marginal propensity to consume is an increasing function of the rate of interest. Some features of the solution depend upon the distribution of X; for example, if X is normally distributed with mean μ and variance σ^2, then (7.15) implies

$$\alpha = \mu - R(r-1)\,\sigma^2 - \log(r\rho)/[R(r-1)]. \tag{7.16}$$

Noting that β depends solely on r (from (7.14)), (7.16) shows that the consumption function shifts upwards in response to a rise in μ, a fall in σ^2 (for $r > 1$) and a decrease in R (for $r > 1$ and $r\rho < 1$); if $r\rho$ is greater than unity, then an increase in R could cause a downward shift in the function. Clearly the implications of (7.16) in particular, and (7.15) in general, depend crucially on whether $r\rho$ is greater or less than unity; this is a condition which has an obvious economic interpretation.

Let us now turn to examine the case of rate of return uncertainty. To keep our analysis simple we will assume that income is zero in every time period, though the consumer is endowed with some initial wealth. We continue to use Y_t to denote consumption in time t, and Z_t to denote wealth at the beginning of period t. However, we now let X_t denote one plus the rate of return (that which was denoted by r above) on end-of-period t savings. Thus,

$$Z_{t+1} = X_t(Z_t - Y_t). \tag{7.17}$$

In this case (7.17) is the appropriate specific form of the function h introduced in (4.32); that is

$$h(X_t, Y_t, Z_t) \equiv X_t(Z_t - Y_t). \tag{7.18}$$

The solution is, once again, given by (4.46) and (4.47) using the specific form (7.18). From these, we get

$$U'(Y^*) = \rho E\{V'[X(Z - Y^*)]\,X\} \tag{7.19}$$

and

$$V(Z) = U(Y^*) + \rho E\{V[X(Z - Y^*)]\}. \tag{7.20}$$

If (7.20) is differentiated throughout with respect to Z, and if the resulting expression is simplified using the optimality condition (7.19), we get

$$V'(Z) = \rho E\{V'[X(Z - Y^*)]\ X\} = U'(Y^*). \qquad (7.21)$$

This should be contrasted with (7.11), the analogous result for the pure income risk case; the interpretation is identical. Combining (7.19) and (7.21) gives the following equation for $Y^*(.)$:

$$U'(Y^*) = \rho E(U'\{Y^*[X(Z - Y^*)]\}\ X). \qquad (7.22)$$

This is the same expression as found by Levhari and Srinivasan (1969), and discussed in Hey (1979a, pp. 77–8). For general properties of the solution, the reader should consult Levhari and Srinivasan. Here we confine attention to a particular case: namely the case of a constant *relative* risk-aversion utility function $U(x) = a - bx^{-R+1}$ (see section 3.3). For this case it is straightforward to verify that the optimal strategy is given by

$$Y^*(Z) = \beta Z \qquad (7.23)$$

where the parameter β is given by

$$(1 - \beta)^R = \rho E(X^{1-R}) \qquad (7.24)$$

(as long as the distribution of X is such as to make β positive and less than unity). The comparative static implications of this result should be immediate; some discussion of them can be found in Hey (1979a, p. 78).

The material of Section 4.4 can also be used to derive the optimal strategy in a finite (or random) horizon world. We leave such derivations to the reader. However we note that in the finite (or random) horizon counterparts of the two models discussed above, the solution is of a similar form. In the case of pure income risk, the optimal consumption function for an individual with a constant absolute risk-averson utility function remains a linear function of wealth; and in the case of pure rate-of-return risk the optimal consumption for a constant relative risk-aversion utility function remains proportional to wealth. In both cases, however, the parameters of the functions change as the horizon approaches.

We now turn to a simpler passive problem: the supply of labour in an uncertain world. Two variants are considered – wage rate uncertainty and exogenous income uncertainty. First, some general notation. Consider a one-period problem in which utility is a function of labour supplied L, and total income (denoted by M to avoid confusion). Income is made up of wage income wL, where w is the wage rate, and exogenous income M_0; thus $M = wL + M_0$. The problem is to choose L so as to maximise expected utility $Eu(L, M)$. Consider first the case where the wage rate w is certain but M_0 is random. Using the notation of Chapter 4 (where X denotes the random variable and Y the control variable), we have

$$X \equiv M_0$$
$$Y \equiv L$$

and

$$U(X, Y) \equiv u(Y, wY + X) \equiv u(L, M). \tag{7.25}$$

Here

$$U_{XY} = u_{12} + w u_{22}$$

and

$$U_{XXY} = u_{122} + w u_{222}. \tag{7.26}$$

Signing the terms in (7.26) leads immediately to the usual comparative results.

Alternatively, if M_0 is certain but w is random, we have

$$X \equiv w$$
$$Y \equiv L$$

and

$$U(X, Y) \equiv u(Y, XY + M_0) \equiv u(L, M). \tag{7.27}$$

In this case, the comparative static effects are determined by the signs of

$$U_{XY} = u_{12} + X u_{22}$$

and

$$U_{XXY} = u_{122} + X u_{222}. \tag{7.28}$$

Note that (7.26) and (7.28) are, in fact, the same; this facilitates analysis. Further treatment of this problem can be found in Hey (1979a, Chapter 13), wherein references to the literature can also be found. A comprehensive analysis is given by Burdett and Mortensen (1978).

This essentially completes our analysis of household problems of the passive type. Brief though our treatment has necessarily been, we hope that we have provided sufficient evidence to convince the reader that the general methods of Chapter 4 have widespread applicability. Before we conclude this section, however, we mention several other problems of the passive type which the reader may find interesting to investigate further. The most obvious problem is that of *optimal insurance*. There are numerous studies of this problem, ranging from the relatively simple decision of whether to take out insurance with respect to a known risk with a given monetary value, to considerably more complicated decisions relating to the insurance of irreplaceable goods (including human life)in the presence of moral hazard. (Other problems connected with insurance, such as that of adverse selection, should more properly be considered as market problems.) A useful starting point is Arrow (1971), while Parkin and Wu (1972) and Ehrlich and Becker (1972) are also of considerable interest. More recent contributions include Cook and Graham (1977) and Mavromaras (1979) on irreplaceable goods, and Shavell (1979) on moral hazard. A related topic is the 'evaluation of human life'; here a useful survey is Linnerooth (1979) which examines several approaches including that based on Neumann–Morgenstern utility theory.

Neumann–Morgenstern utility theory has also been used (or abused or misused depending upon your point of view) to analyse the problem of *optimal tax evasion*. Early contributions to this topic include Allingham and Sandmo (1972), Kolm (1973), Singh (1973) and Srinivasan (1973), while more recent studies are provided by Nayak (1978) and Weiss (1976). It is to be hoped that such studies help governments to combat evasion rather than encourage previously law-abiding citizens to take evasive action!

Signalling and *portfolio selection* are two areas which have some passive and some active aspects. For the former a useful introduction is the book by Spence (1974), while an excellent recent treatment of the latter can be found in Levy and Sarnat (1977). Finally, we note that several examples of the passive type, and corresponding illustrations of how the methods of Chapter 4 may be used to investigate them, are presented in the pioneering works of Rothschild and Stiglitz (1971), and Diamond and Stiglitz (1974).

7.3 CONSUMER SEARCH, JOB SEARCH AND OTHER ACTIVE PROBLEMS

The main topics to be examined in this section are the two principle applications of search theory in economics – consumer search and job search; in the former, the consumer is searching over certain aspects of goods in order to determine the 'best buy', in the latter, the individual is searching over certain aspects of jobs in order to find the 'best employment'. Clearly the two problems have much in common. We examine them in turn.

The simplest model of consumer search assumes that there is just one uncertain dimension of goods over which the individual is searching; this dimension is usually taken to be the price. Consider, therefore, a very simple model in which the consumer wishes to buy one unit of some good which he knows is sold at a large number of different shops. (We assume that the good is homogeneous, so there are no complications arising from problems of quality perception; such complications will be considered in due course.) The individual does not know the actual prices charged by individual shops, however; these prices he must discover through search. We assume that it costs a constant amount c (>0) to find out for any particular shop the price it is charging for the good in question. (This cost could be considered as the cost of a telephone call plus the value of the time spent telephoning.) Finally, we assume that, although the searcher does not know individual prices, he does know the distribution[2] of prices, as represented by the distribution function $F(.)$. Because of the assumed homogeneity of the good, assuming for the time being that the individual is risk neutral, the problem of the individual is simply to devise a strategy which minimises the sum of the purchase price and search costs.[3]

The problem as described above is precisely of the type discussed in Section 5.2 – as the 'extension to the basic search model'; accordingly, we may turn to Section 5.2 for the solution. Clearly, minimising the sum of purchase price and search costs is equivalent to maximising the 'reward' net of search costs, where the 'reward' is the negative of the purchase price. Thus, if we denote price by X, the reward function of Section 5.2 is simply given by

$$U(X) = -X. \qquad (7.29)$$

This is precisely the example discussed between equations (5.21) and (5.22); from that discussion we see immediately that the optimal strategy is to keep on searching until a price less than the optimal *reservation price* x^* is obtained, where x^* is given by (5.22), that is by

$$\int_{-\infty}^{x^*} F(x)\, \mathrm{d}x = c. \qquad (7.30)$$

The solution to this equation is illustrated in Figure 7.1.

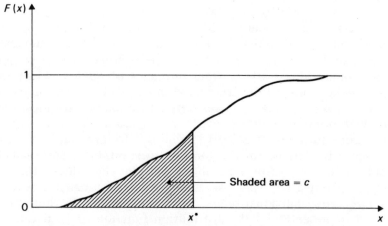

Figure 7.1   The determination of the optimal reservation price

It is clear from this figure that the reservation price is an increasing function of search cost: thus the more expensive it is to obtain price quotes, the less 'choosy' the individual will be. It is also clear that a bodily rightward shift of the price distribution by some amount will cause x^* to increase by the same amount: relative to the distribution search intensity remains unchanged. One further immediate implication of (7.30) is that a Rothschild–Stiglitz increase in risk causes a *decrease* in x^*: search intensity increases with the riskiness of the distribution. (To derive this result, use (3.21) in conjunction with (7.30), or, alternatively, reproduce the argument used in Section 5.2.)

The expected total expenditure (purchase price plus search costs) following this strategy can easily be derived. If we denote it by V, then V satisfies the equation (familiar in form from Chapter 5):

$$V = c + \int_{-\infty}^{x^*} x \, dF(x) + V[1 - F(x^*)].$$

This solves to give

$$V = \left[c + \int_{-\infty}^{x^*} x \, dF(x) \right] \Big/ F(x^*),$$

or, integrating by parts and using the optimality condition (7.30),

$$V = x^*. \tag{7.31}$$

This echoes a similar result (5.10) found in a somewhat different context; it states that the expected total cost (purchase price plus search costs) equals the optimal reservation price. This is an elegant and satisfying result (which, once again, reminds us of the 'indifference properties' of the optimal reservation value in search models). This result implies that all of the comparative static results derived above with respect to x^* hold equally well for V; in particular, the individual prefers to search in riskier distributions (since V is lower). Finally, the expected number of searches following the optimal strategy can be shown to be $1/F(R^*)$ (cf. (5.15)); thus, using (7.31), it follows that the expected purchase price is $x^* - c/F(R^*)$, an expression which could, of course, also be obtained directly.

Although the simple consumer search model discussed above provides a useful starting point for the analysis of the consumer search problem, its actual specification leaves several things to be desired. Its most glaring weakness is its assumption that the amount purchased is fixed, and thus independent of the purchase price and the costs incurred in search. This assumption implies both a zero elasticity of demand and a zero income elasticity of demand – rather an embarrassing combination! A step towards reality can be made by removing the zero price elasticity of demand assumption, but maintaining the zero income elasticity of demand assumption. Under these circumstances, the quantity purchased depends upon the purchase price, though not upon the search costs incurred. To be specific, the quantity purchased will be $q(X)$, where X is the purchase price, and $q(.)$ is the *demand function* of the individual for the good in question. The obvious measure of the 'reward' of the individual is his *consumer surplus* – the area to the left of the demand curve (when drawn with price on the vertical axis) above the purchase price. As is well known, with a zero income elasticity of demand this consumer surplus directly measures the income equivalent of being able to buy at the purchase price (rather than not buy at all). Thus, using $U(.)$ to denote the reward function, we have

$$U(X) = \int_X^\infty q(x) \, dx. \qquad (7.32)$$

From (7.32), we see that $U'(X) = -q(X)$, and so U is a monotonically decreasing function. Using the material of Section 5.2, it follows that the optimal strategy is to keep on searching until a price less than the reservation price x^* is obtained, where x^* is given by (5.21). Thus x^* satisfies

$$\int_{-\infty}^{x^*} F(x) \, q(x) \, dx = c. \qquad (7.33)$$

In the special case when $q(X) = 1$ for all X, (7.33) reduces to (7.30) – our previously obtained result; (7.33) is the natural extension of (7.30). Interestingly, all the comparative statics results that we derived above continue to hold in this more general case. In addition, we can obtain the further result that an increase in demand (an upward or rightward shift in the demand function) causes a decrease in x^*; thus search activity is more intense for goods with a larger demand. Proofs of these results, which are immediate consequences of (7.33), can be found in Hey (1979c).

The method described above can also be employed to analyse the further generalisation obtained by dropping the zero income elasticity of demand assumption. As Cigno (1979) elegantly demonstrates, the appropriate generalisation of (7.33) is

$$\int_{-\infty}^{x^*} \exp \left\{ - \int_{x^*}^x [\partial q(t)/\partial y] \, dt \right\} F(x) \, q(x) \, dx = c \qquad (7.34)$$

where y denotes income. Clearly (7.34) reduces to (7.33) when q is independent of y.

The neatness of the above results is partly a consequence of the assumed risk-neutrality of the searcher. If the searcher is not risk neutral, alternative methods of solution need to be employed. The obvious reward function in such cases would be the indirect utility function of the individual. To our knowledge, such an analysis has not yet been published.

In recent months, a number of extensions to the basic consumer search model have appeared; of particular interest is the extension to incorporate uncertainty over other dimensions of the good. The most obvious candidate is the *quality* of the good. Of course, if price and quality could be observed *simultaneously*, the basic model described above would be appropriate if suitably re-interpreted. For many goods, however, quality cannot be perceived simply by inspection – for such goods experience is necessary. This implies that quality remains uncertain until after purchase. This type of consumer search problem is of the multi-dimensional form discussed in Section 5.4, and the methods described there are appropriate for its solution. Models of this type have been analysed by Hey and McKenna (1981), Lippman and McCall (1980) and Wilde (1980). The first of these is of particular interest in that it shows that the optimal stopping set (with respect to prices) may not be a connected set: depending upon the form of the joint distribution of quality and price, a variety of possibilities exist. For example, 'buy cheap', 'buy medium', 'buy expensive' and various combinations of these could be the appropriate strategy.

We now examine the job search problem. Obviously the broad structure of this problem is identical to that of the consumer search problem, though the detailed specifications are somewhat different. The most immediate difference is that a job, once accepted, can usually be kept for several periods, while the purchase of a good does not commit the consumer to re-purchase it. Thus, the 'natural' formulation of a job search problem appears to be in terms of a dynamic specification.

We begin with the simplest such specification. Consider an individual, initially unemployed, who is searching for an acceptable job. We assume that search can take place only 'off-the-job', that is, while unemployed.[4] Jobs differ with respect to the wage associated with them, but are identical in all other respects. While searching, job offers are received randomly from a known distribution $F(.)$. We define the 'period' to be a sufficiently small time interval for the probability of getting two or more offers in any one period to be effectively zero. The probability of getting an offer in any one period is denoted by q; thus, $(1 - q)$ is the probability that no offer is received. Wage rates are denoted by the random variable X, and the individual evaluates X by means of his Neumann–Morgenstern utility function $U(.)$ which is assumed to be monotonically increasing everywhere. Future utilities are discounted at a constant rate ρ. Finally, we assume that the individual receives unemployment benefit while searching, and that this benefit (net of any search costs) yields utility U_0. The problem of the individual is to devise a strategy which maximises his total expected discounted lifetime utility.

As described, this job-search problem is identical to the general search problem analysed in the first part of Section 5.3; the material of that section is thus directly relevant. From (5.26), we see that the optimal strategy is to keep on searching until a job offer with a wage above the *optimal reservation wage* x^* is obtained, where x^* is given by

$$x^* = U^{-1}[V(1 - \rho)]. \tag{7.35}$$

To find x^*, we need to know V (the maximum expected discounted lifetime utility as viewed from the unemployed state); this is given by (5.29), repeated here:

$$V(1 - \rho) = U_0 + [\rho q/(1 - \rho)] \int_{x^*}^{\infty} U'(x)\,[1 - F(x)]\,\mathrm{d}x. \tag{7.36}$$

The comparative static properties of this basic search model have already been derived in Section 5.3. Interpreted in terms of the specific formulation of this section, they imply some intuitively satisfying predictions for the outcome of the job search process. First, an increase in q (the probability of getting a job-offer in any period) causes increases in V and in x^*; thus, the searcher gets better-off and accordingly becomes choosier about which offers he accepts. A similar consequence results from an increase in U_0; hence an increase in unemployment benefit, or in the evaluation the individual gives it, implies a more prolonged period of search. Thus, paradoxically perhaps, we get the result that a measure designed to soften the impact of unemployment actually causes an increase in the duration of unemployment. (Alternatively, one can view this result as providing a warning against the inference that a rise in unemployment *necessarily* implies a reduction in the welfare of society.) An increase in ρ will also lead the searcher to become more choosy (that is, to increase x^*); accordingly, since investment in search thereby increases, the per period value of the optimal strategy, $V(1 - \rho)$, rises.

Effects of changes in the distribution of wage offers can also be analysed. From (7.36) it is clear that a rightward shift of the distribution will increase x^*; however, if the individual is risk-averse (that is, if U' decreases with x), the rise in x^* will be somewhat smaller than the amount of the shift.[5] The effect of a Rothschild–Stiglitz increase in risk is ambiguous, though the effect of a Diamond–Stiglitz increase in risk (with respect to the reference individual U) can be determined. From Section 3.4, it can be seen that such an increase would increase the value of the integral on the right hand side of (7.36) *if x^* remained unchanged*. Thus, in order to restore equality x^* must rise; this, in turn, implies that V also rises. Once again, we get the result that greater dispersion makes the searcher better off, and leads to a greater search intensity.

The above analysis postulates an infinite horizon. As we have seen several times already in this book, this assumption, combined with the other assumptions which guarantee stationarity, considerably simplifies the task of deriving the solution. Sacrificed realism is the cost of this benefit, however. A step towards reality (while maintaining the simplicity associated with stationarity) is obtained by postulating a random horizon. Specifically, suppose that there exists a constant probability $(1 - \theta)$ that the individual will die at the end of a period given that he was alive at the beginning of it.[6] Then, as we saw in Section 4.4, all the above analysis remains valid as long as ρ is replaced everywhere by $\rho\theta$. Moreover, changes in life expectancy (through changes in θ) can be analysed using our previously derived results on the effects of changes in ρ.

A further step towards reality, which unfortunately destroys the stationarity property, is obtained by postulating a finite (and deterministic) horizon. If all the other assumptions of our basic job search model are retained, we obtain the model described in the second half of Section 5.3. The solution (yielding the optimal strategy of the searcher) is given by equations (5.39), (5.40) and (5.41). The most obvious difference between this and the solution to the infinite horizon problem is that the optimal reservation wage changes through time. To be specific, from (5.45) we see that it falls as the horizon approaches. We thus get the perfectly sensible result that the searcher gets less choosy as time passes, and as the horizon looms larger. Moreover, since the infinite horizon model can be considered as the limiting case of a finite horizon model as the horizon gets further and further away, it follows that the optimal reservation wage in the finite horizon model is always less than in its infinite horizon counterpart. In all other respects, however, the solutions to the two models are similar: in qualitative terms, the comparative static properties derived above for the infinite horizon model carry over to the finite horizon case.

The (deterministic) finite horizon model can also be adapted to incorporate the possibility of death prior to the horizon. Moreover, a variable discount rate can also be introduced. Suppose ρ_t is the discount factor, applied in period t, to utility in period $(t+1)$; thus, the discounted value in period 1 of one unit of utility in period t is $\rho_2\rho_2 \ldots \rho_t$. (If the discount factor were constant at ρ, then this discounted value would simply be the familiar ρ^{t-1}.) Also, let $(1 - \theta_t)$ be the probability that the individual will die at the end of period t given that he was alive at the beginning of the period; thus $\theta_1\theta_2 \ldots \theta_{t-1}$ is the probability that the individual lives at least to period t. The solution to this amended finite-horizon problem is given by (5.39), (5.40) and (5.41) with the following amendments: in (5.39) the sum of powers of ρ on the left hand side becomes

$$1 + (\rho_t\theta_t) + (\rho_t\theta_t\rho_{t+1}\theta_{t+1}) + \ldots + (\rho_t\theta_t\rho_{t+1}\theta_{t+1}\ldots\rho_{T-1}\theta_{T-1}) \quad (7.37)$$

while the ρ on the right hand side becomes $\rho_t\theta_t$; (5.40) remains unchanged; while in (5.41) the same changes apply to the terms corresponding to those in (5.39) discussed above. No new principle is involved – merely some additional notational complexity.

Throughout the above discussion we have tacitly assumed that recall of job offers is possible. In some situations, however, this facility is not available; in some circumstances, the job searcher must announce his decision, as to whether or not he accepts the job, immediately.[7] In the infinite horizon problem, the question of recall is immaterial since the optimal reservation wage remains constant; however, the question is crucially relevant in the finite horizon problem since the optimal reservation wage falls as the horizon approaches. Intuition suggests that the searcher is worse off if recall is unavailable; this is formalised in the material towards the end of Section 5.4. The solution to the basic search model in a finite horizon world without recall is given by equations (5.52), (5.53) and (5.54).

There are numerous variations on the basic (unidimensional, non-adaptive) search model, which we do not have space to explore here. A survey of the most important articles can be found in Hey (1979a), while a more detailed analysis is given by Lippman and McCall (1976a, b). Once again, we draw attention to the splendid paper by Weitzman (1979), which, though not specifically directed towards the *job* search problem, has immediate and important implications for it.

While the bulk of the job search material has been confined to the one-dimensional case (that is wage), a few studies have recently appeared extending the analysis to two or more dimensions. The obvious extension, paralleling that for the consumer search problem, is to include considerations of job *quality* (that is, working conditions, congeniality of colleagues, job satisfaction, etc.). For some jobs, it may be possible to ascertain quality prior to acceptance; in such cases, the material above remains relevant if it is reinterpreted appropriately. For most jobs, however, it is probably the case that one has to experience the job before one can ascertain its quality; for such jobs, at the time of the job offer, there remains uncertainty about the quality dimension. The choice of optimal strategy is of the multi-stage form discussed in Section 5.4: first, the searcher must decide which wage offers he finds acceptable; secondly, once the searcher has accepted an offer, he must decide whether the realised job quality is sufficiently good for him to remain in the job; if not, he leaves the job and starts search afresh. This two-stage problem has been studied independently by McKenna (1979) and by Wilde (1979); the former is of interest since it investigates the circumstances under which the optimal acceptance set at the first stage is a connected set; the latter examines the same problem at a higher level of generality.

Other dimensions of job offers can also be investigated. One obvious aspect of interest is the riskiness of the job – in terms of its security of tenure. One attempt at investigating this problem is Hey and Mavromaras (1981/2), which postulates job offers consisting of a two-component vector: a wage rate and a parameter indicating the security (of tenure). This paper exploits the indifference property along the boundary of the optimal acceptance set to explore the trade-off between wages and riskiness, and to examine how this trade-off is affected by the existence and form of unemployment insurance.

The indifference property (along the boundary of the optimal acceptance set) is a feature of search theory which we have repeatedly emphasised; it greatly facilitates analysis. It should not be viewed too narrowly, however, for it is a feature which appears in any choice situation (whether certain or uncertain) in which there are a finite number of options open to the decision-maker. Consider, for simplicity, a situation in which the decision-maker has two immediate options open to him; let us call these options 1 and 2. There may be *subsequent* choices to be made, but this is irrelevant for the material that follows. Suppose we denote by $V_i(\mathbf{x})$ the *maximum* value of the objective function of the decision-maker, if option i is chosen, when the observed value of some relevant vector $\mathbf{X}$ is $\mathbf{x}$. Then, rather trivially, but nevertheless importantly, the optimal strategy of the decision-maker at this decision point is:

$$\text{if } V_1(x) > V_2(x) \text{ choose option 1;}$$

$$\text{if } V_1(x) = V_2(x) \text{ choose either;} \qquad (7.38)$$

$$\text{if } V_1(x) < V_2(x) \text{ choose option 2.}$$

This rule immediately leads to an optimal acceptance set for each option. In certain special cases, this acceptance set takes a particularly simple form: for example, suppose x is scalar, and $V_1(.)$ crosses $V_2(.)$ once from below at the point x^*; then the optimal acceptance set for option 1 is simply the set of x greater than (or equal to) x^*.

All sorts of problems of discrete choice can be tackled using this approach. For instance, we can incorporate the possibility of 'on-the-job' search into the basic search model (for an example of this, see Burdett (1978)). Alternatively, we can model search (both on and off the job) in which there is a cost, not to searching for jobs, but for changing them (see Hey and McKenna (1979)). Another obvious example is the problem of whether to put in an insurance claim when the policy has some form of 'no claims bonus' scheme (see Venezia and Levy (1980)). All these studies, and many others like them, build on the basic notion outlined above: at each decision point choose the option which has the highest return (on the assumption that one behaves optimally thereafter). Like all significant ideas, it is elegant in its simplicity.

7.4   QUALITY, LEARNING AND OTHER ADAPTIVE PROBLEMS

In order to provide a thorough analysis of household problems of the adaptive type, at least thirty pages of text would be needed – a rather disproportionate number in view of the space devoted to other aspects of household behaviour. Accordingly, we confine ourselves to a brief survey of some of the work done using the general methods described in Chapter 6.

We begin by mentioning briefly one example of the type of learning (in an otherwise passive situation) discussed in Section 6.3. It will be recalled that this section examined a problem in which two variables entered the utility function of the agent – a random variable X and a control variable Y; and in which information about X could be purchased, this information taking the form of observation(s) on random variables whose distributions depended upon X. An obvious example of this type of problem is that of learning, *prior* to purchase, about the *quality* of some good (or, indeed, of some job). Such a problem has been examined by Kihlstrom (1974) who assumes that (varying degrees of) information about product quality can be obtained from a research laboratory. Kihlstrom uses a Bayesian rule (of the type discussed in Sections 6.2 and 6.3); indeed, he uses the specific case of the normal distribution as described in Section 6.2. Unfortunately, we do not have sufficient space to describe his model in detail. His work should, however, be accessible to those readers who are *au fait* with the material of Sections 6.2 and 6.3.

The most obvious instance of learning in an active situation is that of learning about the distribution over which one is searching in a job or consumer search model. Here the material of Section 6.4 is precisely relevant. For example, in the basic job search model where the distribution of wage offers is known to be normal with a known precision but unknown mean, the solution is given by equations (6.37), (6.38) and (6.39). Obviously, the underlying *method* can be generalised to encompass more unknown parameters or more complicated distributional forms, though the mathematics will become progressively more hideous; the task of explicitly deriving the numerical solution will also worsen. A thorough discussion of the problems involved, and a detailed investigation of a particular distribution, can be found in Rothschild (1974). In addition, some interesting specific illustrations (derived with respect to a house-selling problem) are given in Albright (1977).

7.6 CONCLUSIONS

The purpose of this chapter was to demonstrate in general terms how the methods described in Part II of this book may be applied to analyse the decision problems of the household when operating under uncertainty. Clearly, in the space available, we have not been able to provide a comprehensive survey of all the published literature and of all the available results. Nevertheless we hope we have succeeded in conveying the general flavour of such analyses.

As far as passive situations are concerned, we have attempted to demonstrate how a variety of important household problems can be formulated within the broad framework developed in Chapter 4; in addition we have tried to show how useful comparative static propositions can be obtained by invoking the general principles of Chapter 4.

With respect to problems of the active type, we particularly hope that we have conveyed the importance of the indifference property along the boundary of the optimal acceptance set. This property is the key to the analysis of such problems; both its rôle in deriving the solution, and its intuitively sensible nature, should now be obvious to the reader if we have succeeded in our task.

Finally, we hope that we have conveyed the general principles sufficiently well for the reader now to be in a position to carry out his or her own analyses of other household problems.

8 FIRMS

8.1 INTRODUCTION

The purpose of this chapter is to demonstrate how the general methods discussed in Part II of this book may be used to investigate the behaviour of firms operating under uncertainty. Of necessity, we have to be highly selective in our choice of illustrations; accordingly, we restrict attention to a set of examples which share a common theme, and which yield some unambiguous and interesting conclusions.[1] Generally, most of our examples relate to the behaviour of the price-taking firm in one form or another, though occasionally we mention the price-setting firm.

The chapter has three major sections, corresponding to the final three chapters of Part II. Section 8.2, which examines the behaviour of the firm in passive situations of various types, begins with the relatively simple problem of the price-taking firm acting under uncertainty in a static (or one-period) setting. The simplification to a one-period setting is usually achieved by assuming that there are no factors linking together various time periods; one popular assumption is that the product is perishable, so there is no inventory problem to consider.[2] If the product is non-perishable, however, then (in an uncertain world) static solutions are no longer optimal – a dynamic model must be formulated, with inventories playing a key role. Such formulations constitute the majority of the final part of Section 8.2. Section 8.3 briefly examines the firm in some active situations; typically these are search problems of one form or another, the most obvious example being the search for suitably productive workers. (Another is the choice of investment project for the firm – a perfect example of the type of multi-stage optimisation problem discussed in Section 5.4.) Section 8.4 examines the role of learning in the choice of optimal strategy; here some brief mention of price-setting behaviour will be made. Finally, Section 8.5 offers some comments in conclusion.

126   *Microeconomic Themes and Theories*

8.2   OUTPUT AND INVENTORY DECISIONS IN PASSIVE SITUATIONS

We begin our study of the behaviour of the firm under uncertainty with an investigation of the output decision of the price-taking firm operating under output-price uncertainty. The material that follows has several different interpretations, but we introduce it in the familiar guide of the profit-maximising perfectly competitive firm. Moreover, since the analysis will draw heavily on the results of Section 4.3, we tie our present notation to the notation of that section; we hope that no confusion thereby ensues.

Consider, therefore, a profit-maximising firm which is a price-taker in its output market. Suppose that this output price is random and that the firm must decide upon its level of output *before* the uncertainty about the output price is resolved. Suppose further that the cost function $C(.)$ of the firm is known and certain, and that the firm is a Neumann–Morgenstern utility maximiser with utility function $U(Z)$ defined on profits Z. In keeping with our earlier notation, we denote by X the random variable, output price, and by Y the control variable, output. Profits, Z, are related to X and Y by the obvious expression:

$$Z = XY - C(Y). \tag{8.1}$$

The problem of the firm is to choose Y so as to maximise

$$EU(Z) = EU[Z(X, Y)], \tag{8.2}$$

where Z is given by (8.1) and where the expectation is taken with respect to the known distribution of X.

As formulated, this problem is exactly the same as that analysed in Section 4.3. Indeed, the relationship between Z, the argument of the utility function, and X, the random variable, given by (8.1), is linear, and hence is precisely of the form given by (4.23). Thus the material from equation (4.23) to the end of Section 4.3 is entirely relevant. To be specific (8.1) is the special case of (4.23) with $a(.)$ and $b(.)$ given by:

$$a(Y) = Y$$

and

$$b(Y) = -C(Y). \tag{8.3}$$

Clearly $a'(Y) > 0$; thus, using the argument immediately preceding equation (4.25), in a certain world an increase in X (price) leads to an increase in the optimal value of Y (output). This is a familiar result indeed.

The effect of uncertainty on the optimal output level of the firm follows from the result contained in (4.28); to be specific, a mean-preserving introduction in risk leads to a decrease in output if the firm is risk averse, to no change if the firm is risk neutral and to an increase if the firm is risk loving. Furthermore, if the firm is risk averse and if it displays decreasing absolute risk aversion, then, from the material at the end of Section 4.3, it follows that the firm will react to a Sandmo increase in risk by decreasing output.[3]

Some further comparative static results can be obtained. In the material which follows we restrict attention to firms which are risk averse and which display decreasing absolute risk aversion; for such firms we may make use of the result quoted in the paragraph above, and the results (discussed at the end of Section 4.3) which led to it. The reader may like to investigate the corresponding comparative static exercises for firms which display different attitudes to risk.

The relevant first- and second-order conditions (for the maximisation of (8.2)) are given by equations (4.25) and (4.26) respectively, where the functions $a(.)$ and $b(.)$ are defined by (8.3) above. Consider first a bodily rightward shift of the price distribution by an amount α. The effect of this can be investigated by replacing X wherever it appears in the first-order condition (4.25) by $X + \alpha$, and then differentiating the resulting expression with respect to α, and finally putting α equal to zero in the resulting expression.' Such manipulations yield the result:

$$dY^*/d\alpha|_{\alpha=0} = (-1/D)E\{U'(Z)a'(Y^*) + U''(Z)[a'(Y^*)X$$
$$+ b'(Y^*)]a(Y^*)\}. \tag{8.4}$$

Clearly the first term in the curly brackets is positive everywhere; the second term has a positive expectation by virtue of the material in Section 4.3. Since D (defined in (4.26)) is necessarily negative, it follows that the right hand side of (8.4) is positive. Hence, a rightward shift of the price distribution causes the firm to expand output. In this sense, the upward-sloping supply curve of the perfectly competitive firm under certainty remains valid.

Consider now an upward shift of the cost function. The effect of this can be investigated in a similar fashion to that used above:

replace $C(Y)$ ($\equiv -b(Y)$ from (8.3)) wherever it appears in (4.25) by $C(Y) + \beta$; differentiate the resulting expression with respect to β; finally, put $\beta = 0$. This yields:

$$dY^*/d\beta|_{\beta=0} = (1/D)E\{U''(Z)[a'(Y^*)X + b'(Y^*)]\}. \qquad (8.5)$$

From our previous results it follows that the right hand side of (8.5) is negative, and so an increase in fixed costs causes the firm to decrease output. As the reader will recognise, this is a result in stark contrast with the well-known proposition that, in a certain world, changes in fixed costs have no effect on output.

The paragraph above considered an additive shift in the cost function; a multiplicative shift (by a factor γ) can also be investigated. Using the by now familiar method, we obtain

$$dY^*/d\gamma|_{\gamma=1} = (-1/D)E\{U'(Z)b'(Y^*) + U''(Z)[a'(Y^*)X$$
$$+ b'(Y^*)]b(Y^*)\}. \qquad (8.6)$$

Since $b(Y^*) < 0$ and $b'(Y^*) < 0$, it follows from our previous results that the right hand side of (8.6) is negative. Thus, a multiplicative increase in the cost function causes our firm to decrease output.

As we argued in Section 4.3, the unambiguous nature of the above comparative static results essentially derives from the linear relationship between the random variable and the argument of the utility function. One further important property results from this linearity. Suppose tax at the rate t is levied on Z (the profit of the firm); its objective then becomes to maximise the expected value of $U[Z(1 - t)]$. As is obvious, the first-order condition (4.25) becomes:

$$E\{U'[Z(1 - t)][a'(Y^*)X + b'(Y^*)]\} = 0. \qquad (8.7)$$

Differentiation of (8.7) with respect to t yields

$$dY^*/dt = E\{U''(Z_n)Z_n[a'(Y^*)X + b'(Y^*)]\}/[D(1 - t)], \qquad (8.8)$$

where D remains as given by (4.26), and where Z_n denotes net profits (that is $Z_n \equiv Z(1 - t)$).

One way of unambiguously signing the right hand side of (8.8) is to make some assumption about the *relative risk aversion* of the firm. Before doing so, however, let us introduce some further notation. Let $\bar{Z}_n$ denote the value of Z_n when the random variable X is such that $a'(Y^*)X + b'(Y^*) = 0$, and let $\bar{R}_n$ denote the value of the relative risk-aversion index when $Z_n = \bar{Z}_n$. Thus

$$\bar{R}_n = -\bar{Z}_n U''(\bar{Z}_n)/U'(\bar{Z}_n).$$

Now suppose that relative risk-aversion is increasing (decreasing) everywhere. Then

$$-Z_n U''(Z_n)/U'(Z_n) \gtreqless (\lesseqgtr)\bar{R}_n \text{ according as } a'(Y^*)X + b'(Y^*) \gtreqless 0.$$

Hence

$$U''(Z_n)Z_n[a'(Y^*)X + b'(Y^*)] < (>) - \bar{R}_n U'(Z_n)[a'(Y^*)X + b'(Y^*)].$$

$$(8.9)$$

Taking expectations, and using the first-order condition (8.7) to show that the expected value of the right-hand side of (8.9) is zero, it follows that the numerator of (8.8) is negative (positive). We have therefore shown that, for a firm which displays increasing (decreasing) relative risk aversion, an increase in the rate of profits tax will cause the firm to decrease (increase) output. Once again, we have a result in stark contrast with the familiar certainty proposition (and one that has profound implications for welfare economics).

The material above is relevant for any competitive firm which is a Neumann–Morgenstern utility maximiser with respect to the single argument profit, and which has to choose output before the uncertainty about output price is resolved. In particular, in view of the way that the discussion is presented, the material is relevant whatever the form of the production process and irrespective of whether some (though not all) of the inputs into the production process are fixed; all that matters is that marginal cost is everywhere positive, and that, at the optimum, the second-order condition (4.26) is satisfied. Thus, for example, the results remain valid whether capital and labour inputs are both variable or whether one of them is fixed. Of course, the implications of the results for the demand for factors do depend crucially on the specific 'rules of the game' in operation. (For some discussion of factor demand under output price uncertainty, see Hey (1979a, Chapter 21).)

If, in contrast, some of the inputs were sufficiently flexible for output to be chosen *after* the resolution of the output price uncertainty, the material above would no longer be directly applicable. To be specific, profits Z would no longer be a *linear* function of price

X; indeed, under reasonable assumptions, one would expect profits to be a convex function of price. For a full discussion of such considerations, see Epstein (1978).

The above material can also be applied to firms other than those which have profits as the sole argument of their utility functions. Consider, for example, the *labour-managed firm*. In a certain world, such a firm is assumed to operate so as to maximise net income per worker; if, in keeping with our standardised notation, we denote this variable by Z, then we have

$$Z = (\text{revenue} - \text{costs})/(\text{number of workers}). \qquad (8.10)$$

In an uncertain world, Z is the sole argument of the utility function of the labour-managed firm. Consider the behaviour of such a firm in the random-price competitive environment discussed above. The random variable which it faces remains the output price X; the decision variable of the firm is output or, entirely equivalently,[4] output per worker. As we shall see, the latter is more convenient in this particular case; therefore, denote by Y the decision variable, output per worker. Finally, denote by $C(Y)$ the minimum (non-labour) cost per worker of producing output per worker Y; under the usual assumptions about production processes the function $C(.)$ is a strictly increasing convex function. In terms of this notation, (8.10) can now be written

$$Z = XY - C(Y), \qquad (8.11)$$

and thus the problem of the labour-managed firm (operating in a random-price competitive environment) is entirely analogous to that of the profit-maximising firm.[5] Thus, all the results derived in this section concerning the optimal choice of the profit-maximising firm's output apply equally to the optimal choice of output per worker of the labour-managed firm. Similarly, all the results apply to the optimal choice of output per unit of capital of the joint-stock firm (a joint-stock firm, in a certain world, maximises net revenue per unit of capital). For full details, and further discussion, see Hey (1981b).

The basic framework discussed above – one in which output decisions must be made before the output price is known – is a familiar framework for many real-world goods; obvious instances include many agricultural products for which a considerable length of time elapses between planting and harvesting. Also common for such products (because of this uncertainty) is the existence of *forward markets*; such markets enable producers (if they so wish) to eliminate output price uncertainty by contracting, *at the time of the output decision*, to sell the appropriate quantity at a given price (the forward price) for delivery at the future date. The firm, therefore, has the choice of selling its output in the forward market at a certain price, and/or selling its output in the future spot market at an uncertain price. How does this affect our analysis?

The firm now has two decisions to make: how much output to produce and where to sell it. Let us use Y_1 to denote total output, and Y_2 to denote the amount sold in the forward market (that is, the amount hedged). By the nature of forward markets, Y_2 is un-restricted, in particular, the firm can indulge in speculation ($Y_2 > Y_1$ or $Y_2 < 0$) if it so wishes. If X continues to denote the uncertain future spot price, and if $\bar{x}$ denotes the (fixed) forward price, then profit Z is given by:

$$Z = X(Y_1 - Y_2) + \bar{x}Y_2 - C(Y_1). \qquad (8.12)$$

If profit is the sole argument of the utility function of the firm, then the problem of the firm is to choose Y_1 and Y_2 so as to maximise (8.2) where Z is given by (8.12). The first-order conditions are:

$$E\{U'(Z)[X - C'(Y_1^*)]\} = 0 \qquad (8.13)$$

and

$$E[U'(Z)(\bar{x} - X)] = 0. \qquad (8.14)$$

Equation (8.13) will be recognised as the first-order condition relevant to the no-forward-market problem – namely (4.25). The inclusion of (8.14) makes a significant difference, however: add (8.13) and (8.14) together, and then note that both $\bar{x}$ and Y_1^* are constant. This yields

$$[\bar{x} - C'(Y_1^*)]E[U'(Z)] = 0,$$

from which it follows that

$$\bar{x} = C'(Y_1^*). \qquad (8.15)$$

We thus get the delightful result that the optimal output (Y_1^*) of the firm is that output that would be produced in a world with a known fixed price $\bar{x}$.

This does not imply, however, that the firm simply treats the forward market as a surrogate spot market: only under very special circumstances is the whole output sold in the forward market. Consider condition (8.13); using cov (X_1, X_2) to denote the covariance between X_1 and X_2, this can be written

$$E[U'(Z)](\bar{x} - EX) = \text{cov}[U'(Z), X]. \qquad (8.16)$$

For this to be satisfied, we require

$$\text{cov}[U'(Z), X] \gtreqless 0 \qquad \text{according as } \bar{x} \gtreqless EX. \qquad (8.17)$$

Now if the firm is risk averse[6] it follows from (8.12) that

$$\text{cov}[U'(Z), X] \gtreqless 0 \qquad \text{according as } Y_1^* \lesseqgtr Y_2^*. \qquad (8.18)$$

Combining (8.17) with (8.18) we find that optimality requires

$$Y_1^* \lesseqgtr Y_2^* \qquad \text{according as } \bar{x} \gtreqless EX. \qquad (8.19)$$

Thus, if the forward price equals the expected spot price (as viewed by the firm) then the firm will sell its entire output in the forward market. If the forward price is lower, however, the firm will hedge less than its entire output; if the forward price is higher, the firm will speculate by selling forward an amount greater than its output, expecting to purchase the balance in the future at a low spot price. Clearly the existence of the forward market makes a significant difference to the behaviour of the firm; the full implications are explored in the papers by Holthausen (1979) and Feder, Just and Schmitz (1980). The general case can be investigated using the methods described in Chapter 4.

We now leave the static one-period model of firm behaviour, and move on to consider dynamic models. The crucial feature of these dynamic models is the explicit incorporation of inventories: in the static models described above, it was implicitly assumed that the product was immediately perishable – so that no inventory problem existed; we now make the opposite extreme assumption – that the product is totally imperishable, so inventories never 'decay'.

Our main objective is to construct a dynamic version of the basic random-price (expected-utility-of) profit-maximising model discussed above. For expository reasons connected with the mathematics of the solution, however, we begin by examining a simpler inventory problem. This simpler problem, termed for obvious reasons the 'retailer's problem', envisages a retailer who faces a random demand for some good which he stocks. The retailer buys the good from the wholesaler at a fixed unit price of c and sells it at a fixed unit price p ($>c$). The retailer must order stock in advance of the realisation of demand, and no further stock can be ordered after demand is known.[7] For the moment, we assume that there is no storage cost. The retailer's objective is taken to be a simple one of maximising expected discounted lifetime profits (over an infinite horizon), using a constant discount rate ρ.

In order to solve the retailer's problem, we utilise the methods described in Section 4.4. Moreover, as should now be becoming familiar, we tie our notation to that used in Section 4.4. To that end, let X denote the random variable, demand; let Y denote the amount of the good ordered by the retailer from the wholesaler at the beginning of the period; and let Z denote the initial stock of the good held by the retailer before the amount Y is ordered. Finally, let $V(Z)$ denote the maximum expected discounted lifetime profit as viewed from a position where the initial (pre-order) inventory is Z. The periods are linked together through the variable Z; to be specific, we have

$$Z_{t+1} = \begin{cases} -X_t + Y_t + Z_t & \text{if } X_t < Y_t + Z_t \\ 0 & \text{if } X_t \geqslant Y_t + Z_t. \end{cases} \qquad (8.20)$$

This equation is the specific counterpart of the general $h(.,.,.)$ function introduced in equation (4.32).

Since sales are the smaller of demand, X, and final stock, $Y + Z$, it follows that the $V(.)$ function can be expressed as:

$$V(Z) = \max_{Y \geqslant 0} \left\{ \int_0^{Y+Z} [px + \rho V(-x + Y + Z)] dF(x) + [p(Y+Z) \right.$$

$$\left. + \rho V(0)][1 - F(Y+Z)] - cY \right\}, \qquad (8.21)$$

where $F(.)$ is the distribution function of X. The optimal $Y^* \equiv Y^*(Z)$ is the value of Y for which the maximum is achieved.

Applying the usual first-order condition to the term in the curly brackets on the right hand side of (8.21), we find that Y^* must satisfy

$$\int_0^{Y^*+Z} \rho V'(-x+Y^*+Z)\, dF(x) + p[1-F(Y^*+Z)] - c = 0.$$

$$(8.22)$$

One thing is immediately clear from (8.23): since Y^* always appears in (8.22) in the form Y^*+Z, it follows that there exists an optimal value of (post-order) stock Y^*+Z; if Z is below this value, then the optimal strategy is simply to order enough to replenish the stock to this value. If we denote the optimal post-order stock by I^*, then I^* is given by (from (8.22)):

$$\int_0^{I^*} \rho V'(-x+I^*)\, dF(x) + p[1-F(I^*)] - c = 0. \qquad (8.23)$$

Further, for $Z \leqslant I^*$, we have from (8.21) that

$$V(Z) = \int_0^{I^*} [px + \rho V(-x+I^*)]\, dF(x) + [pI^* + \rho V(0)][1-F(I^*)]$$
$$- c(I^*-Z)$$

From this it is clear that

$$V'(Z) = c \qquad \text{for } Z \leqslant I^*. \qquad (8.24)$$

We need not investigate the case of $Z > I^*$, for, if the retailer at the very beginning started out with zero stock, he would never find himself with $Z > I^*$ if he behaved optimally.

Finally, combining (8.23) and (8.24), we see that I^* satisfies

$$\rho c F(I^*) + p[1-F(I^*)] = c,$$

which solves to yield:[8]

$$I^* = F^{-1}[(p-c)/(p-\rho c)]. \qquad (8.25)$$

The implications of this are straightforward.

One simple extension is of interest: suppose that there is an inventory storage cost of h per unit (per period), payable after storage. As the reader should be able to verify, the basic structure of the derivation of the optimal strategy remains unchanged; the only modifications are that an additional term $-\rho h(-x + Y + Z)$ appears in the first square bracket in (8.21), and consequently that the value of I^* is given by

$$I^* = F^{-1}[(p - c)/(p - \rho c + \rho h)] \qquad (8.26)$$

rather than by (8.25). Clearly I^* decreases as h increases.

Our digression, through the retailer's problem, is now over; its purpose was to introduce the reader to the idea of an optimal beginning-of-period (post-order) inventory. We now return to our competitive world.

Consider, therefore, the problem faced by the competitive firm with which we introduced this section, but suppose now that the product of the firm is *not* immediately perishable; indeed assume, on the contrary, that inventory never decays. As before, the firm faces a random price for its product; we assume that this price distribution, which is known, is the same in every time period. In all other respects, the environment is 'competitive'; in particular, the firm can sell any amount it wishes at the realised price(s). To keep our analysis simple, we assume that the objective of the firm is the same as our retailer; thus the firm is risk neutral.

The firm now has two decisions to make each period: how much to produce and how much to sell. To simplify our exposition, we begin by initially ignoring the first and concentrating on the second. Thus, suppose the firm has a given stock of output and cannot produce any more. What is its optimal sales strategy?

Some notation will help: let X denote the random variable, price; let Y_2 denote sales (later we will use Y_1 to denote production); and let Z denote beginning-of-period (later pre-production) inventory. Finally, let $V(Z)$ have its usual meaning: the maximum value of expected discounted lifetime profits given initial inventory Z. Clearly, in our no-production world,

$$Z_{t+1} = -Y_{2t} + Z_t.$$

We assume (to make matters interesting) that the sales decision is taken *after* the realisation of the output price. Thus, we have that

$$V(Z) = E \left\{ \max_{0 \leqslant Y_2 \leqslant Z} [XY_2 + \rho V(-Y_2 + Z) - \rho h(-Y_2 + Z)] \right\},$$
(8.27)

where the expectation is taken with respect to the distribution of X, and where, as in the retailer's problem, h denotes the per period unit storage cost. Note that V is a function but h is a scalar.

The solution to the maximation problem on the right hand side of (8.27) is rather unusual in that it is a corner solution. Rather than derive this rigorously from first principles (which would be rather tedious), we simply state the solution, and the implied value of $V(.)$, and then verify that (8.27) is indeed satisfied by our stated solution.[9]

It turns out that $V(.)$ takes the particularly simple linear form

$$V(Z) = x^*Z,$$
(8.28)

where x^* is a scalar whose value will be determined shortly. Thus for X equal to any specific x, the maximand on the right hand side of (8.27) is linear in Y_2, namely

$$Y_2(x - \rho x^* + h) + \rho Z(x^* - h).$$
(8.29)

The value of Y_2 that maximises this is one of the extremes: 0 if the coefficient of Y_2 is negative; Z if the coefficient of Y_2 is positive. Thus,

$$Y_2^* \equiv Y_2^*(Z) = \begin{cases} 0 & \text{if } x < \rho(x^* - h) \\ Z & \text{if } x \geqslant \rho(x^* - h) \end{cases}$$
(8.30)

We thus get the beautifully simple rule: sell nothing if the price is less than $\rho(x^* - h)$; sell all if the price is above $\rho(x^* - h)$. Using familiar terminology: the retailer, in deciding on his sales strategy, should use a reservation price rule, with reservation price equal to $\rho(x^* - h)$.

It remains to find x^*. Substituting (8.30) and (8.28) into (8.27), we get

$$x^*Z = \int_0^{\rho(x^* - h)} [\rho(x^* - h)Z] \, dF(x) + \int_{\rho(x^* - h)}^\infty xZ \, dF(x)$$
(8.31)

The variable Z cancels throughout (which, of course, it should if our claim that (8.28) is the solution is correct); after simplification (8.31) gives

$$x^*(1 - \rho) + \rho h = \int_{\rho(x^* - h)}^{\infty} [1 - F(x)]\, dx. \qquad (8.32)$$

This equation is of a form familiar from the material on the determination of reservation values; the reader may like to dwell on the reasons why we get a solution to a passive-type problem resembling those for active-type problems. The reader may also like to explore the comparative static properties of the solution (one obvious result is that a Rothschild–Stiglitz increase in risk of the distribution of X leads to an increase in x^*, and hence to an increase in the reservation price).

Let us now incorporate production. Let Y_1 denote the amount produced, and let $C(Y_1)$ denote the cost of producing it. The variables X and Y_2 continue to have the same meaning, and Z is now taken to be the pre-production inventory. The decision on Y_1 must be taken before X is known, and Y_2 continues to be chosen after X becomes known. The equation for $V(.)$, previously (8.27), now becomes

$$V(Z) = \max_{Y_1 \geqslant 0} [-C(Y_1) + H]$$

where   (8.33)

$$H \equiv E\left\{ \max_{0 \leqslant Y_2 \leqslant Y_1 + Z} [XY_2 + \rho V(Y_1 - Y_2 + Z) - \rho h(Y_1 - Y_2 + Z)] \right\}$$

Although this appears considerably more complicated, its solution is a straightforward generalisation of the 'no-production' and 'retailer's' problems discussed above. Once again, $V(.)$ is linear in Z, but now in the form

$$V(Z) = x^*Z + k, \qquad (8.34)$$

where, in fact, x^* takes the same value as in the no-production case and where k is a constant to be determined below. The reader can easily verify that the optimal sales strategy (that is, that which yields the maximum in H) is again given by (cf. (8.30)):

$$Y_2^* = Y_2^*(Y_1^* + Z) = \begin{cases} 0 & \text{if } x < \rho(x^* - h) \\ Y_1^* + Z & \text{if } x \geqslant \rho(x^* - h) \end{cases} \quad (8.35)$$

Thus the maximand for the optimum choice of Y_1 is simply

$$- C(Y_1) + x^*(Y_1 + Z) + \rho k.$$

The maximum of this occurs when[10]

$$x^* = C'(Y_1^*); \quad (8.36)$$

thus optimal production is that which equates marginal cost with x^*. Finally, substituting (8.34), (8.35) and (8.36) into (8.33), k is given by

$$k(1 - \rho) = - C(Y_1^*) + x^* Y_1^*. \quad (8.37)$$

The solution is simple and attractive. Optimal production is constant, and independent of the pre-production stock level – a result in sharp contrast with the retailer's problem. Optimal sales are either all or nothing – depending upon whether the price is sufficiently high. The model is instructive.

Some of the extreme features of the model result from the assumption of risk neutrality. If, in contrast, risk aversion was assumed, the optimal sales strategy would cease to be of the all-or-nothing form, and optimal production would depend on initial stock levels. For further details, the reader should consult the two path-breaking (and relatively early but strangely ignored) papers by Zabel (1967, 1971).

8.3 PRODUCTIVITY SCREENING AND OTHER ACTIVE PROBLEMS

Although the literature on active behaviour by individuals is very well-developed, there is strangely little on active behaviour by firms. Of the few existing studies, one of the more interesting is the work by McKenna (1980) on productivity screening. The basic idea is simple: when firms hire workers, though they may employ some initial screening or interviewing procedure, there inevitably remains some residual doubt about the productivity of applicants. Accordingly, many firms adopt some form of probationary period, with the implication that workers will be sacked if their productivity is not 'satisfactory'. The methods described in Chapter 5 can be used to discover how 'satisfactory' should be defined.

The basic uncertainty is about productivity; let us, therefore, use X to denote the revenue product of a worker. Before hiring, X is a random variable. (Its distribution may be affected by various initial screening devices, but we ignore this possibility). After hiring, the value of X for the hired worker is revealed, and at the end of the probationary period the firm must decide whether the realised value is 'satisfactory'. Suppose the objective of the firm is to maximise total expected discounted net revenue from each vacancy, where an infinite horizon and a constant discount rate ρ is assumed. If the wage is w, and if there is a fixed probability $(1 - \theta)$ that the worker will die (or otherwise quit the firm) at the end of any period, then the value of the objective function of the firm if a worker with productivity x is kept on at the end of the probationary period is $(x - w)/(1 - \rho\theta)$. If we denote by V the maximum value of the objective function as viewed from before a vacancy has been filled, then the optimal strategy is to accept those workers for which (cf. (5.25))

$$(x - w)/(1 - \rho\theta) \geqslant V. \qquad (8.38)$$

As is immediate from (8.38), this defines an optimal reservation productivity level x^* given by $(x^* - w)/(1 - \rho\theta) = V$; that is

$$x^* = w + (1 - \rho\theta) V. \qquad (8.39)$$

It remains to find V. The precise value of V depends upon the particular 'rules of the game' in operation. For any given specification, the derivative is straightforward, though tedious. Since such a derivation would add little, we omit it; the interested reader could refer to McKenna (1980) for full details, as well as a solution to the optimal choice of w (this latter being essentially a problem of the passive type).

It appears rather strange that the methods of Chapter 5 have not been employed more extensively to model the behaviour of firms. It would seem that in many instances firms do, in fact, face situations of the active type. One obvious such candidate is the investment decision – particularly if at each stage the firm is faced with a finite number of investment possibilities. The multi-stage optimisation techniques discussed in Section 5.4 seem ideally suited for such a problem; perhaps we shall see the application of such methods in the near future.

8.4   LEARNING

Adaptive behaviour by the firm is also a relatively neglected area of study despite its potential importance. A few interesting studies have appeared in recent years, however. We may fruitfully begin our analysis by returning to the basic model of Section 8.2, which envisaged a competitive firm operating in a random-price environment. If we initially confine attention to the case of a perishable good, we may analyse the rôle of learning in such a model. (Obviously, learning has a rôle only in a dynamic model; the dynamic model considered here is simply a collection of one-period static models except in so far as the learning is concerned.) The first investigation of such a problem was by Turnovsky (1969) who envisaged an unchanging price distribution, the precise nature of which the firm was initially unsure, and about which the firm learns as time passes. Turnovsky showed how Bayesian methods could be used to analyse this learning process; indeed, he used the specific illustration of the normal distribution discussed in Section 6.2. The crucial feature of this process is that at any one point in time the firm has some subjective assessment of the (unchanging) price distribution; each period it gets an additional observation from the price distribution, and uses this to update its subjective assessment. Note crucially that, by the very nature of this process, the observations that the firm gets are independent of the actions of the firm; thus, the amount of information that the firm obtains cannot be affected by its own actions. It follows from this that the firm can ignore any potential information gain when it makes its output decision – indeed, it can simply choose output each period in the myopic manner described in Section 8.2, using its current subjective assessment of the distribution in the optimality conditions. Of course, the subjective assessment changes through time, but in no other way does the learning potential affect the behaviour of the firm. A similar conclusion, in a more explicitly dynamic framework incorporating inventories, is derived by Zabel (1969).

As the discussion of Chapter 6 showed, in order for the learning potential to affect behaviour of economic agents, the choice of decision variable had to affect not only the objective function of the agent directly, but also indirectly through the amount of information obtained. Clearly, in the price-taking competitive environment discussed above, such an indirect effect cannot exist. In order to generate such an effect we need to consider an alternative environment.

Return then to the 'retailer's problem' discussed in Section 8.2. Suppose that the distribution of demand is constant through time, but that initially the retailer is unaware of its precise position. It will be recalled that we used X to denote demand, Y the retailer's order and Z the pre-order inventory level. If in any period X is less than $Y + Z$, the retailer obtains an observation from the distribution of X which he can use to update his subjective assessment. If, however, X turns out to be greater than $Y + Z$, then the retailer does *not* get an observation on X (unless he can somehow observe the demands of all those customers who went away unsatisfied); all he knows is that the value of X was greater than $Y + Z$. It is clear in this example that the choice of decision variable of the retailer has some influence on the amount of information he receives: the higher he sets $Y + Z$, the more information he is likely to get.

Although we do not have the space to develop a formal solution here, the interested reader may refer to an almost identical problem investigated by Krouse and Senchak (1977). They examine a price-taking firm producing a perishable commodity facing a random demand, about which the firm learns through time. After considering the general problem, Krouse and Senchak explore a rather degenerate special case in which the true demand is constant, though the actual value is unknown. Thus, $F(.)$ takes the form $F(x) = 0$, $x < a$; $F(x) = 1$, $x \geqslant a$, where a is unknown. The firm's initial subjective assessment of a is represented by an exponential distribution with lower bound α and parameter θ. The learning process works as follows: if in any period X turns out to be greater than[11] Y, the firm knows that a is greater than Y, but does not know by how much; thus a is updated to Y. If, however, X turns out to be less than Y, that value of X is immediately revealed as the value of a. Formally, we have:

$$
\left.
\begin{array}{lll}
\text{if } X_t > Y_t & \text{then } \alpha_{t+1} = Y_t & \text{and } \theta_{t+1} = \theta_t = \theta; \\
\text{if } X_t \leqslant Y_t & \text{then } \alpha_{t+1} = X_t & \text{and } \theta_{t+1} = \infty.
\end{array}
\right\} \quad (8.40)
$$

Krouse and Senchak derive the optimal strategy for both adaptive and non-adaptive behaviour (using the methods described in Chapters

5 and 6). Their results are as follows:

Non-adaptive solution

$$Y_t^* = \alpha_t + (1/\theta) \ln (p/c)$$

Adaptive solution

$$Y_t^* = \begin{cases} \alpha_t + (1/\theta) \ln [p/c + \rho\theta (Y_{t-1}^* - \alpha_{t-1})] & \theta < \infty \\ \alpha_t & \theta = \infty. \end{cases}$$

In this expression p and c denote (constant) revenue and cost per unit and ρ is the discount rate. Adaptive behaviour clearly differs from non-adaptive behaviour; in particular, the adaptive output is always greater than the non-adaptive output. Although this result is specific to this particular example, it does illustrate the general statement made earlier to the effect that the optimal adaptive decision takes into account the information potential; in this example, the larger the value of Y, the more information the firm is likely to get.

A similar example to that discussed above, though in a different setting, is the model by Cyert and Degroot (1971) of learning about the 'kink' in duopoly (or oligopoly) models. As we discussed in Hey (1979a, pp. 145–50), Cyert and Degroot have made a number of notable contributions incorporating learning in duopoly and oligopoly models. Also, in conjunction with Holt (Cyert, Degroot and Holt, 1978) they have constructed an interesting model of learning in an investment problem. This model is of particular interest for our purposes since it uses the specific case of Bayesian updating illustrated in Section 6.2. Specifically, Cyert, Degroot and Holt (1978) envisage a two-period world in which the firm must decide its investment strategy. The return from the investment made in the first period yields information which is of value in determining the optimal value of second-period investment. Although the precise details cannot detain us here, the basic idea is that the firm has some project open to it which yields profit W which is normally distributed with mean X and precision r. X is unknown but r is known. In the first period the firm can invest in some proportion Y_1 of the entire project; the way the authors characterise this procedure, the profit Z_1 from investing in a proportion Y_1 is normally distributed with mean XY_1 and precision r/Y_1. Thus Z_1/Y_1 is normally distributed with mean X and precision rY_1. Once the realised value of Z_1/Y_1 is observed, the firm can use this information to update its perception of X. Specifically, suppose the prior distribution on X is normal with mean m and precision p, then (cf. (6.15)) the posterior distribution, after $Z_1 = z_1$ is observed, is normal with mean

$$[pm + (rY_1)(z_1/Y_1)]/(p + rY_1) = (pm + rz_1)/(p + rY_1)$$

and precision $p + rY_1$.

Clearly the higher the value of the first-period investment (Y_1) the greater the posterior precision, and hence the greater the informational content. The reader is referred to Cyert, Degroot and Holt (1978) for further details.

8.5   CONCLUSIONS

Throughout this chapter we have concentrated almost exclusively on the behaviour of price-taking firms. This concentration has enabled us to follow a consistent theme throughout the chapter. It has inevitably meant, however, that large areas of the theory of the firm under uncertainty have had to be omitted. On the credit side, though, it has enabled us to present a large number of concrete results: it is probably fair to say that in the omitted areas, specific results are rather less plentiful.

The general methods discussed in Part II of this book are, of course, equally applicable to other types of firms. Readers interested in pursuing such applications should consult first the survey articles mentioned in note 1. Mention should also be made of the recent article on the behaviour of the monopolist by Lim (1980).

The relative amounts of space devoted in this chapter to the three types of behaviour (passive, active and adaptive) probably reflects fairly accurately their relative coverage in the literature. The reader would be correct in drawing from this the inference that, whereas the passive theory of the firm operating under uncertainty has been reasonably comprehensively covered, there remains much to be done in the important areas of active and adaptive behaviour.

9 OTHER ECONOMIC AGENTS

9.1 INTRODUCTION

The word 'other' in the title of this chapter has at least two distinct interpretations. Since we have so far explored the behaviour under uncertainty of firms and households who obey the axioms of Neumann–Morgenstern utility theory, the set of 'other economic agents' include all those who are neither firms nor households and all those who are not Neumann–Morgenstern utility maximisers. This chapter, which therefore represents somewhat of a digression from the main theme of this book, examines the behaviour of such agents.

The material in this chapter is ordered by the degree of departure of the agents from the Neumann–Morgenstern axioms: we begin with other agents who do in fact act in total agreement with them, and proceed to the opposite extreme of total disagreement at the end of the chapter, passing on the way agents who are part way along the spectrum. This spectrum is divided into sections as follows: the first substantive section (9.2) examines fully-fledged Neumann–Morgenstern agents; Section 9.3 investigates three important classes of problem in which the behaviour of the agents could, in certain (but occasionally rather forced) circumstances, be constructed as being in agreement with the Neumann–Morgenstern axioms; the final substantive Section (9.4) briefly reviews some alternative theories of behaviour under certainty, which conflict with, or otherwise deny, the Neumann–Morgenstern approach. Finally, Section 9.5 offers some comments in conclusion.

9.2 OTHER NEUMANN–MORGENSTERN AGENTS

There are clearly numerous economic agents who do not fit neatly into either of the two boxes labelled 'households' and 'firms' which were the object of study in Chapters 7 and 8; there are also numerous theories which could equally apply to both boxes as well as to other agents. The purpose of this brief section is to show how the material of Part II may be used to analyse such cases. We give one example of a passive-type problem, one of an active type, and a final example which may be considered as a mixture of the two types.

The passive example is drawn from the study by Baron (1976) on the invoicing strategy of an exporter in a world of fluctuating (and hence uncertain) exchange rates. The purpose of Baron's article is to investigate whether the exporter should invoice his exports in the currency of the importer or in his home currency. The exporter is assumed to face a constant and known demand curve for his product, $Q(.)$, the argument of which is the price paid by the customers in the importing country; the cost, in the exporter's currency, of satisfying demand Q is $C(Q)$. The exporter faces uncertainty in the form of a fluctuating exchange rate, and must choose his optimal selling price to maximise his expected utility of profit. In keeping with our standardised notation, we denote the exchange rate by X, the selling price by Y, and profit by Z. We consider first the situation if the exporter invoices in the currency of the importer. Here we have

$$Z = XYQ(Y) - C(Q(Y)) \qquad (9.1)$$

and the exporter's problem is to choose Y so as to maximise $E[U(Z)]$.

As formulated, this is exactly the same as the general problem analysed in Section 4.3. Indeed, the relationship between Z and X is linear; thus the material from (4.23) to the end of Section 4.3 is entirely relevant. To be specific, (9.1) is the special case of (4.23) with $a(.)$ and $b(.)$ given by:

$$a(Y) = YQ(Y)$$

and $\qquad\qquad\qquad\qquad\qquad\qquad\qquad\qquad\qquad$ (9.2)

$$b(Y) = -C(Q(Y)).$$

In a certain world, the effect of a change in X on the value of Y^* (the value of Y which maximises Z) is determined by the sign of a'. From (9.1) it is clear that X times $a'(Y)$ is simply marginal revenue, and since this must equal marginal cost at the optimum, *where both marginals are calculated with respect to price*, it follows that a' must be *negative* in the relevant range. Thus, $dY^*/dX < 0$ in a certain world: an increase in the exchange rate causes the exporter to decrease the price (as invoiced in the importer's currency).[1] Without further ado, we can use the material of Section 4.3 to conclude that the risk averse (neutral, loving) exporter will increase (keep unchanged, decrease) his price, and hence decrease (keep unchanged, increase) his trade, in response to a transition from a fixed exchange-rate regime to a floating-rate regime (with expected rate equal to the previous fixed rate). This result (quoted by Baron (1976, p. 430)) is just one of many that can be obtained using the material of Section 4.3.

Consider now the situation if the exporter invoices in his home currency. Following Baron, we simplify by assuming a linear demand schedule (with intercept α and slope $-\beta$) and a linear cost function (with slope c and intercept which we ignore). For reasons which should become obvious, we now define X as the reciprocal of that used above: in other words, X is now the exchange rate as measured by the number of units of the importing currency per unit of the home currency. Moreover, we define Y as the price as invoiced in the home currency. Profit is now given by

$$Z = YQ(XY) - C(Q(XY)),$$

or using the linearity case defined above, by

$$Z = (Y - c)(\alpha - \beta XY) = X[-\beta Y(Y - c)] + \alpha(Y - c). \quad (9.3)$$

Once again, we have a linear relationship between Z and X; thus, once again, we can use the material of Section 4.3 to determine the optimal choice of Y by the exporter. The reader should easily be able to verify Baron's results, in particular the conclusion that risk aversion on the part of the exporter leads to a lower price under floating rates than under a fixed rate (subject to the same qualification as that imposed above[2]). Further inferences including those relating to the optimal choice of invoicing strategy, can also be derived.

A very interesting application of the active optimisation rules of Chapter 5 is given by Baldwin and Meyer (1979) in their model of liquidity preference under uncertainty. Their model (which differs in detail but not in principle from those of Chapter 5 by being set in continuous rather than discrete time) postulates a decision-maker facing a random inflow of investment opportunities with random rates of return; the opportunities are presented sequentially to the decision-maker, and at the time of presentation the rate of return on the particular investment is known. The problem is made interesting by postulating that at any one time, the individual can invest in just *one* opportunity; thus there is a potential opportunity cost of accepting an investment in terms of the lost possibilities that may present themselves before the accepted investment has matured. In order to make their model simple, Baldwin and Meyer postulate a Poisson process[3] with parameter λ for the arrival of new opportunities, and a Poisson process with parameter μ for the departure rate of accepted opportunities; thus, the time between new arrivals has an exponential distribution with mean $1/\lambda$, and the time to maturity of accepted opportunities has an exponential distribution with mean $1/\mu$. The rate of return on investments is a random variable X with distribution function $F(.)$.

From the formulation of the problem it is clear that the optimal strategy is of a reservation form: accept those X which are sufficiently large, and reject all others. To derive the optimal reservation value x^*, we pursue a method of solution proposed in Section 5.2: begin by assuming an arbitrary reservation value x, and denote by V_x the value of the objective function using this arbitrary reservation value. Baldwin and Meyer's postulated objective function is simply the average rate of return; this can be calculated as follows. Since new arrivals follow a Poisson process with parameter λ, and since a proportion $1 - F(x) = \int_x^\infty dF(t)$ of new arrivals are acceptable, the flow of acceptable new arrivals follows a Poisson process with parameter $\lambda \int_x^\infty dF(t)$. Further, since departures follow a Poisson process with parameter μ, it follows that, on average, the individual holds an investment a proportion $\lambda \int_x^\infty dF(t)/[\mu + \int_x^\infty dF(t)]$ of the time, and does not hold an investment the remaining $\mu/[\mu + \lambda \int_x^\infty dF(t)]$ of the time. The average rate of return on an acceptable investment is simply $\int_x^\infty t\, dF(t)/\int_x^\infty dF(t)$, and the rate of return on no investment is zero. Thus, V_x is given by

$$V_x = \left[\int_x^\infty t\, dF(t) \Big/ \int_x^\infty dF(t) \right] \left\{ \lambda \int_x^\infty dF(t) \Big/ \left[\mu + \lambda \int_x^\infty dF(t) \right] \right\},$$

that is

$$V_x = \lambda \int_x^\infty t\, dF(t) \Big/ \left[\mu + \lambda \int_x^\infty dF(t) \right]. \qquad (9.4)$$

The optimal value of x, x^*, is the value which maximises V_x. Using standard techniques, we find x^* is given by

$$x^*\mu = \lambda \int_{x^*}^{\infty} [1 - F(x)] \, dx, \qquad (9.5)$$

and, of course (as the reader should have predicted),

$$V \equiv V_{x^*} = x^*. \qquad (9.6)$$

Equations (9.5) and (9.6) characterise the solution: from them it is clear that x^* (and thus the average rate of return) is an increasing function of λ and a decreasing function of μ; moreover, a Rothschild–Stiglitz increase in the riskiness of X leads to an increase in x^*. Other inferences are discussed at length in Baldwin and Meyer (1979).

Our final example of this section is of a rather different type; however, it illustrates an important class of problems which economists are currently investigating. This class concerns the behaviour of agents in auctions or in other types of bidding situations – such as tendering or estimating. Many important transactions are carried out through auctions of various kinds; for example, bidding for leases for oil-exploration rights, and tendering for building and other contracts for government departments. An interesting theoretical study of some of the possibilities is given in Wilson, R. (1979). Of particular concern in this paper is the question of the relative merits of 'unit' and 'share' auctions; in a 'unit' auction the item is sold to the bidder submitting the highest bid (at a price equal to that highest bid); in a 'share' auction the bidders receive shares of the item at a sale price that equates the demand and supply of shares. Amongst other results, Wilson concludes that a share auction may yield a significantly lower price than the unit auction; indeed, the sale price in the former could be as low as one-half of the sale price in the latter. Although we do not have the space to go into details, it may be of interest to note that Wilson's method of investigation consists of deriving mutually optimal bidding strategies – such a strategy has the property that, if all except one of the bidders uses it, then it is optimal for the remaining bidder to use it also. This removes one aspect of uncertainty normally present in a bidding situation; one aspect explicitly considered by Wilson is uncertainty about the value of the item being auctioned. There remains much of interest to investigate in this field;

the interested reader might like to refer to the conference proceedings edited by Amihud (1976) and the survey by Engelbrecht-Wiggans (1980).

9.3   PSEUDO-, PARTIAL- AND EXTENDED-NEUMANN–MORGENSTERN AGENTS

This section reviews three alternative approaches to decision-making under certainty. Two of these three could be regarded, under certain rather special circumstances, as being consistent with Neumann–Morgenstern utility theory; the third could be regarded as being a 'natural extension' of Neumann–Morgenstern utility theory. The first of the three, mean-variance portfolio analysis, continues to enjoy immense popularity in financial circles; the second, the 'safety-first' approach, has attracted relatively little interest in its original pure form, though later modifications have generated increasing interest; the third, 'ordinal certainty equivalence', is a relatively recent innovation, whose potential has yet to be realised. We examine the three in order of decreasing popularity.

Portfolio choice analysts have extensively employed mean-variance techniques for many years, despite numerous onslaughts from 'pure' Neumann–Morgenstern practitioners. The appeal of mean-variance techniques for the analysis of portfolio problems is clear: since it is assumed that the expected utility of the decision-maker is simply a function of the mean and standard-deviation (or square-root of the variance) of the return on the portfolio, and since the mean and variance of the return on any portfolio are simply linear functions of the means and of the variances and covariances of the returns of the individual stocks, then the latter information is all that is required by the decision-maker for him to arrive at his optimal portfolio choice.

Clearly the second part of the argument above is indisputable: if the portfolio consists of Y_i units of stock i, which has random return X_i, and there is a total of I stocks from which to select, then the mean return $(Z \equiv \Sigma_{i=1}^{I} Y_i X_i)$ on the portfolio is

$$EZ \equiv E \left[\sum_{i=1}^{I} Y_i X_i \right] = \sum_{i=1}^{I} Y_i(EX_i);$$

furthermore, the variance of the return is

$$\text{var}\, Z \equiv \text{var}\left[\sum_{i=1}^{I} Y_i X_i\right] = \sum_{i=1}^{I} Y_i^2\, \text{var}\, X_i + 2 \sum_{i=1}^{I} \sum_{j=1}^{i-1} Y_i Y_j\, \text{cov}(X_i, X_j).$$

Thus, if EX_i, $\text{var}\, X_i$ and $\text{cov}(X_i, X_j)$ are known for all i and j, then EZ and $\text{var}\, Z$ can be calculated for any portfolio composition (that is, for any set of Y_i).

The disputable item is the assumption that the expected utility of the decision-maker is a function of the portfolio mean and variance alone. There are two circumstances under which this assumption is reconcilable with Neumann–Morgenstern utility theory: the first is when the utility function of the individual is quadratic; the second is when the rate of return on each stock (that is, each X_i) is normally distributed. Let us examine these possibilities in turn.

Suppose the utility function of the individual is quadratic, that is

$$U(z) = a + bz + cz^2, \tag{9.7}$$

where Z, as before, is the return on the portfolio. Then clearly

$$EU(Z) = a + bEZ + cE(Z^2) = a + bEZ + c(EZ)^2 + c\, \text{var}\, Z,$$

and so expected utility is indeed a function of EZ and $\text{var}\, Z$ alone. Consider the implications of (9.7) as a utility function, however: if, for example, the individual is risk averse, then c must be negative; but this implies that utility reaches a maximum (at the point $z = -b/2c$), and for increases in z above this value, utility decreases. Of course, one could restrict attention to z in the range zero to $-b/2c$ (assuming $b > 0$), so as to keep marginal utility positive in the relevant range. But even in this range, absolute risk aversion $(= -U''(z)/U'(z) = -2c/(b+2cz))$ is increasing with z – an unlikely phenomenon. On several criteria, therefore, a quadratic function appears unsuited as a utility function.

Suppose instead that each X_i is normally distributed (while the utility function of the individual is unrestricted). It follows, from the properties of the normal distribution, that Z is also normally distributed (for any given set of Y_i). Since a normal distribution has just two parameters (its mean and its variance), it follows that the expected utility of Z is a function of just the mean and variance of Z. Moreover, the normal distribution is the only distribution with this property: for no other two-parameter family is a linear combination of family members itself within the family.

The route to reconciliation of mean-variance analysis with Neumann–Morgenstern utility theory through the assumption of normality is more attractive than the route through a quadratic utility function. Unfortunately, the normality route has one severe drawback: in practice it would appear that returns are not normally distributed – indeed, the lognormal distribution appears empirically more suitable. Of course, one need not attempt the reconciliation at all. One can simply deny the validity of the Neumann–Morgenstern axioms, and alternatively assert the existence of an indifference map in mean-standard deviation space. Indeed, this is what many mean-variance practitioners do; after all, the issue at stake can ultimately be resolved only empirically – theoretical arguments alone cannot decide the issue. Although this is undoubtedly true, there is a further theoretical argument which would appear to cast severe doubt on the existence of an indiffference map in mean-standard-deviation space. This argument starts from the assumption of *préférence absolue*: which states that, if y_1 is preferred to y_2 then (x, p, y_1) is preferred to (x, p, y_2) (where (x, p, y) denotes a gamble which yields an outcome of x with probability p and an outcome of y with probability $1 - p$). This assumption appears totally innocuous. As Borch (1969) has shown, however, it implies that, if two points in mean-standard-deviation space lie on the same indifference curve, then the two points must in fact coincide; thus, it is impossible to draw indifference curves in mean-standard-deviation space.[4]

Nevertheless, mean-variance analysis remains extensively used by portfolio choice analysts, and looks likely to continue to be so for some time. The reader interested in pursuing the topic further could well begin by studying Goodhart (1975, pp. 30–42).

Interestingly, our second pseudo- (or partial-) Neumann–Morgenstern approach has also been applied in portfolio choice theory; this approach is the 'safety-first principle'. In its original pure form, as proposed by Roy (1952), the principle states that, if the decision-maker's reward Z is related to a random variable X and a control variable Y by some function $Z = Z(X, Y)$, then Y should be chosen to as to minimise $P(Z < 0)$ – the probability of a loss. The basic idea behind this principle is appealing: losses are unattractive, and therefore it is reasonable to try and minimise the probability of ending up with a loss. Of course, the zero threshold is arbitrary – the principle could equally well apply to the minimisation of the probability that Z is less than some threshold value $\bar{z}$; the principle could then be used to analyse the avoidance of bankruptcy.

In its pure form, the safety-first principle *is* reconcilable with Neumann–Morgenstern utility theory, but this reconciliation requires that the utility function takes the special form:

$$U(z) = \begin{cases} a & z \leqslant \bar{z} \\ a + b & z > \bar{z} \end{cases} \qquad (9.8)$$

where b is positive and where $\bar{z}$ is the relevant threshold. From (9.8) it is clear that the expected utility of any prospect Z, which has distribution function $G(\,.\,)$ is given by:

$$EU(Z) = \int_{-\infty}^{\bar{z}} a \; dG(z) + \int_{\bar{z}}^{\infty} (a + b) \; dG(z),$$

that is,

$$EU(Z) = (a + b) - bG(\bar{z}). \qquad (9.9)$$

From (9.9) it is seen that maximisation of $EU(Z)$ is equivalent to minimisation of $G(\bar{z})$, that is of $P(Z \leqslant \bar{z})$. Unfortunately, the utility function (9.8) is rather strange, as the reader will realise. (One rather odd implication of the function is that it suggests that an individual with such a function will prefer a gamble of the form $(\bar{z} + c - d, \frac{1}{2}, \bar{z} - c - d)$ to a certainty of $\bar{z} - d$, where c and d are positive; such risk-loving behaviour seems to contradict the intuition behind the principle of 'safety-first'.)

Additionally, the pure form of the safety-first principle may imply some rather odd behaviour: for example, an individual acting according to this principle (with $\bar{z} = 0$) would apparently prefer the gamble $(-£10\,000, 0.49, £1)$ to the gamble $(-£1, 0.51, £10\,000)$ simply because the former has a lower probability of loss. The problem, of course, is that the principle in pure form ignores all aspects of the risky prospects other than the probability of loss. To get round this objection, several alternatives have been proposed (see Arzac, 1976), including the following:

1. maximise EZ subject to $P(Z \leqslant \bar{z}) \leqslant \alpha$ (where $\alpha \geqslant 0$);
2. maximise $\bar{z}$ subject to $P(Z \leqslant \bar{z}) \leqslant \alpha$ (where $\alpha \geqslant 0$);
3. maximise $[EZ - \lambda P(Z \leqslant \bar{z})]$ (where $\lambda > 0$);
4. maximise $\{EZ + \phi[P(Z \leqslant \bar{z})]\}$ (where $\phi', \phi'' < 0$).

Criterion 1 seeks the maximisation of expected return subject to a satisfactorily small probability of ending up with less than the threshold value $\bar{z}$; criterion 2 maximises the threshold value below which the return lies with a satisfactorily small probability; criterion 3 maximises the expected return less some multiple of the probability of the return lying below the threshold; criterion 4 is a non-linear extension of 3. These various criteria each have their own advantages and disadvantages. Only one of them (criterion 3) is consistent with Neumann–Morgenstern utility theory, and then only when the utility function takes the special form:

$$U(z) = \begin{cases} -\lambda + a + bz & z \leqslant \bar{z} \\ a + bz & z > \bar{z}. \end{cases} \quad (\text{where } b, \lambda > 0) \right\} \quad (9.10)$$

Although this may be regarded as an improvement over (9.8), it still implies some rather odd behaviour – particularly in the neighbourhood of the threshold.

A number of studies have investigated various safety-first principles; notable among these are papers by Roy (1952), Pyle and Turnovsky (1970) and Levy and Sarnat (1972) on the portfolio choice problem, and papers by Day, Aigner and Smith (1971) and Arzac (1976) on the theory of the firm. Several of these authors discuss the question of the compatability of their approach with Neumann–Morgenstern utility theory, and (for the portfolio choice authors) with mean-standard-deviation analysis. The predictions of the various approaches are also compared, and their empirical validity discussed. A more recent paper (Bigman and Leite, 1978) applies the same principles to international trade theory.

The third and final approach discussed in this section is termed the 'ordinary certainty equivalence' (OCE) approach by its originators (see, in particular, Selden (1978)). Since, as Selden demonstrates, the Neumann–Morgenstern utility function emerges as a special case of the OCE approach, the latter can be considered as an extension of the former. Briefly, the OCE approach proceeds as follows: consider a decision problem concerning choice over consumption pairs, where the first element of the pair is consumption this period, and the second element is consumption in the next (and final) period; suppose the first element is certain, but the second is uncertain. In this scenario, Neumann–Morgenstern utility theory specifies a utility function defined over these consumption pairs, and choice is simply determined by the maximisation of the expected value of this utility function. In contrast, the OCE approach works in two stages: first, a second-period utility function is used to reduce the uncertain second-period prospects to certainty equivalents; second, these second-period certainty equivalents are combined with the certain first-period vaues and evaluated using a conventional (certainty) ordinal preference function. The benefit of using this approach, according to Selden, is that it enables a clear distinction to be made between risk attitudes and time preference: under Neumann–Morgenstern utility theory these two characteristics are inextricably interlinked. Undoubtedly he is correct, but whether it matters, or whether the OCE approach leads to better predictions, remains to be seen. An application of this approach is given in Selden (1979). An alternative approach, but addressed to the solution of a similar dynamic choice problem, is presented by Kreps and Porteus (1978, 1979a, b). Clearly, there are strong arguments for extending Neumann–Morgenstern utility theory from the essentially static framework to a more explicitly sequential (or dynamic) framework.

9.4   NON-NEUMANN–MORGENSTERN AGENTS

We now move on in this final substantive section to consider theories of behaviour under uncertainty which are essentially antithetical to Neumann–Morgenstern utility theory. Four alternative approaches are briefly discussed, ranging from an approach which (like Neumann–Morgenstern utility theory) admits the existence (and indeed necessity) of probability as a guide to decision-making, through to an approach which denies the meaning (or usefulness) of the concept of probability in any genuinely uncertain choice problem. Of necessity, we are forced to be brief; thus, much interesting detail will have to be omitted. We apologise to authors whose ideas are thereby rather cursorily treated; the brevity does not accurately reflect the importance of the issues.

We begin with *Prospect Theory*, a relatively new approach to decision-making under risk, launched in the paper by Kahneman and Tversky (1979). Kahneman and Tversky present Prospect Theory as an alternative to Neumann–Morgenstern utility theory; moreover, it is an alternative based on the results of a large number of empirical studies investigating the validity of the Neumann–Morgenstern approach. In the course of these studies, an embarrassingly large number of violations of the basic axioms were observed. These violations can be grouped under three main headings, termed by Kahneman and Tversky, the 'certainty effect', the 'reflection effect' and the 'isolation effect'. The certainty effect is well illustrated by the famous Allais paradox, which was explored in modified form by the authors as follows. First, individuals were asked whether they preferred a gamble which yielded 2500 (units of Israeli currency) with probability 0.33, 2400 with probability 0.66 and 0 with probability 0.01, or a certain reward of 2400. Of the seventy-two questioned, 18 per cent opted for the gamble and 82 per cent for the certainty. Then the same respondents were asked whether they preferred a gamble which yielded 2500 with probability 0.33 and 0 with probability 0.67, or a gamble which yielded 2400 with probability 0.34 and 0 with probability 0.66. Of the seventy-two, 83 per cent chose the first, and 17 per cent the second. Moreover, 61 per cent of the respondents made the modal choice in both problems. To be consistent with Neumann–Morgenstern utility theory, the first option is preferred to the second option in the first problem if, and only if, the first option is preferred to the second option in the second problem. The observed violation has been interpreted by several authors as indicating an over-weighting of certainty.

The 'reflection effect' is a description of the phenomenon noted repeatedly by Kahneman and Tversky: that when pairs of prospects with positive returns are replaced by pairs of prospects which are the 'mirror images' of the original prospects (in that 'plusses' are replaced by 'minusses', but magnitudes are left unchanged), preferences generally tend to be reversed. For example, if a certainty of 3000 is preferred to a gamble yielding 4000 with probability 0.8 and 0 with probability 0.2, then a certainty of − 3000 is considered as *less* preferred than a gamble yielding − 4000 with probability 0.8 and 0 with probability 0.2. Of course, this 'reflection effect' is not inconsistent with Neumann–Morgenstern utility theory – it simply reflects a general tendency for risk-averse behaviour with respect to gains and risk-loving behaviour with respect to losses. When taken in conjunction with the further observation that individuals do not appear in practice to assess the *absolute* value of returns, however, but rather the gains and losses relative to some (possibly changing) reference point, it reflects an undermining of the conventional wisdom.

The 'isolation effect' refers to the general tendency for decision-makers to disregard components that alternative prospects share, and instead to concentrate on the components that distinguish them. The implication of this observation is, unfortunately, that the final choice of the decision-maker may depend crucially on the way that alternatives are presented to them. As an illustration of this phenomenon, Kahneman and Tversky quote the following example. In situation one, the respondents are asked to imagine that they are first given 1000 and then required to choose between a gamble which gives a 50–50 chance of winning 1000 or nothing, and a certainty of 500. In situation two, the respondents are asked to imagine that they are first given 2000 and then required to choose between a gamble which gives a 50–50 chance of losing 1000 or nothing, and a certain loss of 500. Although the end-products in the two situations are entirely the same, 84 per cent chose the second option in the first situation and 69 per cent the first option in the second.

A number of other observations are reported by Kahneman and Tversky: these include a general tendency for respondents to over-weight very small probabilities but to under-weight medium to large probabilities; the total effect of this phenomenon is that the total weight attached to all the probabilities is some number *less* than unity.

One obvious implication of these various observations is that, in practice, people make inconsistent choices: intransitivities inevitably result. Thus, by suitably presenting and re-presenting various pairs of options, a cynical experimenter could trap an individual into giving up option A and a little money for option B, then giving up option B and a little money for option C, and (finally?!) giving up option C and a little money for option A. Of course, economic theorists do not like intransitivities – they make life rather ambiguous. So what should be done?

It appears there are two choices. First, educate people in the eternal verities of Neumann–Morgenstern utility theory, so that *inter alia* they cease making intransitive choices. In one sense, this would lead to an obvious welfare gain. Secondly, construct a new theory in the light of observed behaviour, even though that behaviour exhibits intransitivities. This second route is the route followed by Kahneman and Tversky, with Prospect Theory being the outcome. As yet, no application of Prospect Theory to a particular economic problem has appeared in the literature (to our knowledge); we await such an application with interest. Of the various novelties that it will inevitably contain is the recognition that the predictions of the theory (in respect of the comparative static effects) will have to be conditional – conditional on the particular ways that the parameter changes have been effected and perceived. The predictions of this type of theory might thus be stochastic rather than deterministic. This might represent an important step towards reality.

The possibility, mentioned above, that choice might be stochastic rather than deterministic, lies at the heart of an alternative approach to dynamic decision-making under uncertainty. This approach, which we could term the flexibility/robustness approach, has been described in the most detail by Pye (1978), although Pye's particular version of this approach differs quite significantly from earlier writers on the topic (for example, Rosenhead, Elton and Gupta (1972)). The framework in which the flexibility/robustness approach is presented in Pye (1978) is the familiar sequential dynamic decision-making framework. Specifically, the framework postulates alternating moves (choices) by the decision-maker and responses (random occurrences) by 'nature'. After a finite number of such pairs, an end-point is reached which gives some reward to the decision-maker, the value of the reward depending upon the route followed (that is, the specific sequence of choices and responses). Readers will be familiar with this kind of problem being represented diagrammatically by means of a 'tree diagram'. Under the conventional (Neumann–Morgenstern) wisdom, the problem of the decision-maker is (optimally) solved by use of the backward induction methods described in Part II (especially Chapter 4) of this book. Specifically, start at the horizon (the end-point), and suppose that the decision-maker makes the final move; the optimal move is simply determined by the attainable end-point with the highest utility. Of course, the attainable set, and hence the optimal move, will depend on where 'nature' and the previous moves of the decision-maker had left him; we thus arrive at the natural concept of an optimal strategy *conditional* on the present state of the decision-maker. By working backwards in the, by now, familiar fashion, the decision-maker can determine his optimal strategy at each stage of the problem, conditional on where he is at that moment.

One crucially important implication of this conventional wisdom is that choice at any stage, although conditional on the state at that stage, is otherwise *deterministic*. Indeed, the decision-maker can predict, in advance of arriving at some stage, *precisely* what he would choose if he arrived at that stage in such-and-such a state. No randomness is involved. The crucial point of Pye's approach is to deny this deterministic response. (By so doing he is probably also denying the validity of the backward induction methodology, though this is not clear from his paper.) In contrast, he assumes that the response of the decision-maker may be stochastic: in other words, the decision-maker may not be able to predict precisely (but rather only stochastically) what choice he will make at some stage if he arrives at that stage in such-and-such a state. We must admit we find this basic notion attractive – indeed, it does seem to describe rather well our everyday experience. (Could you say now what you would do in 10-years time if you found yourself then in such-and-such a situation?) There are two problems, however: how do we reconcile the intuitive appeal of this notion with the logic of the backward induction argument outlined above?; how might we use this notion to improve our understanding of decision processes? We put the first question on one side for the moment, and look briefly at Pye's answer to the second. In essence, Pye equates greater uncertainty (as to what the decision-maker might do in a given state) with greater *flexibility*. (To be precise, he uses the *entropy* of the probability distribution of the stochastic choice as a measure of flexibility.) Robustness is then derived in terms of either flexibility alone, or some traded-off combination of flexibility and return. The latter implies that, for a given return, the choice which retains the greatest flexibility is the most robust, and that, for a given degree of flexibility, the choice which has the highest return is the most robust. On a superficial inspection, these are attractive ideas; however, on closer examination, problems appear. Not least of these is the derivation of the probability distribution(s) relating to the stochastic choice(s). One of Pye's suggestions in this respect envisages probabilities as being proportional to expected rewards – a rather strange idea in that it apparently resurrects backward induction, though in an illogical fashion. Clearly, there are unsolved problems here.

Let us return to our first question: how can we reconcile stochastic choice with the logic of backward induction? We suspect the answer is that we cannot. If so, what must go – our intuition or backward induction? This is clearly a very large question – one on which many pages have been written; obviously we are unable to do justice to it in the space available. We suspect the key lies in our notion of Foggy Economics (described in Hey (1979a, pp. 233–4)): looking into the future mentally is like looking into the distance visually on a foggy day – the further ahead one looks the less clear it is, and after a certain point one can see nothing. Nevertheless, one can see one's immediate surroundings, and thus make a move in a direction which seems reasonable; moreover, as one moves, a little bit more is revealed about the unknown. In a foggy world, we suspect backward induction cannot work; on the contrary one must work forwards. Under such circumstances it is hardly surprising that one is not certain now about what one will do at some point in the distance (future). Fog creates randomness.

In addition to the notion of random choice, one particularly important idea emerges from the above discussion – the idea that, since it is impossible (under the stated circumstances) for the decison-maker to determine his *optimal* strategy using backward induction, he must instead be content with simply using a *reasonable* strategy (based on some forward, and partial, analysis). Of course, the randomness of choice and the reasonableness of the chosen strategy are inter-related: what appears reasonable to one person at one point in time will differ from what the same individual may regard as reasonable at some other point in time, or what some other individual regards as reasonable at the first point in time (even in the same given state). Randomness is inevitable.

This denial of the possibility of optimality, and the preference for reasonableness, has been propounded vigorously for a number of years by a group of economists termed (disparagingly?) 'behaviouralists' by the profession. Notable amongst their number is the recent Nobel prize winner, Professor Simon. In many of his writings (see, for example, Simon (1978)), he has argued forcibly that most decision problems faced by economic agents are simply too *complicated* for agents to act optimally – individuals (or even large corporations) do not have the computational ability to solve the problems. (This is a slightly different argument from our 'foggy economics' argument, but it leads to the same general conclusions.) The example *par excellence*, which can usually be guaranteed to silence any sceptic, is the game of chess. According to the logic of backward induction, the game is, in principle, soluble – and hence solved. Since White has an undeniable advantage, the game, when played optimally, must end in a win for White or a draw. Thus, after (or even before) White's (optimal) opening move, the game may as well be terminated! Peculiarly, people continue to play chess – are they not aware of backward induction? (There is, of course, a respectable counter-argument to the complexity argument: many people are amazingly skillful at doing tasks that no robot could be programmed to do – for example, professional golfers achieve unbelievable accuracy; thus, people act *as if* they can solve very complex problems. True; but no economist has yet explored the interesting implications of the fact that some people are better golfers than others!)

Behavioural economists have produced a number of interesting analyses based on the assumption that economic agents act reasonably rather than optimally. (Acting reasonably could, of course, include the procedure of first reducing a complex problem to a similar simple problem, and then acting optimally with respect to the simple problem.) As we have already argued, the inevitable implication of adopting this approach is that the resulting predictions are necessarily stochastic. Indeed, many of the behavioural models are presented in the form of stochastic processes; good examples can be found in Radner (1975), Radner and Rothschild (1975) and Nelson and Winter (1975). References must also be made to the many works of Simon, including his seminal paper (Simon, 1955) on rational choice.[5]

The behavioural models referred to in the paragraph above, although based on reasonable (rather than optimal) behaviour, and although their predictions are stochastic (rather than deterministic), nevertheless produce predictions. Naturally, these predictions are of the form 'if this parameter changes, then there will be a general tendency for the following response to occur', but they are predictions none the less. Our final approach to decision-making under uncertainty would appear to deny even this possibility. This final approach is expounded in the many works[6] of the prolific writer, Professor G. L. S. Shackle. For him, the outcome of a *genuine* choice by an individual is, of necessity, unpredictable; almost definitionally perhaps, the decisions of an individual are what make him individual, and thus distinct from other human begins. Moreover, in sharp contrast to the Neumann–Morgenstern approach and to most of the other approaches discussed in this chapter, the concept of *probability* is of little value in a genuine decision problem. According to Shackle, it is *possibility*, and not probability, that is important; from possibility comes Shackle's pivotal and unique concept of *potential surprise*. (The occurrence of an event deemed perfectly possible by an individual will not cause the individual any surprise; on the contrary, a large amount of surprise will be experienced by the occurrence of an event deemed to be impossible.) Crucial to Shackle is that possibility is not simply probability in disguise. Clearly, to many people the idea of potential surprise is an intuitively sensible one; it is also one that is (damagingly?) lacking in the conventional Bayesian-augmented Neumann–Morgenstern framework. Proper Bayesians are never surprised; or, if they are, Bayesian analysis tells us nothing about how they react. But then Shackle does not either – but perhaps that is the essence of surprise?

We feel that probability is relevant, and indeed crucial, to the decision-making of individuals under uncertainty; at the least, it appears that decision-makers act *as if* they attach probabilities to the various *perceived* possibilities (though this set may well not coincide with the actual set of possibilities). Consider the following choice problem, where the entries in the table are denominated in the utility of the individual making the choice (the utility function having been derived prior to this problem):

		outcome	
		A	$\bar{A}$
choice	1	u	0
	2	1	1

Suppose event A is some event, the occurrence of which the decision-maker may or may not perceive as being totally uncertain. For most individuals, if u was zero they would choose 2, while if u was very high, they would choose 1; thus, it seems reasonable to assert that there will be some value of u, say u^*, at which the individual is indifferent between the two choices. If so, the individual is acting *as if* he was attaching probability $1/u^*$ to event A.[7] This inference appears indisputable; what is interesting is whether the inferred probability depends upon the specific utility values chosen in the experiment. What is even more interesting is the question we have rather begged: how does the individual arrive at his set of perceived possibilities? This recognition that this is a serious question, and does not have a trivial answer, may well lead to a reconciliation between Neumann–Morgenstern theorists, behaviouralists of various types and Shackle.

9.5 CONCLUSIONS

Our basic conclusion is hinted at in the final sentence of the paragraph above. We suspect that the actual process of decision-making proceeds as follows: first the individual, of necessity, reduces a complex problem to a related simple one (in so doing, he carves out part of the world which he thinks relevant and ignores the rest); second, he then optimises with respect to the simple problem; and possibly third, he may then modify this solution in view of the perceived differences between his simple model and the real problem. Neumann–Morgenstern utility theory admirably tackles the second of these; the first and third are partially tackled by the other approaches discussed in this chapter. Perhaps, in due course, we will see the construction of unified models which reunite all three parts.

10 MARKETS

10.1 INTRODUCTION

The first three chapters in this part of the book focused attention on the decisions made by individual economic agents acting under uncertainty. During these three chapters, the behaviour of all other economic agents, as manifested in the environment facing our particular individual, was treated as exogenous to the problem in hand. In this chapter, the final one of this part, we begin the process of analysing the simultaneous interaction of the decisions made by more than one economic agent; specifically, we examine the behaviour of *individual* markets. In the next part of the book, we continue this analytical process: by examining the simultaneous interaction of several markets in Chapter 11, and finally by investigating the behaviour of the macroeconomy in Chapter 12.

This chapter, then, is concerned with individual markets. In particular, we examine the important question of whether, in a market containing a number of sellers and buyers acting under (possibly varying amounts of) uncertainty, an equilibrium state of some kind exists; moreover, we ask whether there is any relationship between the kind of equilibrium state that exists and the 'rules of the game' in the specific market under consideration. In addition, we investigate whether our analysis sheds any light on the question of how, and the process by which, the market might adjust when out of equilibrium.

Most of the material in this chapter is contained in the two major sections, 10.2 and 10.3. The distinction between these two sections concerns the *perceptions* of the market participants of the *quality* of the good (or goods) being traded in the market. Section 10.2 considers the simplest possible case – that when the true quality of the good is correctly perceived by all participants. In contrast, Section 10.3 examines markets in which the quality of the good varies and (more importantly) in which perceptions of the quality also vary; much of this section will be devoted to the important special case in which each participant on one side of the market knows the true quality of the good he or she is trading, whereas the participants on the other side are (at least initially) ignorant of the true qualities. (Familiar examples include used car markets, insurance markets and labour markets.) As we shall see, the existence of such *informational asymmetries* may well provide an incentive for the introduction of *screening* and *signalling* devices: the former adopted by the initially ignorant participants, and the latter by the informed participants.

After these two major sections, Section 10.4 provides a relatively brief summary of other market models, while Section 10.5 offers some comments in conclusion. As a whole, the chapter differs from earlier chapters in that it concentrates more on general issues and less on specific models. This shift of emphasis is necessitated, as should become clear, by the nature of the material.

10.2   MARKETS WITHOUT QUALITY UNCERTAINTY

We begin our analysis of markets by considering, in this section, markets in which the quality of the good (or goods) being traded is fully and correctly perceived by all the participants (and potential participants) in the market. For clarity of exposition we restrict attention, without loss of generality, to markets in which a single homogeneous good is being traded; the analysis is applicable to markets with heterogeneous goods if 'prices' are interpreted as quality-adjusted prices. Most of the section will be concerned with *atomistic* markets – that is, those in which the numbers of traders on the two sides of the market are both very large (essentially infinite); atomistic markets are thus 'perfectly competitive' markets without the 'perfect knowledge' assumption. At the end of the section there will be a very brief discussion of markets in which there is monopoly on one side of the market; as we shall see, the results of the analysis of atomistic markets have interesting implications for monopolistic markets.

Consider, then, a market, for a homogeneous good, in which there are very large numbers of both potential buyers and potential sellers. How does the trading process in such a market operate? If we look to the real world for an answer, we see a variety of processes in operation. In some markets, the sellers take an active rôle in that they publicly announce prices at which they are willing to sell, while buyers take an essentially passive rôle in that they either buy at the announced price(s) or they do not. In other markets, the reverse situation applies – in that buyers take the active rôle while sellers take the passive rôle. In other markets, a set (of one or more) trading specialists (who are ultimately neither buyers nor sellers of the good) intermediate between buyers and sellers in one of a variety of forms; for example, the jobber on the stock exchange announces a pair of prices at which he is willing to buy and sell respectively the good in question – his return from providing this intermediation service arises from the gap between the buying and selling prices. In other markets, trade is arranged through some kind of auction process. In others, a system of tendering or estimating may be in operation. In others, there may be no centralised system in existence; instead, trade occurs through a shifting set of bilateral exchanges between individual buyers and sellers, or between individual (and possibly varying) coalitions (or sets) of buyers and sellers. The list of real-world practices contains many possibilities.[1]

Casual empiricism suggests that the actual real-world trading process that exists for a specific good is not entirely unconnected with the particular characteristics of the good in question: it is rather difficult to imagine stocks and shares being sold by the corner shop; equally difficult is to imagine greengroceries being bought by Aberdeen housewives on the London Stock Exchange! Clearly some forms of trading process are more efficient for some goods, while other forms are more efficient for other goods; that is, the question of the 'best' trading process is itself a problem for economic analysis. A complete analysis of markets would, therefore, determine the optimal trading process for each good, as well as the actual details of the operation of that trading process. Unfortunately, as yet a complete analysis does not exist: up to now, economists have largely ignored the first of these two aspects, and instead concentrated their attention on the second of the two. For obvious reasons, we shall do likewise (while noting that the first aspect remains a vital and important topic for research, not only in its own right, but also for the light that it may shed on the second aspect).

Our analysis will, therefore, take the 'rules of the game' (that is, the form of the trading process) as given, and focus attention on the outcome of the 'game'. Of the various possibilities discussed in the penultimate paragraph, most of the published literature has concentrated on the first possibility; we shall do likewise. Suppose, therefore, that the market is organised in such a way that individual sellers announce (individual) prices, while buyers react essentially passively, in that either they buy at the announced price(s) or they do not. The first obvious point to note about such a market is that, with individual sellers setting prices, there can be no presumption that, at any given time, the same price is being charged by all sellers. On the contrary, the presumption must be that, at any given time, a non-degenerate[2] distribution of prices *may* exist. Two sets of questions naturally present themselves. First, can such a non-degenerate distribution of prices persist?; if so, what are the properties of this non-degenerate equilibrium?, if not, to what single price does the distribution degenerate? Second, if the actual distribution at a given time is not an equilibrium distribution, how does the distribution change?; and does the distribution converge to a (possibly degenerate) equilibrium distribution? As should be clear, the first set of questions relate to the existence, uniqueness and nature of equilibrium price distributions; the second set relate to the adjustment processes of disequilibrium distributions and to the stability, or otherwise, of equilibrium distributions.

Although much of the original interest in market models of this type was motivated by a desire to answer the second set of questions, and thus to arrive at theoretically satisfactory models of price adjustment processes,[3] most of the recent literature has been devoted to the first set of questions. Thus, ironically, a body of literature initially directed towards the description of disequilibrium processes has ended up describing equilibrium states! Be that as it may, some important and interesting literature has emerged.

Let us, therefore, begin by concentrating on the first set of questions: specifically, does an equilibrium distribution of prices exist, and if so, what form does it take? To begin to answer this, we must look in more detail at the behaviour of the individual agents on the two sides of the market. Consider first the (potential) buyers. According to the 'rules of the game', they are price-takers, at least with respect to the prices they actually encounter. They may be presumed to know that there is a distribution of prices across sellers for the good in question. Above this, the amount of information about the distribution or about the prices charged by individual sellers, that a buyer initially has, or is able to obtain (possibly at a cost), depends upon the precise specification of the model under consideration. As a model-builder 'playing God', the theoretician has considerable freedom over the details of the information structure he imposes on the actors in his model. As might be expected, however, as a general rule the more realistic the information structure, the less tractable is the resulting model. (As an inevitable consequence, the published literature so far has been concerned with

relatively simplistic, and unreal, informational structures.) Let us
list some of the possibilities:

1. that each buyer knows the price charged by each seller;
or
2. that each buyer can purchase (at a cost possibly varying across
   buyers) a complete list of the price charged by each seller;
or
3. that each buyer knows the *distribution* of prices across sellers,
   but not *individual* prices, and:
   (a) can purchase exact information about individual prices (at a
       cost possibly varying across buyers and across sellers); and/or
   (b) can obtain (possibly inexact) information about individual
       prices (possibly at a possibly varying cost) from other buyers
       (who have previously become 'informed' through some
       combination of (a), (b) and (c)); and/or
   (c) may have (possibly inexact) information about individual
       prices obtained from earlier time-periods;
or
4. that each buyer neither knows the distribution of prices across
   sellers, nor individual prices, and (a) and/or (b) and/or (c) above;
or
5. some combination of 1, 2, 3 and 4 applied to individual sets of
   buyers.

The most usual situation in the real world is that a potential
buyer, upon his first contact with the market, has some fairly vague
impressionistic evidence gained from contacts with friends and
acquaintances and from experience with purchase of related goods;
this information (depending upon its degree of vagueness) will be
augmented by the individual by some search and research. Purchase
may then take place. If the good is one that an individual purchases
more than once in his lifetime, then the amount of information
about prices that the individual possesses may be expected to
increase through time; though this depends heavily on the frequency
of re-purchase relative to the temporal stability of the price distribution. At a market level, there is a constant flow of buyers into and
out of the market – with the outflow being (almost necessarily)
more informed than the inflow. The real-world situation, therefore,
consists of a combination of 1–4 above.

For any assumed informational structure, the next task of the
model-builder is to derive the optimal[4] strategy of each buyer with

respect to any given price distribution. (Or, if elements of learning through time, that is 3(c) above, are involved, with respect to any given time sequence of price distributions.) For some of 1–4 above, the optimal strategy is fairly easily derived – using, *inter alia*, the techniques of Part II of this book. For example: under 1 there is no problem to examine; under 2 the individual will purchase the (complete) information if the expected benefit of buying at the lowest price rather than at a randomly chosen price is greater than the cost of buying the information; under 3(a), the problem of the individual is a standard one in search theory. However, for some of 1–4 – notably 3(b), 3(c) and possibly 4 – the derivation of the optimal strategy may be rather difficult. As we remarked earlier, this has led to the inevitable consequence of a concentration in the published literature on relatively simple informational structures; in particular, to our knowledge no-one has yet published a model with fully optimal behaviour under temporally dependent price distributions. This is a pity, as this appears to be the usual case in practice.

Once the behaviour of the buyers has been derived, the model-builder can turn his attention to the sellers. Each seller has two decisions to make (each time period): the price to be charged, and the quantity to be produced. A considerable simplification, however, can be achieved if the 'rules of the game' are so defined that the second of these two decisions can be deferred until all uncertainties (about demand) have been resolved. Most published models have adopted this simplification (either by assuming that production takes place after demand is known, or by postulating a constant marginal cost of production). In the absence of this simplification, not only would the derivation of the optimal strategy of the sellers be more difficult, but also the assumed environment surrounding the buyers would have to be changed (to incorporate the possibility that sellers become 'sold out' – in which case search would not be only over prices, but also over the availability of the good). With this simplification, the only decision remaining to the sellers is that of the price (each time period).

To simplify our exposition, let us concentrate attention initially on static (or time-independent) models: these are essentially models in which either the set of buyers is totally changed each trading period, or, despite being in the market for several periods, buyers do not learn. Static models have the great advantage (as far as the model-builder is concerned) that sellers do not acquire 'price reputations' through time. Consequently, in choosing their optimal price in any one period, they neither have to consider any 'legacy from the past', nor have to worry about the implications for the future. All they have to think about is the present.

In view of the postulated large number of sellers in such atomistic markets, the natural concept of an equilibrium is that of a *Nash equilibrium*. To investigate whether a Nash equilibrium exists, the model-builder proceeds by deriving the optimal price of each seller *conditional on the prices of every other seller and the search strategies of every buyer being taken as given*. This makes life much easier, particularly since it removes the problem of examining (strategic) reactions. To derive the optimal price of any seller is thus relatively straightforward (at least in principle): given any distribution of prices over the other sellers, and given the search *strategies* of the buyers with respect to the *total* distribution of prices across sellers, the seller in question can determine the (possibly random) demand for his good for any price that he charges. Given his objective function (which may be to maximise the expected utility of profits), he can then determine his optimal price.

A Nash equilibrium distribution of prices exists if the price of each and every seller is his optimal price, given the remaining distribution, and given the search strategies of the buyers.

As should be clear from the above discussion, the question of whether a Nash equilibrium exists depends crucially on the informational structure imposed on the buyers. Even under the restriction that the resulting model is static, there are a number of possibilities. We do not have space to go into detail here; however, we can refer the reader to several recent examples. (Some earlier ones are discussed in Hey (1979a, Chapters 25 and 26).)

Salop and Stiglitz (1977) impose information structure 2 on the buyers; additionally they suppose there are two groups of buyers who differ in the amount it costs them to buy the complete price list. In this model, buyers either choose to become completely informed, thus buying at the lowest existing price, or to remain uninformed, thus buying at a randomly chosen price (no search behaviour is allowed in the model). As is common in such models, all buyers buy one unit of the good (irrespective of the purchase price – as long as it is below some limit price). Salop and Stiglitz demonstrate that if a Nash equilibrium exists, then it is either a single-price equilibrium (either at the competitive price or at the monopoly (limit) price), or a two-price equilibrium (with the lower price being the competitive price and the upper price no larger than the monopoly price). No n-price equilibria exist, for $n > 2$. Additionally, Salop and Stiglitz show that it is possible that no Nash equilibrium exists; they liken this possibility to Akerlof's 'lemons principle' – something we will discuss in detail in the next section.

A paper by Wilde and Schwartz (1979) is similar to that discussed above in that there are two groups of buyers; but here one group always buys from the first seller encountered, while the second group buys from the cheapest of a sample of size n (where n is predetermined) sellers. Within this framework, they demonstrate the possible existence of a non-degenerate price distribution; like Salop and Stiglitz this may have a mass-point at the competitive price, but the rest of the probability may be spread over a set of prices.

A further paper in the same vein is that by Braverman (1980). The same informational structure as that used by Salop and Stiglitz is imposed, but the cost of becoming informed is distributed continuously across buyers. In many respects, his results are similar to those of Salop and Stiglitz. A slight variant on a theme is provided by Butters (1977); as part of his model, he postulates 'ads' being sent out by sellers. Additionally, this paper is of interest in that it presents an argument (p. 466) to the effect that under information structure 3(a) above, if the cost of search is strictly positive for all buyers, then there can only be one equilibrium – a degenerate one at the monopoly price. The essence of his argument is that the lowest-priced seller always has an incentive (until the monopoly price is reached) to raise his price by an amount equal to the lowest search cost; by so doing, no buyers are lost, and profits are thereby increased.

All of the above models assume that quantities are not a problem – in that supply can always be adjusted to equal demand.[5] A paper in which quantities are explicitly considered is that of Carlton (1978). In contrast with the papers discussed above all prices are assumed known by all buyers; the only uncertainty concerns the availability of the good (since in this model demand is random while supply is predetermined). Carlton demonstrates the possibility of a non-degenerate price distribution; however, as he remarks, in this equilibrium, different prices are associated with different degrees of availability – in this sense the 'good' for sale is not homogeneous.

Before concluding, we ought to mention the important paper by Pratt, Wise and Zeckhauser (1979), who demonstrate the possible existence of non-degenerate price distributions under a variety of different informational structures; they also show the possibility of multiple equilibria. Mention must also be made of one of the pioneers in this area, Franklin Fisher, who continues to produce significant contributions; one of his latest being Fisher (1981). Amongst his earlier work, Fisher (1976) should be singled out for its insightful discussion of the main problems in this area.

The above discussion has concentrated on essentially static models; as we have already remarked such models have formed the vast majority of published work in this area. There are some welcome exceptions, however, particularly in the work of Sutton (1980a, b). These papers present a stationary (as distinct from static) equilibrium distribution model, with explicit modelling of buyer and seller dynamics.

There has also been a small amount of work on alternative trading processes (but still within the same market structure). The most notable is the work by Bradfield and Zabel both jointly and separately (Bradfield, 1979; Bradfield and Zabel, 1978; Zabel, 1979) on markets where trade is co-ordinated by trading specialists.

Although the above material is primarily concerned with atomistic markets, the analysis has had an interesting spin-off for the treatment of monopolies. As Salop (1977) and Stiglitz (1977) have pointed out, it may pay a monopolist to be 'noisy' (for instance by charging a variety of prices for the same good). By exploiting the fact that a buyer may be reluctant (for cost reasons) to become fully informed, the monopolist may be able to increase his profits by creating discrimination through uncertainty.

We have now discussed the problems, and surveyed some of the attempts, involved with answering the first set of questions related to markets – those concerned with existence, uniqueness and nature of equilibrium. As we have seen, there are a bewildering number of possibilities: depending upon the information structure, a degenerate distribution (at either the competitive or the monopoly price) may exist, a non-degenerate distribution (with one or more mass points, and possibly no 'non-mass' points) may exist, multiple equilibria (of various types) may exist, or no equilibria may exist. Under such circumstances, a general conclusion appears impossible!

As far as the second set of questions are concerned (those relating to disequilibrium states and adjustment processes), very little work has been done. Clearly this is because of the problems involved with fully specifying optimal behaviour in disequilibrium states. Even if the adjustment process is itself an equilibrium adjustment process, the demands on the computational abilities of the agents are immense. To compute an optimal response (which, of necessity, is of a dynamic nature) requires each agent to solve a dynamic optimisation problem given the adjustment processes of all the other agents.

The mind boggles! Of course, if the adjustment process itself is not in equilibrium, then the analysis must go back one stage; but this compounds the computational problems still further. No wonder theorists like to deal with static equilibrium states!

Nevertheless, if disequilibrium exists in the real world, economists should attempt to model it. As we have argued, describing *optimal* behaviour in disequilibrium is desperately complicated. But perhaps this is an argument for dropping optimality rather than for ignoring disequilibrium?

10.3 MARKETS WITH QUALITY UNCERTAINTY

Throughout the above section we adopted the simplifying assumption that the good being traded was homogeneous, or, equivalently, that all traders correctly perceived the true quality of the goods. In this section, we drop this simplification; to be specific, we examine markets in which the quality of the goods being traded varies, and, more importantly, in which perceptions of the true qualities vary amongst participants. Thus, the essential feature of the markets under consideration in this section is that there is *asymmetrical information* amongst the participants.

We will devote virtually all of this section to one particularly important case of informational asymmetry – that in which the agents on one side of the market are fully informed about the true quality of the good they are trading, while agents on the other side are ignorant (at least initially). The classic example, featured in the title of Akerlof's (1970) seminal paper, is the used car market; in this, the sellers of used cars might be presumed to know the quality of the car(s) they are selling, though the buyers (in the absence of any screening or testing device) are unlikely to be able to ascertain the true quality by inspection alone. Another important example is the labour market; in this, the sellers (the individuals offering their labour services) know their own skills and productivity (at least in a general sense), though the buyers (again in the absence of any screening or testing device) are usually unable to perceive quality by inspection alone. One final example is the insurance market; in this, the buyers might be presumed to have a considerably better knowledge of how bad a risk they personally are than do the sellers (the insurance companies).

If we compound the problems of Section 10.2 by introducing the complication of informational asymmetries without any corresponding simplification elsewhere, we are likely to get an impossibly complex model. We will, therefore, follow the literature in adopting the simplification that all buyers and all sellers are (costlessly) fully informed about the prices being charged. In the light of this assumption, price dispersion originating from ignorance of prices cannot exist. Consider now a market in which the sellers of the good know the true quality of the good they are selling, but in which the buyers cannot distinguish quality by pre-purchase inspection. (The opposite situation, in which sellers are ignorant and buyers are informed is analytically identical.) Under our assumptions, if an equilibrium (price distribution) exists, it must be just a single price: because of our assumption of costless information about prices, the only equilibrium distribution must necessarily be a degenerate one. Put another way – because buyers cannot distinguish between goods of different qualities, they must all trade at the same price.

Thus, in equilibrium, *if it exists*, a single price must prevail – because of the informational asymmetry. As Akerlof (1970) eloquently points out, however, this fact may be sufficient to ensure that an equilibrium can *not* exist! The argument is straightforward: if it exists, the equilibrium price must depend, *ceteris paribus*, on the *average* quality of the goods being traded. This essentially means that the sellers of the low quality goods are being subsidised by the sellers of the high quality goods. But it is quite likely that the sellers of the top quality goods are losing so much of the value of their goods that they would prefer not to sell their goods at that price. Accordingly, the top quality sellers might withdraw from the market. Inevitably, their doing so would lower the average quality of the goods remaining in the market; this, in turn, would lower the equilibrium price. The process could then continue, with a continual withdrawal of the top quality sellers, until possibly no sellers were left. The market could cease to exist.[6]

Whether the market will disappear or not depends on the particular good in question, and upon the underlying demand and supply schedules. In a particularly important article, Rothschild and Stiglitz (1976) demonstrate the non-existence of this type of equilibrium in a simple insurance market; let us examine their model in some detail. Rothschild and Stiglitz investigate insurance against the occurrence of an accident which reduces the income of the individual from W to $W-d$. An insurance contract is a pair (a_1, a_2) specifying a premium, a_1, and a payment by the insurance company, $a_1 + a_2$, if the accident occurs. Thus, if an individual takes out the contract (a_1, a_2), he will have income $W - a_1$ if the accident does not

occur, and income $W - d + a_2$ if the accident does occur. The 'good'
being traded is the contract (a_1, a_2). The 'quality' of the good
depends upon the probability, p, of the individual experiencing the
accident. The contract is actuarially fair if $a_1 = p(a_1 + a_2)$, that is, if
the premium equals the expected payout. As far as an individual is
concerned, since his p is fixed, the quality of the contract increases
as a_2 increases relative to a_1; as far as the insurance company is concerned, the quality of any given contract (a_1, a_2) improves as p falls.
From the point of view of the company, individuals with high p
values are poor quality, those with low p values high quality.

In this insurance example, informational asymmetry enters in that
the insurance company (in the absence of any screening device)
cannot distinguish between low quality (high p) and high quality
(low p) contracts. If a single type of contract is to be offered to all
individuals, the same problem as in the Akerlof paper may arise: for
any contract aimed by the insurance company at the average p, the
low risk people may find it unattractive; this may drive out the low
risk individuals, thereby increasing the average risk and hence the
premium. As before, the high risks may drive out the low. In the
special case of just two risk groups, Rothschild and Stiglitz show that
such an eventuality must happen.

The sellers of insurance, however, have an option open to them
which the sellers of used cars generally do not: they can offer a
variety of contracts, and design them in such a way that specific
contracts appeal to specific risk groups. To illustrate this possibility,
consider the insurance model discussed above, and suppose that there
are just two groups of potential insurees – a high-risk group and a
low-risk group, with respective accident probabilities of p^H and p^L
(where $p^H > p^L$, of course). If a standard contract (a_1, a_2) is offered
to everyone, an equilibrium will not exist. If two contracts, denoted
by (a_1^H, a_2^H) and (a_1^L, a_2^L) for reasons which will shortly be obvious,
are offered, however, and if the various preferences and parameters
are such that the former is preferred by the high-risk group and the
latter by the low-risk group, then, as long as the contracts are
profitable to the company, an equilibrium will exist. For obvious
reasons, Rothschild and Stiglitz call such an equilibrium a *separating
equilibrium*. The insurance company has overcome its informational
ignorance by providing an incentive for the buyers to practise *self-
selection* – that is, to reveal their true qualities by their behaviour.
(The most obvious example of this is the practice of offering reduced
premiums for increased deductibles.) Thus, the non-existence of a
pooling equilibrium, and hence the potential disappearance of the

market, may be averted by the encouragement of self-selection. There are circumstances, however, in which even separating equilibria do not exist (for details see Rothschild and Stiglitz 1976)).

Self-selection is not the only way of overcoming the difficulties introduced by informational asymmetries. Since the sellers of the high-quality goods would benefit if they could convince potential buyers of the true quality of their goods, they have an incentive to provide convincing evidence. Clearly, simply announcing that their goods are high quality will not in general be sufficient (except in markets which exist for many periods, and in which reputations can be made or destroyed), since sellers of low-quality goods can do likewise. Offering a *guarantee* is one obvious route; a less obvious route is through the use (and jealous protection) of *brand names*. All such devices are instances of *signals* of product quality. Interestingly, much of the early work done on signalling (particularly that by Spence (1974)) was done in the context of labour markets. Good quality workers have incentives to obtain signals of their quality: obvious examples include the obtaining of educational qualifications of one form and another, and the completion of apprenticeship programmes. Of course, to be effective, there must be some connection between the possession of a signal and the possession of the actual quality that the signal is meant to indicate – if it is equally easy (or equally costly) for all grades of quality to obtain a given signal, the resulting signal is likely to be rather worthless! Thus, as a *signal* of intelligence, a degree is useful only if it is harder for a less intelligent person to get a degree than a more intelligent person.

Unfortunately, we do not have sufficient space to go into more detail here; the interested reader could begin with the book by Spence (1974). Before we leave the subject of signalling, however, we should note that, although it may provide a route to establishing equilibrium in an informationally asymmetrical market, it may well be inefficient in a welfare sense. Unless the acquisition of a signal has some other positive benefit (as one would hope in the case of a degree!), the cost of acquiring the signal may be simply a welfare loss.

The other side of the coin to signalling is *screening* – the adoption of quality-testing devices by the initially uninformed. An example in the used car market is the inspection service by the Automobile Association. Screening is also practised in the labour market through the use of interviews, personality assessments, examinations and probationary periods. All these devices reduce uncertainty on the part of the initially uninformed; as such they may well lead to the existence of equilibrium. As with signalling, however, they may also represent a welfare loss.

In the real world there are a whole variety of devices used to reduce uncertainty in such situations (and, indeed, a whole variety of devices used to increase uncertainty or to mislead the uninformed!); some of these we have discussed above. Doubtless the reader can add to our list. Before we conclude, we ought to mention one final method, which has been the subject of recent study by economists, namely the adoption of *minimum quality standards*. This is a method widely practised by professional organisations – doctors, lawyers, actuaries and the like – who require potential members of the profession to undergo a series of tests before being admitted to membership. In essence, this procedure indicates, to potential purchasers of the services of the profession, the minimum quality level; it thereby protects the service from self-destruction (by 'quacks'). An excellent exploratory analysis is contained in the paper by Leland (1979). The theme has been taken up and extended in two papers by Shaked and Sutton (1979 and 1980).

The issues discussed in this section are important ones, and it is unfortunate that we do not have the space to explore them in more detail. In addition to the references noted above, the interested reader could refer to the Symposium on the Economics of Information in the 1976 volume of the *Quarterly Journal of Economics* (and a similar symposium in the October 1977 issue of the *Review of Economic Studies*), as well as the recent papers by Riley (1979a, b) and Wilson (1979).

10.4 OTHER MARKET MODELS

We have attempted in the two preceding sections to provide some framework for the analysis of markets. Even within the relatively restrictive framework that we have adopted, there is a bewildering variety and diversity of models. Outwith our framework there is even more diversity. All we can hope to do in this section is to provide the reader with some indication of the kinds of market models that have been the subject of study; no attempt at comprehensiveness can be made. (Some further discussion can be found in Part V of Hey (1979a).)

Our partial catalogue might fruitfully begin, within the *Review of Economic Studies* symposium mentioned above, with the paper by

Wilson (1977). His model postulates a sealed-tender auction for a single item, and represents one of a large set of auction and bidding models recently surveyed by Engelbrecht-Wiggans (1980).

Another important set of models consists of those devoted to the labour market. A subset of these models contains the *implicit contracts literature* initiated by Azariadis (1975); Baily (1974) and Gordon (1974). Closely related is the literature on temporary layoffs, originating in the work of Baily (1977) and Feldstein (1976). Such labour market models differ quite crucially from the market models discussed in Sections 10.2 and 10.3 in that they specifically focus attention on long-run dynamic issues; this reflects the crucial feature of labour as a traded commodity – in most societies, labour contracts (whether explicit or implicit) are usually of a more long-term nature than contracts for other goods. A useful survey of the types of labour market models mentioned in this section is given by Pissarides (1981). The analysis of themes related to those discussed in Section 10.3 (that is, those concerning the quality of labour) has been begun by Grossman (1977). In particular, he provides a preliminary exploration – crucial to markets in which the same participants appear for several time periods – of the question of *reputations*, both of the reliability of workers and the integrity of firms. Much remains to be done in this area, however.

As we have remarked several times, the bulk of the literature on markets has concentrated on *static equilibrium* analysis, with all participants acting *optimally* (at least with respect to the information structure imposed on them). As we have also remarked, these two things (static equilibrium and optimality) tend to go hand-in-hand. Outside a static equilibrium framework, it is very difficult to define optimal behaviour (and even more difficult to imagine real-life people actually deriving the optimal strategy); within a static equilibrium framework, it is rather difficult to maintain that economic agents do anything other than optimise. Thus, dispensing with static equilibrium tends to imply dropping optimally, and vice versa.

Recent years have witnessed a small, but growing, number of publications aimed at breaking out of the 'static equilibrium optimality' framework. Of necessity, as we have partially argued above, these models tend to be stochastic (and occasionally Markov) models, in which 'behavioural' rather than 'optimising' assumptions are used to specify agents' behaviour. Behaviour is based on reasonable rules of thumb; this tends to imply stochastic rather than deterministic choice.[7] An excellent recent example is provided by Smallwood and Conlisk (1979), who examine a model in which buyers are uncertain about product quality (defined in a relatively simple manner as the probability of the good 'breaking down' in use). The authors postulate that buyers, who stay in the market many time periods, will continue to purchase a particular good (brand) until a breakdown (of the good, not the buyer!) occurs; at this point a switch to another brand may be made. As a general rule, the more reliable brands will end up with the most buyers; but, because buyers do not behave optimally, the most reliable brands do not end up with *all* the buyers. (This process is very similar to the psychological model of learning described in Section 6.5.) Because of the nature of the model, both disequilibrium states and equilibrium states can be modelled; the latter takes the form of a stationary stochastic process. This represents quite a marked distinction from the models of Section 10.2. A similar type of model is presented by Satterthwaite (1979).

10.5 CONCLUSIONS

Although the 'behavioural' (or evolutionary) models briefly discussed in the concluding paragraphs of Section 10.4 represent a very tiny fraction of the total output of market models, they would appear to constitute an important step in the right direction. Their great advantage, in view of the complexity of modelling fully optimal behaviour in disequilibrium states, is that they allow some light to be shed on the important problem of modelling adjustment *processes*. Their great disadvantage is that, of their very nature, they do not lead to simple general predictions; on the contrary, they tend to be rather bulky, large and 'messy', with highly specific predictions conditional on highly specific parameter values. But perhaps this reflects the economic world in which we live?

PART IV

MACROECONOMIC IMPLICATIONS

11 GENERAL EQUILIBRIUM AND DISEQUILIBRIUM

11.1 INTRODUCTION

This chapter provides an important bridge between the micro-economic material of the preceding part of the book and the macro-economic material of the succeeding chapter: whereas general equilibrium theory can be considered as the study of the simultaneous interaction of all the economic agents in the economy, macro-economics is (or, at least, should be) essentially a highly aggregated version of general equilibrium theory.

Of course, the focus of interest necessarily varies: at the level of generality espoused by general equilibrium theory, broad questions concerning, for example, the behaviour of aggregate unemployment and output cannot fruitfully be explored; likewise, because of the complexity of the analysis of a many-market model, the detailed questions concerning the functioning of markets which were examined in Chapter 10, cannot (yet) be answered within a totally general equilibrium framework.

The focus of this chapter is on the introduction of time and uncertainty into the conventional (certainty) general equilibrium model. To motivate the material of the chapter, it may be useful to begin by outlining this conventional model; we will then be in a position to describe and appraise the problems involved with the incorporation (or recognition) of uncertainty. For expositional reasons, we use the simplest version of the general equilibrium model as our vehicle for discussion; this version relates to a pure exchange economy in a timeless (or one-period) world.

Consider then a simple economy in which there are I individuals (or individual decision-making units), indexed by i. Suppose that there are in existence a total of J goods and services which potentially yield utility[1] to some or all of the individuals; let these goods and services (or just 'goods' for short) be indexed by j. In this pure exchange economy there is no production; individuals are simply endowed with initial stocks of the various goods: for reasons which should become clear (in relation to our wish to use a standardised notation wherever possible) we denote by $\bar{Y}^i_j$ the initial endowment of good j held by individual i. Of course, $\bar{Y}^i_j$ will be zero if individual i has no initial endowment of good j. By $\bar{\mathbf{Y}}^i$ we denote the vector $\{\bar{Y}^i_1, \bar{Y}^i_2, \ldots, \bar{Y}^i_J\}$. Individual i is assumed to have a well-defined utility function $U^i(.)$ defined over the vector of *final consumption* $(\mathbf{Y}^i + \bar{\mathbf{Y}}^i)$ where $\mathbf{Y}^i$ denotes the vector of *net* trades $(Y^i_1, Y^i_2, \ldots, Y^i_J)$.

We now consider the problem faced by the typical individual. To improve clarity (and since no confusion thereby results) we omit the superscript i during our analysis of this problem. Our typical individual is presumed to be a price-taker in all markets; we denote by $\mathbf{X} = (X_1, X_2, \ldots, X_J)$ the vector of given prices. The problem of the individual is thus the familiar one of choosing net trades $\mathbf{Y}$ so as to maximise utility $U(\mathbf{Y} + \bar{\mathbf{Y}})$ subject to the usual budget constraint, which we write in the form $\mathbf{X} . \mathbf{Y} = 0$, where $\mathbf{X} . \mathbf{Y}$ denotes the vector product $\Sigma^J_{j=1} X_j Y_j$. The Lagrangean for this problem is

$$L(\mathbf{Y}; \mathbf{X}) \equiv U(\mathbf{Y} + \bar{\mathbf{Y}}) - \lambda \mathbf{X} . \mathbf{Y},$$

and the first-order conditions are the familiar

$$U_j = \lambda X_j \qquad (j = 1, \ldots, J)$$

and

$$\mathbf{X} . \mathbf{Y}^* = 0$$

where the subscript j on the utility function denotes (as usual) the partial derivative with respect to the jth argument.

These first-order conditions yield excess demand functions

$$\mathbf{Y}^* = \mathbf{Y}^*(\mathbf{X}; \bar{\mathbf{Y}}) \qquad (11.1)$$

for the J goods, as functions of the price vector $\mathbf{X}$ and the initial endowment $\bar{\mathbf{Y}}$. One important property[2] of these excess demand functions is that they are homogeneous of degree zero in prices, $\mathbf{X}$.

Let us now move on from considerations of the typical individual to considerations of particular markets. Since the total excess demand (or desired net trades) for good j is given by $\Sigma^I_{i=1} Y^{i*}_j$, then equilibrium in the market for the jth good requires that

$$\sum_{i=1}^{I} Y_j^i{}^* = 0. \tag{11.2}$$

General equilibrium accordingly requires that (11.2) holds for all $j = 1, \ldots, J$. One of the more important aspects of general equilibrium theory is that of demonstrating the existence (or otherwise) of a price vector $\mathbf{X}$ for which such requirements are met. In this simple pure-exchange economy fairly minimal restrictions on the utility functions are sufficient to ensure the *existence* of general equilibrium in this sense. (An obvious further question, once existence has been demonstrated, is that of *uniqueness*: does just one such equilibrium exist, or are there several?) We do not propose to go into details of such existence proofs – suffice it to say that numerous proofs exist elsewhere (for an excellent source, see Arrow and Hahn (1971)).

Although these proofs of existence of equilibrium in simple exchange economies are important (in the rather negative sense that in their absence much of economic theory would be rendered pointless), as reflections of reality the models leave much to be desired. Even though the model can *formally* incorporate[3] time (by calling the same good at different points in time different goods) and geographical dispersion (by calling the same good at different places different goods) and, indeed, uncertainty (by calling the same good in different states of the world different goods), the logic of the model requires that all prices be determined, and all contracts entered into, at the 'beginning of time'. The rest of 'economic history' then simply consists of the execution of the various pre-arranged contracts.

Notwithstanding the rather obvious points that not all individuals are born on the same day, not all individuals die on the same day, and not all individuals are particularly good at taking lifetime decisions on the day that they are born, the requirement that all contracts be arranged at the 'beginning of time' has a number of difficulties. Not trivial are the problems involved with contracting for the delivery of all demanded goods at all relevant places and at all relevant future times, but such problems pale into insignificance compared with those of contracting for *contingent* deliveries – contingent on all possible states of the world. If this clever device of contingent contracts is to eliminate completely the problem of incorporating uncertainty into general equilibrium theory, all possible sources of uncertainty must be accounted for – including uncertainty over (future) endowments and uncertainty over (future) tastes. Imagine your arranging a contract for delivery of four pints of milk on 16 December 1999 if you are feeling under the weather, but a delivery of just two pints if you are feeling normal! Imagine too the problem of satisfying the deliverer of your true state of health when that date arrives! A not-insignificant moral hazard problem would appear to exist.

Clearly such considerations are absurd. In the real world, one cannot contract at the 'beginning of time' for the delivery of all goods at all points in time and in all states of the world. Although some futures markets exist, generally one has to await the passage of time, and indeed the resolution of the intervening uncertainty, before one can enter into specific contracts for delivery at a particular date. The problem, using the terminology of general equilibrium theorists, is that the set of markets which exist at any one time is *not complete*. Thus only a subset of all possibly desirable contracts can be entered into at any one time – depending upon which markets exist at that time. Of course, the question of which particular markets do exist, and why other markets do not, is itself crucially important. As we have indicated above, the presence of moral hazard may be a sufficient reason for non-existence of certain contingent markets; another reason could be the high transaction costs involved with drawing up the relevant agreement – this could well outweigh the potential benefits, particularly if individuals are sufficiently unsure about their own future tastes that they value the flexibility endowed by remaining unconstrained by future commitments.

The point we are making is simple: in the real world, not all contracts are made at the 'beginning of time'; on the contrary, trade is carried out *sequentially* through time. Markets open (when the economic need arises, and conditions permit their existence) fulfil their purpose, and then close. A complete analysis of this process would not only describe the sequence of trades actually carried out *given a particular time-sequence of markets*, but would also explain the reasons for a particular time-sequence existing in the first place. Hitherto, economists have focused their attention on the first of these two aspects, and largely ignored the second.[4] We shall do likewise.

The rest of this chapter discusses *sequential* general equilibrium. The bulk of the material is contained in Sections 11.2 and 11.3: the difference between these two sections being that, in the former, trade is assumed to take place at market-clearing prices (in the markets that actually exist at that time) – thus no economic agents experience quantity constraints; in contrast, Section 11.3 explores the implications of non-market-clearing prices, particularly as regards the impact of the quantity constraints that inevitably result. As will become clear, this material paves the way for the macroeconomics of Chapter 12, particularly with respect to the problem of unemployment (which may represent a quantity constraint on the suppliers of labour). The remaining sections of the chapter are relatively minor (in terms of space rather than importance): Section 11.4 looks at stochastic models of general equilibrium; in some ways this provides an introduction to the ideas on general *dis*equilibrium discussed in Section 11.5. Finally, Section 11.6 offers some comments in conclusion.

11.2   GENERAL EQUILIBRIUM WITHOUT QUANTITY RATIONING[5]

We consider in this section economies in which sequential trading takes place: as time passes, markets come into existence, fulfil their purpose and then disappear. As we have noted above, the question of which particular markets exist at any one particular time is itself strictly a problem for economic analysis. Such an analysis remains to be performed, however. We shall, therefore, take the time-sequence of markets as given.

Throughout this section we will assume that, in each time period, trade takes place only at market-clearing prices (in the markets that actually exist, of course). Since we continue to maintain the price-taking assumption of Section 11.1, this implies that no traders experience quantity constraints: all agents can in fact buy or sell the exact amount that they want. As should be clear, this combination of assumptions makes life much easier for the analyst; in particular, it means that much of the general equilibrium apparatus assembled for the analysis of the simple (timeless) problem discussed in Section 11.1 can be salvaged, and brought to bear on the more complicated problem examined in this section.

To make our exposition as simple as possible, we start with the extreme assumption that the 'time-sequence of markets' (which is given) consists solely of *spot* markets for delivery of goods in that period. We remain within our pure-exchange model, and assume that all individuals receive (like manna from heaven) an endowment of goods each period; by $\bar{Y}^{it}$ we denote the vector of initial endowments of individual i in period t. To simplify our exposition still further we make the assumption that all goods (with one exception) are perishable, and thus become worthless unless consumed within the period. The one exception is a good which is totally *im*perishable, but which is also totally valueless as far as providing *direct* utility to any individual is concerned; this good, for obvious reasons, we call *money*.

The set of goods which constitute the initial endowment may well vary from period to period. For expositional convenience, however, we will index goods in each and every period by j, and assume j takes values from 1 to J every period. (Strictly speaking J should be subscripted with a t, and good j in period t may well be different from good j in some other period. Allowing for this possibility appears to complicate unnecessarily our notation.[6]) We will treat the good 'money' outside this scheme, and let $\bar{Z}_t^i$ denote the endowment of money to individual i in period t.

Our simple sequential pure-exchange economy thus works as follows: each period, individuals receive an endowment of (some of the) goods available in that period; money may be part of this, and each individual may have some money left over from the previous period; however, because of the perishability of all goods (except for money), there are no stocks of goods left over from previous periods; likewise, none of the goods of this period can sensibly be left unconsumed (as they will simply perish); trade takes place at market-clearing prices; consumption occurs and the period ends; the process then continues.

In one sense, the workings of this economy are almost the same as a sequence of equilibria of the 'timeless' economy discussed in Section 11.1. Indeed, the various periods are almost independent of one another. They are not totally independent, however: there is the crucial linking factor of *money*. In our simple economy, money fulfils the important rôle of allowing purchasing power to be transferred from period to period: if, for example, an individual has a very large endowment this period but knows that he will have a very small endowment next period, he can (if his time preference for consumption so requires) 'buy' money this period (that is, save) and use it to increase his consumption next period. Without money, and in the presence of total perishability of goods but in the absence of futures markets, the individual would not be able to re-distribute his purchasing power over time.

Let us look in more detail at how the process operates. First, we must specify whether we are in a finite or infinite horizon world; we confine attention to the former (though the arguments also apply to the latter) and let T denote the total number of periods in our world. For simplicity, we assume that all individuals begin their decision-making life in period 1 and end it in period T. Consider a typical individual; as before, we omit the superscript i to improve clarity. Suppose the utility function of this individual, defined over the set of vectors of final consumptions in the T periods, is additively separable, and can be written in the form[7] (cf. (4.31))

$$\sum_{t=1}^{T} \rho^{t-1} U_t(\mathbf{Y}^t + \bar{\mathbf{Y}}^t). \tag{11.3}$$

To analyse this sequence economy we employ the technique of backward induction (see Section 4.4). Begin with the final period, T. Our typical individual enters this period with a stock of money Z_T 'left over' from the previous period, and starts the period with an initial endowment $\bar{\mathbf{Y}}^T$ of goods and $\bar{Z}_T$ of money. Since the values of $\mathbf{Y}^t + \bar{\mathbf{Y}}^t$ for $t = 1, \ldots, T-1$ have all been determined, the problem of the individual is to choose a vector of net trades $\mathbf{Y}^T$ and an end-of-period stock of money Z_{T+1} so as to maximise $U_T(\mathbf{Y}^T + \bar{\mathbf{Y}}^T)$ subject to the constraint that $Z_{T+1} = Z_T + \bar{Z}_T - \mathbf{X}^T . \mathbf{Y}^T$ where $\mathbf{X}^T$ denotes the price-vector prevailing in period T. Since period T is the final period, the optimal value of Z_{T+1} is trivially zero, and the problem of the individual reduces to the familiar one of choosing $\mathbf{Y}^T$ so as to maximise $U_T(\mathbf{Y}^T + \bar{\mathbf{Y}}^T)$ subject to $Z_T + \bar{Z}_T = \mathbf{X}^T . \mathbf{Y}^T$. This problem (except for the addition of money) is identical to that outlined in Section 11.1; its solution leads to excess demand functions (cf. (11.1))

$$\mathbf{Y}^{T*} = \mathbf{Y}^{T*}(\mathbf{X}^T; \bar{\mathbf{Y}}^T, Z_T + \bar{Z}_T) \tag{11.4}$$

for the J goods as functions of the price vector $\mathbf{X}^T$, the initial endowments $\bar{\mathbf{Y}}^T$ and the total money holding $Z_T + \bar{Z}_T$.

Aggregation of these individual excess demand functions leads to market demand functions. As before (see Section 11.1), equilibrium in the market for the jth good requires that (cf. (11.2))

$$\sum_{i=1}^{I} Y_j^{iT*} = 0 \tag{11.5}$$

while *general* equilibrium requires that (11.5) holds for all j. If $\mathbf{X}^T$

is a price vector for which general equilibrium obtains, the $\mathbf{X}^T$ is a market-clearing price vector. The same arguments which were used to establish *existence* of general equilibrium for the timeless economy can be used to establish existence of general equilibrium in period T. Of course, the price-clearing vector $\mathbf{X}^T$ will depend not only on tastes (that is, the U_T^i) and initial endowments (the $\bar{\mathbf{Y}}^{iT}$ and $\bar{Z}_T^i$) as in the timeless economy, but it will also depend upon the stocks of money (the Z_T^i) carried over from the previous period.

Before continuing our induction we ought to draw attention to the fact that we appear to have ignored the price of money. In fact, we have simply taken money to be the numeraire, and accordingly set its price equal to unity. This procedure seems innocuous.[8]

Returning to the individual level, the maximum level of final period utility depends upon $\mathbf{X}^T$, $\bar{\mathbf{Y}}^T$ and $\bar{Z}_T$, in addition to Z_T. Substituting the excess demand functions (11.4) back into the final-period utility function emphasises this. If the individual knows with certainty what the market-clearing $\mathbf{X}^T$ is going to be, and if he knows with certainty the endowments $\bar{Y}^T$ and $\bar{Z}_T$ he is going to get, the individual could calculate the maximum achievable final-period utility given any stock of money Z_T left over from period T, namely

$$U_T(\mathbf{Y}^{T*} + \bar{\mathbf{Y}}^T) = U_T[\mathbf{Y}^{T*}(\mathbf{X}^T; \bar{\mathbf{Y}}^T, Z_T + \bar{Z}_T) + \bar{\mathbf{Y}}^T]. \quad (11.6)$$

In practice, the individual may not have such knowledge. Suppose, instead, that he has a (subjective) assessment of the likely values of $\mathbf{X}^T$, $\bar{\mathbf{Y}}^T$ and $\bar{Z}_T$ and thus can calculate the expected value of final period utility, (11.6). This expected value depends upon Z_T; in keeping with our standardised notation (see Section 4.4), we denote it by $V_T(Z_T)$. Thus

$$V_T(Z_T) \equiv EU_T[Y^{T*}(\mathbf{X}^T; \bar{Y}^T, Z_T + \bar{Z}_T) + \bar{Y}^T], \quad (11.7)$$

where the expectation is taken with respect to the (joint) distribution[9] of $\mathbf{X}^T$, $\bar{\mathbf{Y}}^T$ and $\bar{Z}_T$.

We now move back to period $(T-1)$. The problem of the individual in this period (cf. (4.36)) is to choose net trades $\mathbf{Y}^{T-1}$ and end-of-period money stock Z_T so as to maximise

subject to

$$\left.\begin{array}{c} U_{T-1}(\mathbf{Y}^{T-1} + \bar{\mathbf{Y}}^{T-1}) + \rho V_T(Z_T) \\[2ex] Z_T = Z_{T-1} + \bar{Z}_{T-1} - \mathbf{X}^{T-1} \cdot \mathbf{Y}^{T-1}. \end{array}\right\} \quad (11.8)$$

As should be apparent from the structure of the problem, the trade-off between present and future consumption (given that present period spending is done optimally) determines the optimal value of Z_T, while the trade-off between the various goods in the present (given an optimal saving for the future) determines the optimal value of $\mathbf{Y}^{T-1}$. Carrying out the maximisation specified in (11.8) leads to excess demand functions (cf. (11.4))

$$\mathbf{Y}^{T-1*} = \mathbf{Y}^{T-1*}(\mathbf{X}^{T-1}; \overline{\mathbf{Y}}^{T-1}, Z_{T-1} + \overline{Z}_{T-1}) \qquad (11.9)$$

for the J goods as functions of the price vector $\mathbf{X}^{T-1}$, the initial endowments $\overline{\mathbf{Y}}^{T-1}$ and the total money holding $Z_{T-1} + \overline{Z}_{T-1}$, and to an end-of-period stock demand for money[10]

$$Z_T = Z_T(\mathbf{X}^{T-1}; \overline{\mathbf{Y}}^{T-1}, Z_{T-1} + \overline{Z}_{T-1}) \qquad (11.10)$$

with the same arguments.

Returning to the aggregate level, we can once again repeat the arguments concerned with establishing the existence of a market-clearing vector $\mathbf{X}^{T-1}$ – that is, with establishing the existence of general equilibrium in period $T - 1$.

Now go back to our individual. If (11.9) and (11.10) are substituted back into (11.8), the maximum expected utility over the final two periods can be determined; this will depend upon $\mathbf{X}^{T-1}$, $\overline{\mathbf{Y}}^{T-1}$ and $\overline{Z}_{T-1}$ in addition to Z_{T-1}. As viewed from period $T - 2$ all these (except for Z_{T-1}) may be uncertain. We denote by $V_{T-1}(Z_{T-1})$ the expected value of this maximum final-two-period utility; thus (cf. (11.7)):

$$V_{T-1}(Z_{T-1}) \equiv E\,[\,U_{T-1}(\mathbf{Y}^{T-1*} + \overline{\mathbf{Y}}^{T-1}) + \rho V_T(Z_T)\,] \qquad (11.11)$$

where $\mathbf{Y}^{T-1*}$ is given by (11.9), Z_T is given by (11.10), and the expectation is taken with respect to the (joint) distribution of $\mathbf{X}^{T-1}$, $\overline{\mathbf{Y}}^{T-1}$ and $\overline{Z}_{T-1}$.

The induction can now continue. The general case is as follows. In period t the problem of the individual is to choose $\mathbf{Y}^t$ and Z_{t+1} so as to maximise

$$\left. \begin{array}{c} U_t(\mathbf{Y}^t + \overline{\mathbf{Y}}^t) + \rho V_{t+1}(Z_{t+1}) \\[2ex] \\ Z_{t+1} = Z_t + \overline{Z}_t - \mathbf{X}^t . \mathbf{Y}^t \end{array} \right\} \qquad (11.12)$$

subject to

The solution to this problem leads to excess demand functions

$$\mathbf{Y}^{t*} = \mathbf{Y}^{t*}(\mathbf{X}^t; \bar{\mathbf{Y}}^t, Z_t + \bar{Z}_t), \tag{11.13}$$

and end-of-period money stock demand function

$$Z_{t+1} = Z_{t+1}(\mathbf{X}^t; \bar{\mathbf{Y}}^t, Z_t + \bar{Z}_t). \tag{11.14}$$

Finally, the $V(\,.\,)$ functions are defined recursively by

$$V_t(Z_t) \equiv E\left[U_t(\mathbf{Y}^{t*} + \bar{\mathbf{Y}}^t) + \rho V_{t+1}(Z_{t+1})\right] \tag{11.15}$$

where $\mathbf{Y}^{t*}$ and Z_{t+1} are given by (11.13) and (11.14).

Moreover, the existence of general equilibrium in each period can be established using essentially the same methods as those employed in the analysis of the timeless model of Section 11.1. In this sense, then, general equilibrium theory can incorporate genuine sequential trading.

(An aside, rather too lengthy for a footnote, may be useful at this stage. As far as expectations concerning market-clearing price-vectors $\mathbf{X}^t$ are concerned, our discussion has simply assumed they exist in the mind of the individual. Our analysis does not prevent those expectations being formed in some 'learning' fashion, however; indeed, individuals might have some forecasting model, for future prices, based on past prices, which they use in forming their expectations. Alternatively, they may be highly sophisticated and recognise that the actual market-clearing vectors depend on the (random) initial endowments. If they knew the relationship precisely, they could forecast the true expected value of $\mathbf{X}^t$. This would appear to be what is meant by *rational expectations*.)

The above discussion has shown, we hope, that using the method of backward induction with conventional general equilibrium theory combines to provide a sensible general equilibrium story in a sequential, incomplete-markets world – at least within the particularly simple version described above. What happens, however, when we try to move the model closer to reality?

While maintaining the assumption of complete perishability of goods for the time being, we may usefully take a step towards increased realism by considering the introduction of *forward* (or futures) markets. A one-period-forward market, for example, usually operates by traders agreeing, this period, on a contract for delivery in the next period, at a price to be paid next period, but agreed now.

This device clearly eliminates the relevant (future spot) price uncertainty. How does the existence of such markets affect our analysis? To keep our answer simple, suppose that just one-period-forward markets are in existence (that is, there are no n-period-forward markets in existence for $n > 1$). Under what circumstances will an individual trade in such markets? Well, this must depend upon the relative values of the price in the forward market and the expectation of the future spot price by the individual for that good – as well as the attitude to risk of the individual. The general problem (although considerably more complicated) is not unlike that discussed in Section 8.2. For example, given a sufficiently low (high) forward price, or given a sufficiently risk-averse (-loving) individual (for, after all, the forward price is certain while the future spot price is uncertain), the individual will buy (sell) forward. If so, he will arrive in the subsequent period with certain commitments entered into in the past.[11] These, in turn, will constrain his present trades (including further forward commitments).

In principle, therefore, we can adapt the above apparatus to derive excess demand functions for all individuals in all markets, both spot and forward. In principle, the same apparatus can be used to investigate the existence of general equilibrium. In practice, however, analytical complexity is likely to be somewhat high!

In the discussion of our simple model, we tacitly assumed that no interest was earned on money balances. Our discussion was also rather silent on the question of constraints on the possible values of money balances; implicitly, there was a presumption that Z_t could take negative values. This, of course, implies *borrowing*. Strictly speaking, therefore, we should have specified a series of interest rates and included some analysis of the determination of equilibrium interest rates (which express the equilibrium relative prices of money at different points in time). More importantly, perhaps, we should have included some discussion on the arrangements for borrowing – particularly those concerning the repayment of loans, and the avoidance of default. In the real world, in the presence of uncertainty, lenders usually require some form of collateral; in our abstract world, since no physical collateral exists (as all goods are perishable), a commitment by the borrower to supply future endowments to the lender must be made. (Though with uncertainty, and without a framework of law, the possibility of default may be high.)

If we drop the assumption of immediate perishability of all (non-money) goods, the analysis becomes considerably more complicated. In particular, individuals now have the extra option of storing goods from period to period, and hence indulging in commodity speculation. Whether individuals will take advantage of this option depends, *inter alia*, on the cost of storage relative to the expected price change between periods. Non-perishability of goods, however, does mean that they can be used as collateral for loans.

A further real-world feature that one would like to include in these abstract general equilibrium models is insurance. In a very partial way, insurance is a device for reducing state-of-the-world uncertainty. Obviously, no real-world set of insurance contracts eliminates uncertainty as completely as does the device of complete contingent contracts in the Arrow–Debreu general equilibrium world. Moreover, most insurance contracts are expressed in terms of money. Nevertheless, insurance does offer some potential for reducing state-of-the-world uncertainty (though the existence of moral hazard inevitably reduces this potential).

In the past few paragraphs, we have moved a long way from the simple sequential general equilibrium model discussed at the beginning of this section. The introduction of forward markets, of borrowing and lending, and of insurance, and the recognition of the non-perishability of goods have added a number of complicating 'twists' to the simple story told earlier. In *principle* the analytical apparatus we have assembled during the course of this book should be able to investigate the general problem, especially if we continue to maintain the price-taking and lack-of-quantity-constraints assumptions. As our discussion above has highlighted, such an investigation would have to pay much more attention than is normally the case to the (institutional or other) arrangements for the enforcement of contracts. At a market or economy level such considerations become crucially important.

The complications discussed above have almost hidden the issue with which we started this section: the question of the existence of general equilibrium in a sequence of time periods. Basically, we have examined an economy moving through time; in each time period a number of markets (spot and forward) are in operation, and trade takes place in these markets at market-clearing prices. Because of the changing nature of the economy through time, the market-clearing price vector (and indeed the actual goods over which it is defined) varies from period to period. In this sense, therefore, what we have examined is *temporary general equilibrium*. This obviously represents a step forward from the timeless general equilibrium theory of Section 11.1; nevertheless, it employs throughout the assumption of market-clearing prices (and hence lack of quantity constraints). In a world as uncertain as that described, and in the absence of an omni-potent Walrasian Auctioneer, such an assumption is clearly unpalatable. We explore the implications of its removal in the next section.

11.3 GENERAL EQUILIBRIUM WITH QUANTITY RATIONING

If the price-vector prevailing in some time period is not the market-clearing vector, then, definitionally, some traders will experience quantity constraints. Their optimal strategy will thus no longer be of the form derived in the previous section. In this section, we explore the various possibilities that this implies.

As the reader will appreciate, dropping the market-clearing assumption within the context of the multi-period model discussed above leads to rather unpleasant (notational and analytical) com-plexities. To make progress, within the quantity-rationing context, we therefore need to start from a rather simpler model. Let us revert (at least initially) to the timeless model of Section 11.1.

Two lines of enquiry are available, both of which have been pur-sued in the literature. (A useful recent survey is that by Drazen (1980) on which this section is loosely based. An earlier survey is that by Grandmont (1977a), which sheds light also on the material of Section 11.2.) The first line of enquiry continues to work within the *price-taking* framework employed above; the class of models derived under this approach are usually referred to as *fixed-price* models. The main problem with this approach is, as we shall see, that it implies rather curious behaviour on the part of the economic agents – particularly those who experience the quantity constraints. One wonders: why do they continue to act as price-takers? Why do they not, at least, experiment to see whether changing the price at which they are willing to trade removes the constraint? Such con-siderations have naturally led to the second line of enquiry – which involves the construction of models in which prices are endogenously determined. For reasons which will become apparent in due course, such models could be termed models of general *monopolistic* equili-brium.

We examine these two lines of enquiry in turn; we begin with the historically earlier line – the construction of fixed-price models. Consider the simple (timeless) economy described in Section 11.1, but suppose that the *prevailing* (fixed) price vector is not the market-clearing vector. Continue to assume that all individuals are price-takers, however. In this economy, some individuals will experience quantity constraints – in that they are unable to buy or sell as much of some goods as they would like. How does this affect their behaviour, and the equilibrium state of the economy? Clearly, the answer to this question depends upon three main things: (a) how the individuals perceive the constraints facing them; (b) how they respond to these perceived constraints in terms of their expressed excess demands; and (c) how the quantity constraints are 'resolved' in terms of the rationing of quantities amongst the relevant individuals. We consider these in turn (while recognising that they are necessarily interlinked).

We can express the perceived constraints on trade in the form of lower and upper bounds on the volume of excess demands. For a typical individual (suppressing the superscript i), we denote these lower and upper bounds by $\underline{y}$ and $\bar{y}$ respectively. Thus, the individual perceives that his excess demand for the jth good will be subject to the constraint:

$$\underline{y}_j \leqslant Y_j \leqslant \bar{y}_j. \tag{11.16}$$

We stress that these are *perceived* constraints, and therefore do not necessarily coincide with *actual* constraints; whether they do or not depends on what happens under (b) and (c) above. Before moving on to (b), we should briefly speculate as to where the vectors $\underline{y}$ and $\bar{y}$ might come from. In a general formulation, in which the period under consideration was just one of many, the constraint vectors may be determined by past experience. For a simple example, if the individual had wished to buy Y_j^* of good j in the previous period, but was rationed to an amount Y_j (where $Y_j < Y_j^*$), then the individual may use Y_j as the value of $\bar{y}_j$ in the current period. In such a case it might also be reasonable for the individual to set $\underline{y}_j = -\infty$, on the grounds that it was the buyers of good j who were being constrained, and not the sellers. Of course, whether this procedure *is* reasonable, depends upon the *actual* rationing mechanism in operation in the market in question. (A symmetrical argument would suggest putting $\underline{y}_j = Y_j$ and $\bar{y}_j = \infty$ if the individual had wished to *sell* an amount $-Y_j^*$ in the previous period but had been constrained to selling just $-Y_j$, where $Y_j^* < Y_j$.) It is not clear how the individual might choose $\bar{y}_j (\underline{y}_j)$ if he had always been a buyer (seller) of that good and had never experienced any constraints. Indeed, notwithstanding our simple example, the mechanism by which $\underline{y}$ and $\bar{y}$ are formed remains an interesting open question.

Let us now move on to stage (b): given the perceived constraints (11.16), how does the individual determine his actual stated excess demands Y^*? In the literature, two answers to this question have been suggested, neither of which is entirely satisfactory. One is due to Drèze (1975), and the other to Benassy (1975). Drèze's suggestion is that the actual excess demand vector Y^* of the individual is the value of Y that maximises the utility of the individual, $U(Y + \bar{Y})$ subject to, (i) the usual budget constraint $X \cdot Y = 0$, and (ii) the constraints (11.16), that is $\underline{y} \leqslant Y \leqslant \bar{y}$. Tautologically, the resultant Y^* must satisfy both the budget constraint and the perceived quantity constraints.

The problem with this procedure is that it envisages the individual as meekly accepting the perceived constraints – no attempt to breach any constraint (even when it would increase the utility of the individual) being considered. This would be a sensible procedure if the constraints were true, objectively determined constraints, which under no circumstances could be breached. But they are merely perceived constraints; surely individuals would, at least, try to test them?

This line of reasoning motivates Benassy's alternative approach. He envisages agents choosing each Y_j^* ignoring the perceived constraint for that particular good, but taking into account the perceived constraints for all the other goods (as well as the budget constraint). In this fashion, the chosen excess demands Y_j^* may well violate the perceived constraints; if so, the individual is communicating to the market that he wants to buy (sell) more than he perceives that he will be able to buy (sell). Thus, unlike the Drèze scheme, the Benassy formulation allows some indication of the magnitude of the quantity imbalance to be communicated to the market. Unfortunately, there are a number of problems connected with the Benassy approach. The main problem, at an individual level, is that the vector Y^*, derived by the procedure sketched above, may very well violate the budget constraint. In such a case, if the individual found himself successfully overcoming all the perceived constraints, he might find himself unable to meet all his commitments. How the model might cope with such an eventuality is not clear.

There is a further twist to the tale that we have not yet considered. Depending upon the rationing arrangements, traders may come to notice some relationship between the magnitude of their stated excess demand Y_j^* and their actual trading allocation Y_j. (We will give an illustration of how this might come about in due course.) If this were to be the case, then if an individual could work out the precise relationship between Y^* and Y, he could use this to determine[12] his optimal Y^*.

The relationship between the set of excess demands and the set of actual trades depends upon the rationing scheme(s) in operation. A variety of possibilities exist, and have been explored in the literature. Consider, for simplicity, a single market and suppose that, on aggregate, there is excess demand in that market (the argument for excess supply is symmetrical). If there is some kind of *centralised* rationing device, it might reasonably be expected to operate so that all sellers completed their trades, while the (insufficient) supply is rationed out in some way to the demanders. One rationing device is to allocate the supply in *proportion* to stated demands; another is to satisfy totally a certain proportion of the demanders and let the remainder go totally unsatisfied. Rationing schemes could be deterministic or random.

An important distinction is between manipulable and non-manipulable rationing schemes; the former term refers to schemes in which actual trades are increasing functions of stated net trades; the latter term is confined to schemes in which actual and stated trades are independent (except through the influence of aggregates). Proportional rationing schemes are clearly manipulable. As Drazen (1980, p. 288) points out:

> The problem with manipulable rationing is obvious. If agents desire to 'break' their constraints and each agent is aware that the trade he actually realizes will be proportional to demand expressed, there is an incentive to overbid in order to realize one's desired transaction. If all agents engage in such behavior, the process may be unstable and no equilibrium may exist.

The rationing mechanism in any particular market depends upon the specific trading rules in operation in that market. The majority of rationing mechanisms that have been studied in the literature assume that 'actual trades balance, trade is voluntary, and the short side of the market realizes its transactions' (Drazen, 1980, p. 288). These assumptions imply some *centralised* mechanism; as Grandmont (1977b) has pointed out, this is equivalent to assuming a '*tâtonnement* in quantities'. One is inevitably left wondering: if quantities can be centrally co-ordinated, why not prices as well (so that the problem of quantity constraints need never arise)?!

In addition to this problem, the *fixed-price* approach suffers from a shortcoming noted earlier: it implies some rather odd behaviour by the constrained individuals. (One could also argue that it implies equally odd behaviour by the unconstrained individuals. For example, if you are a seller in a market in which there is excess demand, would it not be more sensible to insist on a higher price for your product rather than continue to take the 'prevailing price' as given?). With quantity constraints, the continued use of the price-taking assumption becomes implausible. Such considerations have led to the rapid growth in the past few years of a body of literature on endogenous price-setting within general equilibrium models. Such models could, quite realistically, be described as models of general monopolistic equilibrium. Arguably the leading exponent of these new models is Hahn, who has published a number of important papers in recent years (for example, Hahn (1977, 1978); there are also several unpublished papers along similar lines in the Economic Theory Discussion Paper series of the SSRC Research Project on Risk, Information and Quantity Signals in Economics at the University of Cambridge).

The key ingredient in Hahn's approach is the notion of *conjectures*. In the context of the quantity-constrained general equilibrium model discussed above, agents are assumed to have conjectures about the way that quantities (or quantity constraints) are related to the price at which the individual offers to trade. (We should emphasise that individual agents have taken over the price-setting rôle; the *deus ex machina* no longer exists, thank goodness!) In a sense, these conjectures are estimated demand and supply curves. In his early work, Hahn worked with a given set of conjectures, and investigated the existence of general equilibrium (of prices and quantities) relative to this set; loosely speaking such an equilibrium consists of a situation in which no individual has any incentive, in the light of his conjectures, to alter any of his prices. Hahn showed that non-Walrasian (or quantity-constrained) general equilibria could exist under such circumstances. This result has important implications for the existence of unemployment in macro models (as we shall discuss in more detail in Chapter 12).

The assumption of *given* conjectures, however, detracts from the significance of this result. In subsequent work, therefore, Hahn and others investigated how conjectures might reasonably be formed. Amongst the many ideas thrown up by this work, the concepts of *rational conjectures* and *infinitesimally rational conjectures* (the former being a global, and the latter a local, concept) have proved to be of value. The basic idea of these concepts is to provide a check on the conjectures held by individuals. Essentially, a conjecture is rational if, when the individual holding it experiments with different prices, he finds that the quantity responses he experiences agree with his conjectures. As should be apparent, requiring this to hold globally is very stringent indeed. Hence, the use of *infinitestimally* rational conjectures; these simply relate to infinitestimally small changes in prices. An alternative way of describing these concepts is to use the analogy of estimated demand curves. Global rationality requires the estimated demand curve and the actual demand curve to coincide; local rationality simply requires that the slope of the estimated demand curve (at the equilibrium price-quantity point) is the same as the slope of the actual demand curve at that point. A full analysis of these important, but conceptually and technically difficult, issues can be found in the admirably readable survey by Drazen (1980).

At this stage in the development of the literature, it is not yet clear what is going to emerge at the end of the day. On the one hand, the models are becoming more realistic (in their assumed environments and their descriptions of the problems faced by economic agents). Yet at the same time, they are becoming increasingly complicated, both at the aggregate and the individual level. At the aggregate level this is not a cause for concern, since a modern large economy is indeed very complex; however, at the individual level, it *is* becoming rather worrying. The latest crop of models (especially those in which the economic agents are supposed to hold conjectures with respect to all the goods which they wish to trade) imply an incredible amount of sophistication in the computational and analytical abilities of the economic actors in the models. While it may be of interest to examine how a world populated with such geniuses would behave, it may be more directly relevant to our world to analyse the performance of models in which the actors have rather more human powers.

11.4   STOCHASTIC GENERAL EQUILIBRIUM

Recent years have witnessed a small but growing strand of literature devoted to the examination of the implications of economic agents behaving *reasonably* rather than *optimally*. Embedded in such studies is the central notion that agents use 'rules of thumb' when taking decisions. One common, but not inevitable, feature of such rule is that they imply *random* behaviour.[13] The natural analytical apparatus to employ for the study of such behaviour is, therefore, the theory of stochastic processes. Accordingly, at the level of generality of this chapter, one naturally comes to think in terms of stochastic models of general equilibrium.

Stochastic general equilibrium can also arise out of models of optimising behaviour. Below, we outline a framework which can be employed for either type of model; because of pressure of space, we proceed at a high level of generality.

Consider an economy whose state at any time t can be described by a vector of exogenous variables $\mathbf{X}^t$ and a vector of variables that are the decisions of the economic agents in the economy $\mathbf{Y}^t$. (The reader may like to envisage the $\mathbf{Y}$ carrying an asterisk superscript in an optimising model, and being without one in a 'rules of thumb' model.) Let $\mathbf{Z}^t$ be the vector containing all $\mathbf{X}^t$ and $\mathbf{Y}^t$ (that is, $\mathbf{Z}^t = (\mathbf{X}^t, \mathbf{Y}^t)$); thus $\mathbf{Z}^t$ describes the economy at time t. When the agents come to take their decisions $\mathbf{Y}^t$ in period t (which have to be made before $\mathbf{X}^t$ is known), they have available as potential information the vector $\mathbf{Z}^{(t-1)} = (\mathbf{Z}^{t-1}, \mathbf{Z}^{t-2}, \ldots)$ which consists of a description of the economy in all past periods. Without any loss of generality we can say that $\mathbf{Y}^t$ will be a function of this 'inheritance from the past' $\mathbf{Z}^{(t-1)}$. If $\mathbf{Y}^t$ is chosen optimally, then this function will be a known deterministic function (determined by carrying out the usual optimising procedure); if, however, rules of thumb are used then the function may contain some random element. To allow for both possibilities, we write the decision function as

$$\mathbf{Y}^t = \mathbf{g}^t(\mathbf{Z}^{(t-1)}, \mathbf{W}^t) \qquad (11.17)$$

where $\mathbf{g}^t$ is a (deterministic) vector function, and $\mathbf{W}^t$ is a vector of random variables (identically zero in an optimising model). We can now write

$$\mathbf{Z}^t = (\mathbf{X}^t, \mathbf{Y}^t) = (\mathbf{X}^t, \mathbf{g}^t(\mathbf{Z}^{(t-1)}, \mathbf{W}^t)$$

or, more compactly,

$$\mathbf{Z}^t = \mathbf{f}^t(\mathbf{W}^t, \mathbf{X}^t, \mathbf{Z}^{(t-1)}). \qquad (11.18)$$

Equation (11.18) summarises how past history, through its effect on $\mathbf{Y}^t$, combines with the exogenous variables of the current period (and possibly some random effect) to form the state of the economy of the current period $\mathbf{Z}^t$.

Now suppose that $\mathbf{X}^t$, the values of the exogenous variables at time t, is *stochastic*. Then (11.18) describes a stochastic process. It also describes a stochastic process even if $\mathbf{X}^t$ is non-random as long as $\mathbf{W}^t$ has a non-degenerate distribution. This stochastic process generates the series $\ldots, \mathbf{Z}^{t-1}, \mathbf{Z}^t, \mathbf{Z}^{t+1}, \ldots$; that is, it generates the states of the economy. In principle, given knowledge of the distributions of $\mathbf{X}^t$ and $\mathbf{W}^t$, and knowledge of the functions $\mathbf{f}^t(\,.\,)$ it is possible to derive the pdf's $h_t(\,.\,)$ which describe $\mathbf{Z}^t$ (for all t). By a *stochastic general equilibrium,* we mean a situation in which $h_t(\,.\,)$ is *independent* of t. Does such an equilibrium exist?

A particularly simple answer to this question is obtained if (11.18) can be written

$$\mathbf{Z}^t = \mathbf{f}(\mathbf{W}^t, \mathbf{X}^t, \mathbf{Z}^{t-1}). \qquad (11.19)$$

In moving from (11.18) to (11.19) two changes have been made: first, the superscript t has gone from $\mathbf{f}$; second, $\mathbf{Z}^{(t-1)}$ has become $\mathbf{Z}^{t-1}$. The first change is legitimate if the same *mechanism* (or rule) for decision-making is used each period; this would be so if no learning took place, or if an unchanging 'rule of thumb' were employed. The second change is innocuous (variables can simply be redefined) *if* the economic system has a memory of a finite and constant length; this would be particularly likely in a 'rule of thumb' model. If we now posit that the process generating the random variable pair $(\mathbf{W}^t, \mathbf{X}^t)$ is a Markov process with stationary transition probabilities, then it follows immediately that the process $\mathbf{Z}^t$ will also have the Markov property (with stationary transition probabilities). In such a case the existence of a stationary (or invariant) distribution is easily determined.[14]

More details of stochastic models of general equilibrium can be found in Grandmont (1977a) (wherein further references can be found) and in Green and Majumdar (1975).

11.5   GENERAL DISEQUILIBRIUM

The reader cannot have helped noticing (notwithstanding the title of this book) that virtually all of the material so far in this chapter has been concerned with *equilibrium* rather than *disequilibrium*. True, much of the material was directed at problems (such as unemployment – an example of quantity rationing) that we would like to imagine are essentially *dis*equilibrium phenomena. Nevertheless, the framework of analysis has been almost always that of equilibrium.

This is no coincidence. Indeed, it is an inevitable consequence of the method of analysis overwhelmingly employed in economics: namely, the optimising model of individual choice. At an aggregate level, optimising and equilibrium necessarily go hand-in-hand: or, to put the same point another way, optimising and disequilibrium are incompatible.

The argument really is quite simple: a genuine state of disequilibrium, almost definitionally, implies that some decision-maker has been frustrated in his plans. But if someone is frustrated, then optimality has not been achieved. Conversely, if optimality is achieved, then no-one is frustrated and hence equilibrium is attained.

The implication, of course, is that if one wants to model genuine disequilibrium, then the optimising model of individual choice must be abandoned. The choice is stark. Perhaps, one might argue, we do not really want to model disequilibrium; perhaps the problem is one of semantics? Consider unemployment, for example. If it does not eliminate itself automatically – that is, if it remains stubbornly at a high level – then perhaps the economy *is* in equilibrium (because no motion is perceived). If so, our equilibrium analysis is appropriate. If unemployment is a genuine disequilibrium phenomenon, however, then it will not persist; there will be a tendency for change (presumably towards a reduction). It will therefore automatically eliminate itself, and so no real problem exists (except during the transition period).

The above argument is plausible. A problem exists only if the transition period is at all long. In a sense this is an empirical issue; but as with any empirical question, the estimation must necessarily be guided by theory. Thus, even if only for this purpose, a disequilibrium theory is needed. And it is here where the behavioural 'rules of thumb' models, mentioned in the previous section, may well come into their own.

11.6 CONCLUSIONS

An immense amount of highly sophisticated work has been carried out in recent years on the general equilibrium problems discussed in this chapter. Without doubt, economists have now a much greater understanding of, and insight into, the technical and conceptual problems involved with the analysis of sequential models of general equilibrium than they did a decade ago. For all its weaknesses, general equilibrium analysis is increasingly a crucial central core for the whole of economic theory. Perhaps most importantly, knowledge has now advanced sufficiently far for economists to be in a position to assess critically what their techniques of analysis can and cannot achieve. Ironically, therein may be the seeds of their own destruction.

12 MACROECONOMICS

12.1 INTRODUCTION

Notwithstanding its title, this chapter makes no attempt to cover the whole of macroeconomics – such a task would clearly be impossible in so small a space. Our objective is a much more modest one: that of describing how the developments in microeconomics discussed in the preceding pages of this book have laid the foundation for the recent fundamental (and ongoing) reappraisal of macroeconomic theory – particularly as regards such (apparently) disequilibrium phenomena as unemployment and inflation.

The student of the history of economic thought will, of course, be aware that many of these recent developments in microeconomics were, in fact, stimulated by increasing dissatisfaction with conventional 'Keynesian' macroeconomics. Of particular importance in this reappraisal of Keynesian economics (and of the economics of Keynes) was the publication of the book by Leijonhufvud (1968). Although primarily exegetical in character and purpose, this book raised (but did not answer) a large number of crucial analytical questions as far as the construction of macroeconomic models was concerned. In the years since the publication of this book, much effort has been expended, and much ink spilt, in trying to answer (or lay to rest) these questions.

It is probably fair to say that the majority of this effort (and the majority of the ensuring analytical progress) has been concentrated in the areas with which this chapter is concerned – namely, the analysis of macroeconomic 'disequilibrium'. It goes without saying that Keynes was particularly concerned with the problem of unemployment – and that his *General Theory* was one of the earlier (and clearly most influential, though not the only) attempts at deriving a macroeconomic model in which chronic unemployment could exist (and indeed persist).

Whether it was an inadequacy in Keynes' own writing, or a flawed and inadequate translation by his disciples of his prose into mathematics (and diagrams) is not the concern of this chapter; suffice it to say that the *IS–LM* framework which finally emerged as the encapsulation of Keynes' main ideas has come under increasingly heavy attack as a vehicle for the explanation of chronic unemployment. In essence, the *IS–LM* framework blames such a phenomenon on one or other of three things: (downwardly) rigid money wages, money illusion or the existence of a liquidity trap. Empirical investigation has found virtually no evidence of the third of these, and precious little evidence of the second (though it is true to say that economic agents do appear to suffer from money illusion for small price changes); as to the first, surely that cannot be a problem when price inflation is running at 10 per cent or more?

Even more damning to the *IS–LM* framework is its apparent lack of a consistent macroeconomic foundation. The main inconsistency arises with respect to the treatment of quantity constraints; as we discussed in Chapter 11, if, for some reason,[1] markets do not clear, then some agents will experience constraints on the quantities that they can trade. The repercussions of this will depend upon the 'rules of the game' of the model under consideration – there might be a 'spillover' effect into quantities demanded or supplied in other markets and/or frustrated traders may take over the price-setting rôle themselves. Clearly, whatever happens, the constraint cannot simply be ignored.

Thus, if we have a macroeconomic (or general equilibrium) model in which there is unemployment in the labour market, then *definitionally* workers are constrained in the quantities of labour that they can supply – and this must inevitably have repercussions in the other markets in the model. Interestingly, the standard *IS–LM* model *does* take this feature partially into account – at least as far as the demand for goods is concerned; note that this latter demand (in more familiar terms, the 'consumption function') has as its argument *realised* income: in a general equilibrium model *without* constraints straints the appropriate argument would be the prevailing price vector.[2] Nevertheless, the consumption function remains essentially an *ad hoc* construct; its microeconomic foundations are neither completely specified nor obviously compatible with the rest of the model.

Although, in the familiar *IS–LM* story of unemployment equilibrium, it is overtly the suppliers of labour who are experiencing quantity constraints, the suppliers of goods might also be experiencing constraints. (Such constraints might prohibit the profitable employment of extra labour.[3]) As we shall see shortly, this is an essential component of the description of a genuinely 'Keynesian' unemployment state. If firms are so constrained, then their behaviour in other markets might thereby be affected; in particular, their demand for labour might change. Note, however, that the demand-for-labour function in the standard *IS–LM* model is the usual 'marginal product of labour' curve; this embodies the implicit assumption of *unconstrained* behaviour.

The standard *IS–LM* model thus displays a curious mixture of unconstrained and apparently constrained behavioural functions; without wishing to overstate the point, the model does not appear to have a particularly satisfactory (and consistent) microeconomic foundation. Moreover, some of its policy implications are unpalatable: for example, if the 'rigid money wage' assumption is invoked as an explanation of unemployment, the policy that immediately comes to mind as the appropriate cure is a lowering of money wages. Clearly, in the context of the standard *IS–LM* model, such a policy change would have the desired effect. But this is something that Keynes would categorically have denied. If Keynes was right, the *IS–LM* model is wrong.

As we hope to show in the course of this chapter, it is the *IS–LM* model that is at fault in its inadequate (or inconsistent) treatment of disequilibrium – as manifested in quantity constraints. A correctly specified 'disequilibrium' model can indeed lead to the policy recommendations advocated by Keynes – without recourse to the three rather dubious assumptions noted above.

The obvious starting point for a macroeconomic model with consistent microeconomic foundations[4] is the general equilibrium theory of Chapter 11. Indeed, in many respects, the material of this present chapter is simply a rather special case of the material of Chapter 11. As we remarked at the beginning of that chapter, macroeconomics is essentially a highly aggregated version of general equilibrium theory – though, of course, the focus of interest differs. At the macroeconomic level, interest is usually centred on broad aggregates – such as aggregate output, aggregate employment and unemployment, the (aggregate) price level and money wage rate, the aggregate stock of money, and so on. Accordingly, the number of goods and services in macro models is usually very small indeed. In this chapter we shall follow convention in restricting attention to just three goods and services: output (goods), labour and money; all three are presumed to be homogeneous. There are thus two markets (the goods market and the labour market) and two 'prices' (the money price of goods and the money wage rate). To simplify our analysis, we assume that the rate of interest is zero, and that there is no lending or borrowing. There are three types of agents in the macro models that we shall describe: firms (who demand labour and supply goods), households (who demand goods and supply labour) and the government (which may demand both goods and labour but is a supplier of neither). For simplicity, throughout most of our analysis, we shall assume that all firms are identical and that all households are identical (so that we need simply analyse one firm and one household, and can ignore distributional effects). In essence, then, we have three 'goods' and three agents.

As well as differing in the number of goods and services under consideration, general equilibrium theory and macroeconomic theory differ in the end-product of their respective analyses: whereas the former is mainly interested in questions of existence and uniqueness (and stability when dynamic elements are introduced), the latter is generally more interested in questions of comparative statics, especially those relating to the effects of governmental policy – given a particular equilibrium, what will be the impact of such-and-such a change in one of the exogenous (especially government controlled) variables?

Despite these differences of focus, the basic 'rules of the game' are the same. Thus, much of the analytical apparatus constructed in Chapter 11 can equally well be used (appropriately modified) in this chapter. Of central importance is the view of the operation of the economy as a *sequence* of time periods; in any one time period, certain markets are open for trading. The trades that economic agents attempt to carry out on these markets depend on their initial endowments (including any inheritance from the past), on their expectations about the future, and, of course, on the 'rules of the (trading) game' in operation. The trades that are *actually* carried out depend on the attempted trades and on the trading rules in operation. The actual trades in part determine the inheritance that will be left over to the following period, when a similar process will be enacted.

At the current level of sophistication of the reformulated macro-economic theory, attention is usually restricted to just *one* period of this sequence of trading periods. Thus, data on the past (the periods prior to the one under consideration), and the set of expecta-tions about the future (the periods subsequent to the one under consideration) are taken to be exogenous to the period under analysis (except in so far as current variables influence expectations). In most of the models that we will be examining, it will be assumed that only spot markets exist in any time period – thus neither labour nor output can be traded forward. As we discussed in Sections 11.2 and 11.3, however, the incorporation of such forward markets should not substantially affect the qualitative implications of the models. As before, we will assume that money is totally imperishable, and that labour is totally perishable (in that I cannot work 48 hours tomorrow and none today!); finally, depending upon the model under consideration, the perishability of output (goods) may be anywhere between (and including) these two extremes.

As far as the trading rules in operation are concerned, we will follow the procedure adopted in Chapter 11 – beginning with the simplest such rules, and gradually increasing the realism (and complexity) as we move towards the end of the chapter. Specifically, we begin with an examination of *fixed-price* models – that is, those in which all agents act as price-takers; first, and very briefly, we discuss models without quantity rationing. These, of course, are Walrasian models – in which the price vector is a market-clearing vector. Secondly, we explore models in which the price vector is not a market-clearing one, and consequently in which agents experience quantity constraints. The analysis of these models will occupy Sections 12.2 and 12.3 – the difference between the two sections being the rationing scheme assumed to be in operation to 'resolve' the quantity constraints: in the former, the rationing scheme is deterministic; in the latter, stochastic. We will clarify this distinction in due course. Section 12.4, amongst other things, looks briefly at what happens if agents unilaterally attempt to 'resolve' their quantity constraints by ceasing to act as price-takers and taking over the price-setting rôle themselves; as might be anticipated, this material is very similar to the 'conjectural equilibria' approach discussed in the second half of Section 11.3. Section 12.4 also contains some brief comments on extensions and alternative approaches. Penultimately, Section 12.5 briefly investigates the questions of (true) macroeconomic disequilibrium and of the adjustment processes while in such states. Finally, Section 12.6 offers some comments in conclusion.

12.2   FIXED-PRICE MODELS WITH DETERMINISTIC QUANTITY RATIONING

The set of models in this category constitutes the core of the 'new' macroeconomics; increasingly such models are becoming standard fare in many postgraduate and undergraduate theory courses.[5] Historically, their initiation may be traced to Patinkin (1956) and Clower (1965), with significant advances being contributed by Barro and Grossman (1971, 1976) and Malinvaud (1977). To the best of my knowledge, the most accessible (and well-refined) recent exposition is that of Muellbauer and Portes (1978), on which this section is very heavily based. Muellbauer and Portes' contribution is important in that it includes inventories in the model (and thereby removes an unfortunate asymmetry of the earlier models) and provides an easily-understood diagrammatic framework for analysis.

The basic model is that described in Section 12.1 above, with the additional assumption that all agents are price-takers. To complete the specification of the model, we need to provide details of the rationing schemes which come into operation if the prevailing price vector is not the market-clearing one. Since most of the literature referenced above has worked throughout with just *a* firm and *a* household, there is an implicit (and sometimes explicit) assumption that, when rationing occurs, all rationed agents are given the same ration (irrespective of their desired trades). This is by no means an innocent assumption, and we shall discuss it at length in due course; however, let us maintain it for the time being.

Given these assumptions, we can work throughout with a firm and *a* household (plus the government, of course). To simplify matters, we assume that the only rôles that the government has are those of demander of goods and supplier of money, and further that the government never experiences any constraints on trade.

We must now introduce some notation. Originally, we had hoped to be able to use a uniform notation throughout the book; up to now, we have achieved this aim (and we hope the exposition and continuity has improved as a consequence). In this final substantive chapter, however, we must finally admit defeat: to continue with our uniform notation would merely confuse the important issues we wish to discuss; therefore, we depart from it. It is somewhat of a consolation to be able to use a notation which is fairly widely adopted by macroeconomists: as this section is heavily based on Muellbauer and Portes (1978), we use their notation, with one or two minor modifications.

We begin with the variables themselves; after introducing them, we will describe the various subscripts and superscripts which qualify their meaning in various ways. For the firm, the flow of output (production) is denoted by Y, while sales are denoted by X; any discrepancy affects inventories, whose end-of-period value is denoted by I. Total sales X are divided into purchases by the household C, and purchases by the government G. The household also provides a flow of labour services L to the firm. End-of-period money balances are denoted by M. Finally, the money wage-rate and the money price-of-the-good are denoted by w and p respectively.

Before completing the notational preliminaries, a few words about the 'rules of the game' should prove helpful. Here we follow Muellbauer and Portes' specification, though variations on this theme are clearly possible. One important detail relates to the distribution of the profit of the firm: we assume that the whole of the profit of one period is given to the household (as a dividend) at the beginning of the following period. This profit is, of course, held in money; for simplicity, it is assumed that the firm has no other motive for holding money. Thus, the profits for this period constitute the end-of-this-period stock of money of the firm. At the beginning of the next period, the whole of this is distributed to the household, and thus becomes part of the initial endowment of the household for that period. As far as physical stocks of the good are concerned, we assume that these are all held by the firm (in the form of inventories), and none are held by the household.[6] We note that whereas the stock of goods may increase or decrease (depending upon the relative size of production and total sales), the stock of money increases each period by the amount of government expenditure G.[7]

We now return to notational matters. Most of our analysis will relate to one period – call it period t – in the sequence of time periods described earlier. Where necessary we will indicate the relevant period by a subscript; if this is missing, it should be presumed that the variable relates to period t. Likewise, subscripts '+ 1' and '− 1' will be shorthand for '$t + 1$' and '$t − 1$' respectively. As far as the flow variables, output and labour, are concerned, we must differentiate carefully between desired (*ex ante*) trades and actual (*ex post*) trades. Since in any market *ex post* demand must equal *ex post* supply (that is purchases must equal sales), we do not need to distinguish between these two quantities: accordingly, if a variable has *no* superscript, it signifies *ex post* trades. Since our model is crucially interested in quantity-constrained situations, however, *ex ante* demand and supply must be carefully distinguished: accordingly, we use a superscript 'd' to denote the former and 's' to denote the latter.

In the type of model discussed in this section, the rationing mechanism is of a particularly simple form: it is postulated that the short side of the market dominates. Thus, the actual quantity traded in any market is the *minimum* of *ex ante* supply and *ex ante* demand. Since we have made the simplifying assumption that the government is never rationed,[8] we may express the operation of the rationing mechanism as follows:

$$C = \min \{C^d, C^s\} \qquad \text{where } C^s = X^s - G, \qquad (12.1)$$

and

$$L = \min \{L^d, L^s\}. \qquad (12.2)$$

Let us now briefly sketch the outlines of the analysis that is to follow. We are going to examine the implications (in the time period under consideration) of different prevailing price-vectors (w, p). Given some (w, p), the firm first works out its desired demand for labour and desired total sales (conditional on its initial inventories and its expectations about the future) assuming that it will experience no constraints; likewise the household first works out its desired supply of labour and desired demand for the good (conditional on its initial stock of money and its expectations about the future) assuming that it will experience no constraints. Now, if it happens that the desired demand for labour of the firm equals the desired supply of labour of the household *and* the desired total sales less government purchases of the firm equals the desired demand of the household for the good, *all well and good*: the price-vector prevailing is the market-clearing one – *the economy is in Walrasian equilibrium.*

If the (w, p) vector is *not* the market-clearing one, however, further calculations have to be made – since the expressed demands and supplies of the paragraph above were derived under the assumption of no constraints on trade. If there are constraints, then the firm and/or household will have to re-work their optimising calculations.

To emphasise this important point, the literature has evolved the distinction between *notional* and *effective* demands and supplies: the former are those calculated under the assumption of no constraints; the latter are those calculated taking actual constraints into consideration. While the meaning of *notional* demands and supplies is clearly unambiguous, there is a certain ambiguity about the meaning of *effective* demands and supplies. As we discussed at the beginning of Section 11.3, there are a variety of ways that the individual agent may take the constraints into consideration when calculating his optimal strategy.

In the context of the model of this section, the resolution of the meaning of effective demands and supplies is straightforward. As we will be seeking quantity-constrained *equilibria*, we will require that perceived and actual constraints coincide. Given, in addition, that there are just two markets in our model, this makes life very simple. For example, if the household finds that its notional supply of labour is larger than the demand for labour of the firm, it will have to recalculate its sales decision under the additional constraint of a less-than-desired level of employment. Of course, one of our two agents may find that it is simultaneously constrained in both markets (in which case, it may have to accept meekly whatever it is offered!). A full quantity-constrained equilibrium occurs when the actual constraints and the constraints used in the calculation of effective demands and supplies coincide.

If we concentrate attention on *non*-market-clearing price vectors, there are four possible cases to consider (since there are two markets and two possibilities – excess demand and excess supply – in each). These are as follows (the reasons for the nomenclature will become clearer as we proceed):

(*K*) *Keynesian unemployment:* sellers rationed in both markets; that is, $C^d < C^s$ and $L^d < L^s$.

(*R*) *Repressed inflation:* buyers rationed in both markets; that is, $C^d > C^s$ and $L^d > L^s$.

(*C*) *Classical unemployment:* buyers rationed in goods market, sellers rationed in labour market; that is, $C^d > C^s$ and $L^d < L^s$.

(*U*) *Underconsumption:* sellers rationed in goods market, buyers rationed in labour market; that is $C^d < C^s$ and $L^d > L^s$.

The household is unable to supply all the labour it wishes in cases (*K*) and (*C*) and cannot purchase all the goods it desires in cases (*R*) and (*C*). The firm is unable to sell all the output it wishes in cases (*K*) and (*U*) and cannot purchase all the labour it desires in cases (*R*) and (*U*). Note that, under the 'rules of the game', it is impossible for both the firm and the household to be *simultaneously* constrained in the *same* market.

In order to analyse these four régimes in more detail, we need to derive the various effective demand and supply schedules. We therefore need to analyse the behaviour of the household and the firm individually. We begin with the former.

For the household (as indeed for the firm) there are four cases to consider: unconstrained in either market; constrained in the labour market; constrained in the goods market; and constrained in both. To determine the optimal strategy of the household in each of these four cases, we need to specify the objective function of the household. Recall that the period under consideration is just one of a sequence of periods; this has the crucial implication that decisions made this period not only affect *directly* the utility of the household in this period, but also *indirectly* affect the future utility of the household – through the bequest to the future of this period, namely the stock of money left over at the end of this period. The precise way that M affects household utility can be determined by the method discussed in detail in Section 11.2 (*viz*, backward induction). The reader should, if necessary, refer back to that section, since, without any further ado, we will use that material to write the total expected lifetime utility of the household as viewed from the beginning of period t as:

$$U(C, L, M; \mathbf{a}) \qquad (12.3)$$

where $\mathbf{a}$ is a vector of parameters (which will be interpreted in due course). We assume that the function U is such that U_1 and U_3 are positive and U_2 is negative (where subscripts denote partial derivatives). It is crucial to note that in (12.3) C and L contribute *directly* to utility and disutility this period, while M contributes to expected utility in subsequent periods. Expectations about future periods (that is, about future endowments and future price vectors) are embodied in the form of the function $U(.)$ – particularly in the way that M enters the function. These expectations are represented by the parameter vector $\mathbf{a}$; a change in expectations, as manifested in a change in $\mathbf{a}$, will shift the utility function. For example, an expected increase in dividends of the next period (which represents the initial incremental endowment of money of the household) would naturally lead to an increase in U at all levels of C, L and M. One particularly important feature of (12.3) should be noted: as written, it implies that current values of C, L and M have no effect on expectations (as represented by $\mathbf{a}$). This is a strong assumption, and one to which we shall return in due course.[9]

The problem in period t for the household, is to choose C, L and M so as to maximise (12.3) subject to any quantity constraints that are in existence, and subject to the usual budget constraint, which can be written in the form:

$$M = M_{-1} + wL - pC. \qquad (12.4)$$

If (12.4) is substituted into (12.3), the maximand becomes:

$$u \equiv U(C, L, M_{-1} + wL - pC; \mathbf{a}). \qquad (12.5)$$

At this point, a diagrammatic representation will prove helpful. In Figure 12.1, we follow Muellbauer and Portes in drawing the iso-utility contours of (12.5) in (C, L) space.[10] Point H is the highest attainable utility level, and thus represents the household's notional (unrationed) demand for the good and supply of labour. The position of point H depends on **a** and upon M_{-1}, w, and p (as well as the form of the utility function) as can be seen from (12.5). We can thus write notional demand and supply as follows:

$$C = C^d(\mathbf{A})$$

and $\left.\begin{array}{c} \\ \\ \end{array}\right\}$ (12.6)

$$L = L^s(\mathbf{A})$$

where

$$\mathbf{A} = \{\mathbf{a}, M_{-1}, w, p\}. \qquad (12.7)$$

Consider now the three constrained cases, beginning with the case of a constraint on the supply of labour. If there is a labour supply ration of L where $L < L^s(\mathbf{A})$, then the effective demand for goods is determined by the tangency of the vertical line at L with the indifference curve at point A in Figure 12.1. As the labour supply ration varies, the effective demand for goods is represented by the line passing through A and H. This can be represented algebraically by the following effective demand curve for goods:

$$C = \bar{C}^d(\mathbf{A}, L)$$

where $\left.\begin{array}{c} \\ \\ \end{array}\right\}$ (12.8)

$$L < L^s(\mathbf{A}) \text{ is the labour supply ration.}$$

The notation in (12.8) emphasises that there is a constraint (indicated by the bar on C^d) and that the effective demand for goods depends on the size of the ration. As the figure shows, and as commonsense clearly requires, $\partial C / \partial L > 0$; that is, the greater the (constrained) supply of labour, the greater the demand for goods.

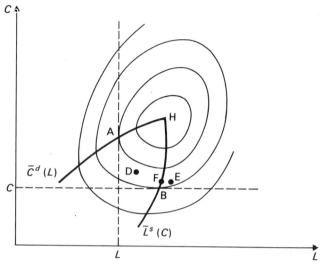

Figure 12.1   The household's indifference map

In an exactly similar fashion, if the household is constrained in the goods market, then its effective supply of labour is traced out by the line passing through *B* and *H*; algebraically:

$$L = \bar{L}^s(\mathbf{A}, C)$$

where

$C < C^d(\mathbf{A})$ is the good ration.

(12.9)

Clearly $\partial L/\partial C > 0$. If the household is constrained in both markets, two possibilities arise. The first is illustrated by the point D in Figure 12.1; in this case the household meekly accepts the situation and 'consumes' the (C, L) pair indicated by D. The second is illustrated by the point E: this is such that $C < C^d(\mathbf{A})$ and $L < L^s(\mathbf{A})$, but E is outside the *wedge* formed by the two constrained functions; in this case, the household would simply move to point F so that the labour supply constraint would no longer be binding. Clearly, the household will never remain at a point outside the wedge. Since this wedge is of vital importance in what follows, we picture it separately in Figure 12.2.

This completes the analysis of the household; we now turn to the firm. Apart from a few modifications necessitated by the 'rules of

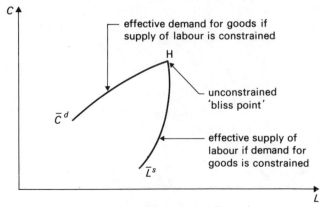

Figure 12.2   The household's wedge

the game' (specifically that the stock of wealth of the firm is held in goods rather than in money), the basic procedure is the same. By an exactly parallel argument, we can write the total expected lifetime utility of the firm as viewed from the beginning of period t as:

$$V(X, L, I; \mathbf{b}) \qquad (12.10)$$

where $\mathbf{b}$ is a vector of parameters encapsulating the firm's expectations about the future. We assume that the function V is such that V_1 and V_3 are positive and V_2 is negative. Equation (12.10) should be compared with (12.3) – its household counterpart. Here again, it is crucial to note that X and L contribute directly to utility and disutility this period, while I contributes to expected utility in subsequent periods. Once again, we draw attention to the fact that the form of (12.10) implies that realised values of X, L and I do not influence expectations.[11]

The problem in period t for the firm is to choose X, L and I so as to maximise (12.10) subject to any quantity constraints, and subject to some appropriate constraint on inventories. Muellbauer and Portes express this latter in the form:

$$I = h(I_{-1}) + Y - X. \qquad (12.11)$$

In this, the function $h(.)$ represents some partial perishing of inventories (to make sense, $h(I) < I$). There are, of course, alternative ways of expressing the idea that the holding of inventories is costly in some sense (see Chapter 8 for a further example), but they all lead to similar implications. If (12.11) is substituted into (12.10), the maximand becomes

$$v \equiv V(X, L, h(I_{-1}) + Y - X; \mathbf{b}).\qquad(12.12)$$

The iso-utility contours of (12.12) are portrayed in Figure 12.3; for parallel reasons, the general picture is similar to that of Figure 12.1. Point F represents the unconstrained optimum, and yields the notional supply and demand:

$$X = X^s(\mathbf{B})$$

and

$$\left.\begin{array}{c} \\ \\ \end{array}\right\}\qquad(12.13)$$

$$L = L^d(\mathbf{B})$$

where

$$\mathbf{B} = \{\mathbf{b}, I_{-1}w, p\}.\qquad(12.14)$$

The effective supply of goods, when labour demand is rationed, is given by the line labelled $\bar{X}^s(L)$ in Figure 12.3; algebraically

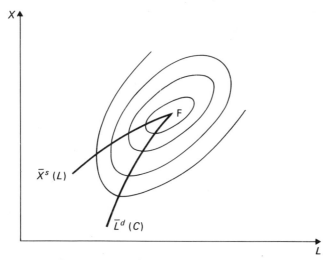

Figure 12.3   The firm's indifference map

$$X = \bar{X}^s(\mathbf{B}, L)$$

where $\left.\begin{array}{c}\\\\\\\end{array}\right\}$ (12.15)

$L < L^d(\mathbf{B})$ is the labour ration.

Similarly, the effective demand for labour, when the supply of goods is rationed, is given by the other line in the figure, and algebraically by

$$L = \bar{L}^d(\mathbf{B}, C)$$

where $\left.\begin{array}{c}\\\\\\\end{array}\right\}$ (12.16)

$C < C^s(\mathbf{B})$ is the goods ration.

Finally, points within the wedge indicate binding constraints in both markets. We reproduce the firm's wedge on its own in Figure 12.4.

We can now proceed to analyse the operation of the economy as a whole. Although the firm's wedge is in (X, L) space, and the household's wedge in (C, L) space, we can easily express both in the same space by virtue of the assumption that the government is never rationed, and hence that

$$X = C + G. \qquad (12.17)$$

Thus, the firm's wedge can be translated into (C, L) space simply by moving it downwards by a vertical distance G. Both wedges can then

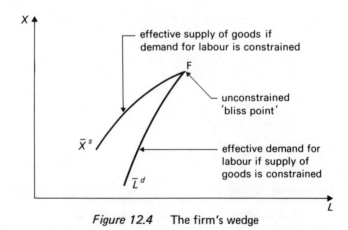

Figure 12.4   The firm's wedge

be portrayed in (C, L) space. In addition to the full Walrasian equilibrium, there are (if we ignore various borderline cases) the four cases that we mentioned earlier. All five are portrayed in Figure 12.5.

The Walrasian equilibrium is characterised by the coincidence of points F and H; trade therefore takes place at this point, and both the firm and the household attain their unconstrained 'bliss' point.

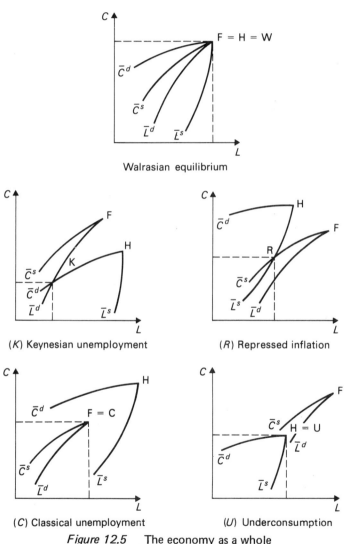

Walrasian equilibrium

(K) Keynesian unemployment

(R) Repressed inflation

(C) Classical unemployment

(U) Underconsumption

Figure 12.5 The economy as a whole

A Keynesian unemployment equilibrium occurs when point F lies northwest of point H; trade takes place at point K, where $\bar{L}^d$ intersects $\bar{C}^d$. At this point, the household is unable to supply all the labour it desires and the firm is unable to supply all the output it desires. The firm is on $\bar{L}^d$, however, and hence does not wish to expand its employment of labour (since it is already employing as much labour as it needs given its constraint on output); similarly, the household is on $\bar{C}^d$ and hence does not wish to expand its purchases of the good (since it is already buying as much as it wants given its constraint on employment). The situation is thus indeed one of equilibrium (at the given (w, p) vector, of course).

A repressed inflation equilibrium occurs when point F lies southeast of point H; trade takes place at point R, where $\bar{L}^s$ intersects $\bar{C}^s$. Although the household wishes to buy more goods, the firm is unwilling to supply any more because of the constraint on the amount of labour it can get. The firm would like more labour, but the household is unwilling to supply any more because of the constraint on the amount of goods it can buy. Once again, *impasse*, or equilibrium (at the given price vector).

In contrast with Keynesian unemployment, Classical unemployment occurs when F is southwest of H; trade takes place at point F ($= C$) which is the 'bliss' point of the firm. The household would like to supply more labour and purchase more goods, but the firm is unwilling to oblige in either respect since it has already achieved bliss. The 'Underconsumption' situation is similar, except that the rôles are reversed.

Given this diagrammatic representation, comparative static exercises are relatively straightforward. Changes in G, **A** and **B** cause shifts in one or both of the two wedges, and the consequent effect on the equilibrium point can thus be analysed. Since space is limited, we confine attention to a brief analysis of the effects of changes in G; a much fuller analysis of the comparative statics effects can be found in Muellbauer and Portes (1978).

Consider, then, an increase in government expenditure G. This has no effect on the household's wedge in (C, L) space, nor the firm's wedge in (X, L) space (assuming that the increase does not change expectations about the future). The firm's wedge in (C, L) space will shift down vertically, however, by a distance equal to the increase in G. If the economy was initially in a Keynesian unemployment equilibrium, the effect will be to move the equilibrium point K northeastwards along $\bar{C}^d$ towards H. Thus, employment and output will expand – a genuinely Keynesian result. If the economy was initially in a Classical unemployment state, however, the effect will be to move the equilibrium point F (= C) downwards by an amount equal to the change in G. Thus, employment and aggregate output will both remain unchanged (and the increased government spending will simply 'crowd out' private consumption). If the initial state was the full Walrasian equilibrium, the increase in government spending would simply move the economy into the Repressed inflation régime.[12]

In manipulating the above apparatus, it is vitally important to remember that all the equilibria discussed are *fixed-price* equilibria. That is, all the notional and effective demand and supply schedules are conditional on some given price vector (w, p) (and indeed conditional on the agents acting as price-takers throughout). The particular vector (w, p) prevailing will, of course, determine which of the regimes the economy is in. If there is a unique Walrasian vector, then the (w, p) space can be divided up into the appropriate segments. This is illustrated in Figure 12.6, which is obtained from Muellbauer and Portes (1978, p. 810) wherein a full explanation of its derivation may be found.

The figure is particularly important in that it emphasises Keynes' point that a reduction in w does not necessarily improve things when the economy is in a Keynesian unemployment state; the reduction

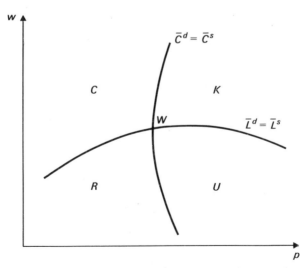

Figure 12.6   The five régimes in (w, p) space

may well move the economy further away from W – the full-employment (Walrasian) equilibrium. The effect of a change in w on employment and output can be analysed using the double-wedge apparatus. As Muellbauer and Portes demonstrate, although a fall in w unambiguously increases unemployment and output when the economy starts from a Classical unemployment state, starting from a Keynesian unemployment equilibrium the effect is ambiguous. This is an important result in that it demonstrates how this 'reformulated' macroeconomics can provide an intellectually satisfying resolution of the debate between the Keynesians and the Classicists.

Before concluding this section, some brief comments on expectations should be made. As we have already remarked, equations (12.3) and (12.10) (and hence the double-wedge diagrammatic analysis), implicitly assume that current values of C, L and G do not influence expectations. This is a strong assumption, particularly since it implies that expectations of the agents about future régime probabilities are independent of the current régime. In practice, dependence is more likely to be the case. For example, it would seem reasonable for the household to hold gloomier predictions about its future employment prospects if it were underemployed this period than it if were fully employed. Likewise, a firm which is unable to sell all it wants this period may well feel gloomy about future sales prospects. If expectations were dependent on the régime of the current period in this manner, then the above analysis would be complicated by the fact that the position of the wedges themselves would be affected by the régime state. Amongst the various problems this gives rise to, is the possibility that, under such circumstances, no equilibria may exist.

12.3 FIXED-PRICE MODELS WITH STOCHASTIC QUANTITY RATIONING

The model discussed above provides many important insights into the functioning of an economy with non-market-clearing prices; it clearly represents a major advance in the understanding of so-called disequilibrium phenomenon by economists. Nevertheless, the story that is told in this model is not entirely convincing – particularly as regards the plausibility of the 'rules of the game' employed.

The major problem arises from the combination of the fixed-price assumption and the specific rationing mechanism adopted. A quantity-constrained equilibrium envisages at least one agent frustrated in his quantity plans. If there were, in fact, just one firm and one household, it is somewhat unrealistic to assume that the frustrated agent would continue to operate as a price-taker: if the household wanted to purchase more goods than were available, surely it would offer to pay a higher price?; likewise, if the household wanted to sell more labour than was demanded, surely it would offer to work for a lower wage? The combination of the price-taking assumption and deterministic quantity constraints is, as we have already argued in Section 11.3, unrealistic, particularly with just one firm and one household.

But, of course, the assumption of a single firm and a single household was simply made for expository reasons. What the model *really* represents is an economy with a large number of identical firms and a large number of identical households. As we have already noted, this is perfectly legitimate as long as all rationed agents receive the same ration. Nevertheless, two problems arise: first, it still appears to be the case that agents have an incentive to take over the price-setting rôle; second, the rationing scheme implied by this requirement has some rather odd implications. We will delay discussion of the first of these two points until Section 12.4; in the meantime, we examine the second.

One immediate problem with this uniform rationing scheme is that it suggests a highly efficient centralised rationing organisation; moreover, it does not appear to conform to any real-world rationing mechanism. In actual labour markets, for example, particularly when institutionalised 'working weeks' are the norm, the usual mechanism when there is an excess supply of labour is that some people become unemployed while the rest stay employed; this is in sharp contrast to the uniform *under*employment envisaged in the model.

Further problems arise when agents are *not* identical. In this situation, demands and supplies will vary from individual to individual. Suppose, for illustration, that there are 10 households with household i wishing to supply i units of labour. Total supply is thus 55 units. Suppose, however, that total demand for labour is just 44 units; how is the demand to be rationed? A uniform scheme would imply 4.4 units for each of the 10 households. But this is not feasible, as it would mean forcing households 1, 2, 3 and 4 to supply more labour than they wished. An alternative is to adopt a *proportional* rationing scheme: since total demand is 4/5 of total supply, let each household supply 4/5 of its desired amount. But this scheme is *manipulable*; as we remarked in Section 11.3, such a scheme will necessarily encourage explosive over-bidding, and thus ensure the non-existence of equilibrium.

A further alternative is to take households sequentially, and continue employing them until the total demand is satisfied. For example, if our 10 households were taken in ascending numerical order, then households 1–8 inclusive would be fully employed (relative to their desired supplies), household 9 would be employed for 1/9 of its desired amount and household 10 would be totally unemployed. If, instead, the households were taken in descending numerical order, households 6–10 inclusive would be fully employed, household 5 would be employed for 4/5 of its desired amount, and households 1–4 inclusive would be totally unemployed.

The fertile mind should be able to imagine many such schemes. The most plausible (especially when manipulable schemes are excluded) seem to be those in which the outcome of the rationing process, at least as viewed by individual agents, is *stochastic*: deterministic schemes, for the reasons discussed above, lead to all sorts of problems. Indeed, when actual real-life examples are examined, one of the most plausible schemes is that in which an agent (on the rationed side of the market) either gets his demand or supply satisfied completely or gets nothing at all; moreover, each agent is uncertain *ex ante* about which outcome will emerge.

Stochastic rationing schemes, of the type discussed above, are beginning to be analysed in the literature; the pioneers include Svensson (1980), Gale (1978), Green (1980) and Honkapohja and Ito (1979). Such schemes have two main advantages: first, they are more realistic; second, they lead to a far more satisfactory definition of effective demand (and supply) than do the (deterministically-based) definitions suggested by Dreze and Clower (discussed in Section 11.2).

To illustrate this latter point, let us return to the problem as described in Section 12.3 for the household. Recall equation (12.5):

$$u \equiv U(C, L, M_{-1} + wL - pC; \mathbf{a}). \qquad (12.18)$$

The various demand and supply functions were determined as follows:

1. max u w.r. to C and L (notional demand and supply);
2. max u w.r. to C s.t. L fixed ($< L^s$) (effective demand);
3. max u w.r. to L s.t. C fixed ($< C^d$) (effective supply).

Consider, instead, a stochastic rationing scheme of the very simple form discussed above; that is

$$C = \begin{cases} C^d \text{ with probability } \Pi_1 \\ 0 \text{ with probability } 1 - \Pi_1; \end{cases}$$

$$L = \begin{cases} L^s \text{ with probability } \Pi_2 \\ 0 \text{ with probability } 1 - \Pi_2. \end{cases} \tag{12.19}$$

Suppose further that the C and L rations are independent. Then the problem for the household is to choose C^d and L^s so as to maximise expected utility, namely:

$$\Pi_1\Pi_2\tilde{U}(C^d, L^s) + \Pi_1(1 - \Pi_2)\tilde{U}(C^d, 0) + (1 - \Pi_1)\Pi_2\tilde{U}(0, L^s)$$
$$+ (1 - \Pi_1)(1 - \Pi_2)\tilde{U}(0, 0) \tag{12.20}$$

where

$$\tilde{U}(C, L) \equiv U(C, L, M_{-1} + wL - pC; a). \tag{12.21}$$

The effective demand (C^d) and effective supply (L^s) that emerge as the solutions of this maximisation problem are not only feasible but also consistent with optimising behaviour. Moreover, this remains true even with more than two markets. This represents a clear improvement on the Drèze and Clower effective demands. A full discussion of these points may be found Svensson (1980) and Honkapohja and Ito (1979), both of which explore the implications of a stochastic scheme similar to, though rather more sophisticated than, (12.19).

A further advantage of stochastic rationing schemes is that they can easily be extended to cover markets in which there is some friction (or inefficiency) in the quantity rationing process. By this, we mean that it is not necessarily the case that all traders on the short side of the market achieve their desired trades. This seems an important feature of the real world, particularly in the absence of a centralised quantity clearing mechanism. For example, in labour markets, vacancies and unemployment often co-exist. Some preliminary analysis along these lines can be found in Green (1980), which also comments on the papers referred to in the paragraph above.

12.4 OTHER MODELS

The past 6 years or so have witnessed a positive deluge of fixed-price macroeconomic models of the type discussed above. With the dust beginning to settle, it is now possible to assess the significance of the contributions made by such models. Despite the fact that they are necessarily much more complicated (even in the relatively simple versions considered here) than the earlier *IS–LM* based models, it is clear that they have provided economists with considerably greater insights into the operation of an economy out of full Walrasian equilibrium. The source of these insights, and hence the main strength in one sense, is, of course, the fixed-price assumption. But, simultaneously, this constitutes their greatest weakness: after all, no-one (except possibly a hardbitten socialist) would be surprised by the suggestion that market imbalance may result if prices are fixed arbitrarily. Clearly, fixed-price models cannot constitute the whole of the macroeconomic story; although they do provide a vitally important chapter.

There appear to be two possible avenues for exploration. The simplest would simply involve 'tacking on' some price adjustment scheme to the basic model of Section 12.2. The end-product would be a discrete[13] model consisting of a sequence of time periods *within* which prices were fixed, and *between* which prices were adjusted by some kind of *tâtonnement* process. (For example, the change of price in each market could be made proportional to the aggregate excess effective demand in that market.) This would imply bringing back the Walrasian Auctioneer playing a somewhat modified rôle. Some discussion of this type of model is contained in Section 12.5.

While this kind of model might prove useful for certain analytical purposes, as a description of the operation of an economy it leaves several things to be desired. First, it reintroduces the *deus ex machina* who obligingly carries out the price adjustment process for purely altruistic reasons. Secondly, it skates over the important question of why the agents in the model should continue to act as price-takers while suffering from quantity constraints. (It is clearly essential to the story told above that the Auctioneer does not perform his job *too* efficiently – for otherwise full Walrasian equilibrium would be attained immediately; but if the Auctioneer is inefficient, then possibly the agents have an incentive to take over the job themselves.) Thirdly, it implies that the agents will continue to act in the manner described in Section 12.2 even though it may no longer be in their interests so to do – in view of the price adjustment mechanism operating: as time passes, agents will learn about the adjustment mechanism, and use this knowledge to predict future prices.

This third point reminds us that the story told in Section 12.2 was the description of just one period in a sequence of time periods;

it is therefore inconsistent with that story to isolate that one period and consider it as being repeated over and over again. True consistency requires that the models of the agents unfold period by period in line with the price adjustment process. But to construct a fully consistent model in which all agents knew the price-adjustment mechanism, and acted optimally with respect to that mechanism, would appear to be a very difficult task indeed.

The second possible avenue for exploration would involve dropping the price-taking assumption. Thus, individual agents would take over the price-setting rôle. One could, for example, postulate that if an agent found that he was unable to buy all he wished of some particular good at the going price, then he would offer to pay a somewhat higher price. This might remove (or, at least, ease) the constraint. We have already discussed at some length (in Chapters 10 and 11) the considerable difficulties that arise with this line of argument; not least are the informational requirements that it imposes on the agents. (In the price-taking framework, agents 'simply' need to know, or have conjectures about, the relevant quantity constraints; in a price-setting framework, however, agents need to know, or have conjectures about, the relevant demand and supply schedules that they face.) Nevertheless, this 'conjectural equilibrium' approach (for references, see Section 11.3) does hold out the promise of a sensible description of a macroeconomy with fully consistent microeconomic behaviour underlying it. Only time will tell whether the promise will be fulfilled.

At first glance, the stochastic rationing approach discussed in Section 12.3 appears to resolve the problem of the implausibility of the fixed-price approach. For example, as far as the simple scheme described in that section is concerned, each agent either gets what he asks for at the prevailing price (in which case he has no obvious incentive to offer to trade at some other price) or he gets nothing (in which case the prevailing price is immaterial). Superficially, the agent has no incentive to take over the price-setting rôle. Unfortunately, this argument presumes that the probabilities involved (of getting all or nothing) are fixed. In practice, they will depend upon the prevailing price. Thus, an agent who gets what he demands with probability $\Pi (0 < \Pi < 1)$, and gets nothing with probability $1 - \Pi$, may be able to improve his utility by increasing Π through an offer to trade at a higher price. The fixed-price assumption is thus implausible even under the stochastic rationing approach.

Before concluding this section, we ought to return briefly to the mainstream fixed-price approach, and mention various extensions to the basic model described in Section 12.2. As the reader will no doubt be aware, this basic model is very simple indeed in structure: there are just two markets (both spot), there is no borrowing and lending, no investment, no financial assets other than money and no foreign trade. Although an improvement on the *IS–LM* framework in many respects, it omits a large number of features that macroeconomists have long considered of vital importance. Some progress has, in fact, been made in incorporating some of these features in the 'reformulated' macroeconomics. Investment and financial assets are introduced (though in a rather special way) by Barro and Grossman (1976). International trade is considered by Dixit (1978), who also explored some aspects of public finance in an earlier paper (Dixit 1976). Nevertheless, much work still remains to be done.

12.5 DISEQUILIBRIUM AND ADJUSTMENT PROCESSES

Until recently, the standard method adopted by economists to model price adjustment processes was simply to append to the normal demand and supply analysis a further equation (or equations) indicating that the change of price was some increasing function of excess demand. For example, in a single market with price denoted by p, and with demand and supply curves denoted by $D(.)$ and $S(.)$ respectively, a price adjustment mechanism of the following form would be appended:

$$\Delta p = f[D(p) - S(p)] \qquad (12.22)$$

where $f' > 0$ and $f(0) = 0$.

The intuition behind such a formulation is straightforward: if there is (positive) excess demand, then the price will tend to rise; if there is (positive) excess supply, then the price will tend to fall. Unfortunately, the economics behind this formulation is not so obvious; indeed, as we discussed in Chapter 10 and in Hey (1979a), the formulation neither represents the optimising behaviour of any agent in the market, nor is consistent with the derivation of the demand and supply curves. Nevertheless, *ad hoc* adjustment processes of the form of (12.22) have been of some analytical value in providing theorists with some rough and ready idea of the 'dynamic' properties of various models. (In addition, it must be said that such crude formulations have also met with a fair measure of empirical success.)

Thus, although the appending of such price adjustment processes to otherwise equilibrium models is of highly dubious theoretical validity, it may enable the theorists to say a little about the dynamic behaviour of his models. Such exercises have been performed with respect to the basic 'reformulated' macro model of Section 12.2. (The reader could refer to Barro and Grossman (1976), Böhm (1976) and Varian (1977a, b) for details.)

Refer to Figure 12.5, and consider, for example, the appending of such an adjustment process (for both prices and wages) to the model represented there. Suppose the economy starts in a Keynesian unemployment state. There is excess supply of labour, the magnitude of which is measured by the horizontal distance between the point K and the $\bar{L}^s$ curve; there is also excess supply of goods, the magnitude of which is measured by the vertical distance between the point K and the $\bar{C}^s$ curve. The operation of the price adjustment mechanism would cause falls in both w and p, the extents being determined by the functional forms and by the magnitudes of the excess supplies. Referring now to Figure 12.6, such an adjustment process could lead the economy to the full Walrasian equilibrium point (W), but is more likely to lead it to either régime C or régime U. Once in the former, the price adjustment mechanism would lead to a fall in w and a rise in p (as can be seen from Figure 12.5); this might take the economy back into régime K, or possibly into régime R. If régime U was entered, both w and p would fall; moving the economy into régime R. From régime R, the price adjustment mechanism would yield higher w and p; thus, moving the economy into either régime C or régime U (or possibly régime W). And so on; the final outcome depending, of course, on the values of the various adjustment parameters involved. As can be seen, however, there is a general tendency for the process to move the economy towards point W.

Such an analysis also draws attention to the possibility that, if the two 'arms' of each wedge are very close together (that is, the wedges are very thin), then the actual difference between effective excess supply and effective excess demand could be very small indeed even though the equilibrium point is well to the south-west of the 'bliss' points F and H. Such a possibility is illustrated in Figure 12.7.

In such a situation, particularly if the adjustment mechanism is at all sluggish, it may take many periods to move the economy away from its Keynesian unemployment state; in this sense, then, chronic unemployment may persist for some considerable time.

Of course, appending these *ad hoc* adjustment processes is, as we have already argued, strictly illegitimate. What are the alternatives?

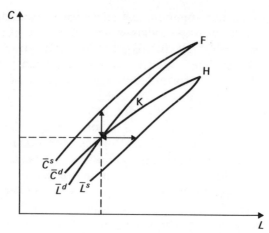

Figure 12.7   Small excess effective demand

The obvious answer is one which takes us back to the preceding section: what is really needed is a model in which agents choose prices as well as quantities. Then we can examine, in a fully consistent framework, the evolution of wages and prices through time. The conjectural equilibrium approach promises such a possibility. But it is important to note the word 'equilibrium'; in no sense will the resulting process describe a *disequilibrium* adjustment process.

This is an important point, and one we should emphasise before concluding this section: all the models discussed in this chapter are essentially equilibrium models – despite the fact that ostensibly disequilibrium phenomena such as unemployment are being analysed. Consider, for simplicity, the model described in Section 12.2. The points W, K, C, U and R in Figure 12.5 are *equilibrium* points under the 'rules of the game' of that model. Remember that w and p are fixed, and all agents are assumed to be price-takers. The only things left to worry about are quantities. In expressing their demands and supplies, agents make some guess about the constraints they are likely to experience; if their guesses are wrong, they have made a mistake, and hence the situation is not an equilibrium state since not all agents are behaving optimally. The points W, K, C, U and R are crucially characterised by the fact that perceived constraints and actual constraints coincide: thus, all agents are behaving optimally. That is why these five points are equilibrium points.

This is an argument we have already used: optimality and equilibrium go hand-in-hand. Thus, departures from equilibrium require the theorist to depart from the use of optimality. And this takes us into the realms of behavioural, evolutionary, models of economic behaviour. Perhaps, paradoxically, the appending of *ad hoc* adjustment processes to essentially equilibrium models is acceptable after all!

12.6 CONCLUSIONS

There can be no doubt whatsoever that the fixed-price models of Sections 12.2 and 12.3 constitute a significant improvement on the *IS–LM* framework as an intellectually honest description of non-market-clearing states. The 'reformulated' macroeconomics has also yielded considerable insights into the appropriate econometric techniques for the modelling of economies out of full Walrasian equilibrium; recent years have witnessed numerous advances in the econometric theory relating to markets in disequilibrium.

Unfortunately, there is also little doubt that the new models are much more complicated to analyse and describe; with the passage of time, however, a number of relatively simple diagrammatic formulations have emerged (most notably that of Muellbauer and Portes presented in Section 12.2). This has significantly increased the adoption and use of the new models.[14] Clearly this process will have to continue in the coming years, as the basic model is enlarged and extended to include all of the various macroeconomic aspects of concern to economists.

PART V

REVIEW AND APPRAISAL

13 THE PAST AND THE PRESENT

13.1 INTRODUCTION

The purpose of this chapter is to overview the book as a whole, and to appraise the present 'state of the art' as far as the economic modelling of 'disequilibrium' is concerned. This chapter thus paves the way for Chapter 14 which concludes our book with a discussion of the possible, probable and desirable future developments in the subject.

This chapter is organised as follows: in Sections 13.2, 13.3 and 13.4 we overview respectively the material of Parts II, III and IV of the book. As far as possible, we confine our comments to an essentially factual appraisal of recent developments; more general critical comments are delayed until the concluding section, 13.5.

13.2 PART II

Notwithstanding the various criticisms that can and have been levelled at it, it is undoubtedly true that Neumann–Morgenstern utility theory has provided a most fruitful foundation for the analysis of economic behaviour under uncertainty. Recent years have witnessed numerous theoretical advances whose *sine qua non* was the existence of Neumann–Morgenstern (NM) utility theory. Clearly it would be foolish to minimise its importance.

The contents of Part II bear witness to its significance. Contained in this part are many important analytical devices which have been developed in recent years, and which are repeatedly and fruitfully used in numerous economic applications. Underpinning the whole analysis of behaviour under uncertainty are the concepts of risk aversion, risk neutrality and risk loving; their encapsulation by the concavity, linearity and convexity of the utility function is a particularly neat but powerful implication of NM theory. Also of repeated applicability is the conjugate notion of 'increasing risk' particularly as developed by Rothschild and Stiglitz. However, it is necessary to remember (as evidenced by the partiality of the Rothschild–Stiglitz ordering) that 'riskiness' is just one aspect of random prospects.

The simple but significant comparative static propositions of Section 4.2 (on the simplest static problem of a passive type) are essentially immediate consequences of the fact that risk-aversion and concavity of the utility function are synonymous. These propositions are important in that they directly provide sufficient conditions for the existence of empirically testable theoretical predictions in simple passive uncertainty problems. The same is true of the comparative static propositions derived in Section 4.3, although they relate to a special case of the general problem (which, of course, is the reason why they are rather 'stronger').

Section 4.4, on dynamic optimisation, introduced a number of key analytical devices, which proved their usefulness in the subsequent pages of the book. For *finite* horizon dynamic problems, the key device was the method of *backward induction*; this method is fundamental to the analysis of optimal behaviour under uncertainty. It employs the obvious, yet profound, fact (termed the 'optimality principle of dynamic programming' in other contexts) that an optimal dynamic plan must be optimal as viewed from all points of time within it. Thus, the optimal decision for any one period must be made conditional on the presumption that the optimal decisions will be made in all future time periods. Obviously, the actual derivation of the sequence of optimal decisions must be made in 'reverse' order – starting from the horizon and working backwards.

Although this technique of backward induction works brilliantly well in finite (whether random or deterministic) horizon problems, by its very nature it cannot be directly employed in infinite horizon problems; for these latter, an alternative technique may have to be used. In Section 4.4, the special case of an infinite horizon problem which was essentially *stationary* was investigated. This led to an enormous simplification: specifically since it meant that the optimal decision in any period was dependent only on the 'inheritance from the past' and not on the 'date' of the period. It requires very stringent restrictions, however, and therefore may not be very realistic.

Although not immediately apparent, there are strong connections between the material on dynamic optimisation in passive situations (the concern of Section 4.4) and the material on optimisation in active situations covered in Chapter 5. To highlight these connections, let us consider the following very simple problem: suppose, at some stage in some decision problem, the individual has to choose one of two options (call them 1 and 2). Suppose, further, that if he chooses *i* then the expected value of the utility of the individual is V_i ($i = 1, 2$) on the presumption that, after deciding between options 1 and 2, *the individual thereafter behaves optimally with respect to all subsequent decisions*. Then the optimal choice is simple: he should choose 1 if $V_1 > V_2$ and 2 if $V_1 < V_2$ (and it does not matter which he chooses if V_1 equals V_2). This is the simplest illustration of the 'principle of dynamic programming' mentioned earlier; in view of its simplicity it is surprising that it has such profound implications.

In essence, this simple idea underlies all the search theory of Chapter 5. It crucially underlies the idea that the reservation value in any search problem is characterised by indifference between continuing and terminating search. This property led to a number of important insights into the implications of optimal search behaviour.

In the light of this principle, once V_1 and V_2 (or their equivalents) are calculated, the problem is solved. Thus, the only real effort is the calculation of the relevant Vs. As should be apparent from our discussion of backward induction, it must be the case that the Vs are calculated backwards: the Vs as viewed from before some decision is taken being calculated in terms of the Vs as viewed from after the decision has been taken (and thus as viewed from before the next decision is taken). In principle, this technique can be applied in any (finite horizon) problem, including those in which learning is involved.

The use of Neumann–Morgenstern utility theory necessitates the use of probability theory (since one of the axioms of NM theory is that individuals combine probabilities in accordance with the usual probability laws). It is therefore natural to employ Bayes' theorem as a description of learning (since Bayes' theorem is essentially the conditional probability definition rewritten). As we saw in Chapter 6, Bayes' theorem has an intuitively satisfying appeal in that it makes clear the way that prior beliefs are changed into posterior beliefs by the incorporation of information. The material of Chapter 6 was also important in that it demonstrated how the value of information in any decision problem could be calculated; moreover, it showed how this value was intimately related to the structure of the decision problem under consideration. (Unlike the situation in so-called Information Theory – in which the 'value of information' is simply a mathematical construct.)

The combination of backward induction and Bayes' theorem, as was shown in Section 6.4, provides a powerful method of modelling learning in active situations. The V functions (defined above) in such situations depend not only on the 'inheritance from the past' but also on the current parameters of the subjective probability distributions of the random variables about which the individual is learning. In calculating the V functions (by the backward process described above), the structure of the problem determined the connections between the 'inheritance from the past' in successive time periods, and Bayes' theorem determined the connections between the parameters (of the distributions) in successive time periods. Thus, once again, Bayes' theorem shows itself as the 'natural' learning model to use with NM utility theory.

At this point, however, we began to express doubts which became rather stronger and rather more insistent as the book proceeded. In essence, our doubts relate to the assumed computational abilities of the economic agents under discussion. While it seems perfectly reasonable to use NM utility theory and Bayes' theorem to model human behaviour in relatively simple decision problems, we are somewhat uneasy about the use of these analytical devices to model behaviour in more complex decision problems. To be specific, the model of learning in active situations described in Section 6.4 implies that the economic agent can actually carry out the highly complex calculations required to determine the values of the various V functions. Given that most electronic computers would find the task difficult, we suspect that the model is assuming rather too much.[1] Perhaps economists should take more heed of those psychologists who argue that actual human behaviour follows simple 'rules of thumb'[2] rather than optimal rules in relatively complex environments?

13.3   PART III

The purpose of Part III was to show how the analytical tools and techniques described in Part II could be applied to investigate a wide variety of microeconomic problems. The first three chapters in this Part were concerned with the behaviour of individual agents; as such they were solely interested in partial equilibrium matters. In contrast, the fourth chapter, concerned with market models, began the process of general equilibrium analysis, which was continued in Part IV of the book.

Chapters 7 and 8, devoted to households and firms respectively, were relatively straightforward applications of the material in Part II. Throughout both these chapters, it was assumed that the economic agents under discussion obeyed the axioms of Neumann–Morgenstern utility theory. As these chapters show, considerable insight into the behaviour of households and firms under uncertainty can be obtained by the use of this theory.

The analysis in Section 7.2 of the behaviour of the household in passive situations was important in that it yielded a number of simple sufficient conditions for the derivation of unambiguous comparative static propositions. Of particular significance were the results relating to increased uncertainty (with respect to future income and the rate of interest). In addition, Section 7.2 contained an interesting special case, which gave rise to a linear consumption function (as a function of wealth).

The material in Section 7.3, mainly on consumer-search and job-search models, related to a part of economic theory which is currently experiencing considerable popularity. The appeal of search theory is obvious: the structure of the problem, and particularly its sequential nature, is one immediately recognisable in all walks of economic life. From this point of view, it is much more attractive than the conventional vision of economic decision-making as a once-and-for-all simultaneous affair. Also of intuitive appeal is the idea of *reservation values*: in many decision problems it is the passing of some threshold value that triggers off specific decisions.

While much progress has been made into the analysis of search problems (of a non-adaptive type), the analysis of household learning is relatively underdeveloped. The paucity of Section 7.4 bears witness to this. Perhaps this is a further symptom of the problem discussed above?

As Chapter 8 demonstrates, the analysis of search behaviour by firms is not so well-developed as that by households.[3] In contrast, the analysis of firms in passive situations is much better developed. Section 8.2 provides a fairly comprehensive study of the price-taking firm operating in both static and dynamic environments. In the latter, inventories play the rôle of the 'inheritance from the past', and are thus the counterpart of the money savings of the household.

In view of our unease about the universal applicability of Neumann–Morgenstern utility theory, it seemed only right that we should include some discussion of alternative approaches. The second half of Chapter 9 contained such a discussion. Without wishing it to appear that we want to have our cake and eat it, we must admit that many of the alternative approaches to decision-making under uncertainty discussed in Chapter 9 have their attractions. Mean-variance analysis is attractive in that it simplifies the informational requirements of economic agents: 'all' the agents need to know are the means and the variance–covariance matrix of the relevant random variables. Safety-first analysis is attractive in that it embodies the idea that individuals try to avoid 'disaster' in some sense. Prospect Theory is attractive in that it attempts to incorporate the actual observed deficiencies of real-life human beings forced to make decisions under uncertainty. The Robustness/flexibility approach is attractive in that it tries to capture the idea that individuals are prepared to forego something in return for flexibility. The Behavioural approach is attractive in that it envisages human beings indulging in 'rules of thumb' when faced with complex decision problems. Professor Shackle's approach is attractive in that it explicitly allows for *surprise* (in contrast with the Bayesian approach which is unable to cope with surprise).

Unfortunately, all of these alternative approaches also have significant disadvantages. Mean-variance analysis violates the intuitively attractive notion of *préférence absolue*. Safety-first analysis, if blindly applied, leads to some manifestly absurd decisions. Prospect Theory necessarily implies intransitivities (and how on earth do we cope with them?). The Robustness/flexibility approach is not yet developed. The Behavioural approach may be deemed to be arbitrary; moreover, it may imply manifestly sub-optimal behaviour. Professor Shackle's approach would appear to deny probability a rôle even when it clearly *is* informative.

In contrast, NM theory (combined with Bayesian learning) is consistent – as long as computational problems are ignored. But what happens if such problems cannot be ignored?

In Chapter 10, we returned to the conventional fold, and examined the operation of markets. Even using NM theory, the analysis of markets proved to be both conceptually and technically difficult. One particular problem, which we encountered for the first time in Chapter 10, but which was to increasingly recur throughout Part IV, was that of the correct modelling of *disequilibrium*. We argued that, if both sides of any market were behaving optimally, then the only situation that could prevail would be an *equilibrium situation* (with respect to the 'rules of the game' of the market under consideration, of course). Definitionally, disequilibrium, which means the existence of a tendency for change, would imply that some economic agent (the one who was inducing the tendency) was dissatisfied, and thus not behaving optimally. Optimality and equilibrium go hand-in-hand.

It is however, important not to equate equilibrium in a market with market-clearing, and disequilibrium with non-market-clearing.

Whether a non-market-clearing situation is a disequilibrium state or not depends upon the 'rules of the game' in operation. We will return to these points in Chapter 14.

13.4 PART IV

The market theme introduced in Chapter 10 was taken up and amplified in Part IV. Chapter 11 provided a general (but rather abstract) framework for the analysis of the simultaneous interaction of several (exhaustive) markets in an economy. Chapter 12 put more flesh on the bones of Chapter 11 by considering an explicitly macroeconomic version of the general equilibrium theory of the latter.

The key analytical device of both these chapters was the investigation of *fixed-price* equilibria. As this term indicates, the 'rules of the game' were such that prices were fixed (and all agents acted as price-takers); the equilibria that were derived were crucially conditional on this feature, particularly since they were manifestly non-market-clearing states. Also of vital importance, in view of the quantity constraints that agents found themselves experiencing in such states, was the precise nature of the rationing mechanism employed to 'resolve' the constraints.

Among the numerous insights that this fixed-price analysis has yielded is the crucial distinction between a Keynesian unemployment state and a Classical unemployment state; moreover, the analysis makes clear why policy measures which are appropriate for one state may be inappropriate for the other. No longer do we have an uneasy compromise between Keynesians and Classicists – now the distinction is clear.

Of course, although the analysis of fixed-price equilibria is an important part of the macroeconomic story, it clearly does not and cannot constitute the whole story. What is needed in addition is some account of how prices adjust. Moreover, this account must be plausible in the sense that it describes the actual behaviour of agents in the economy (rather than some fictitious Walrasian Auctioneer). The conjectural equilibria approach of Professor Hahn and his colleagues appears to be a promising step in the right direction.

13.5 CONCLUSIONS

The rumblings of discontent (with the state of macroeconomics) that initiated many of the theoretical developments described in this book became audible less than a decade and a half ago. Over the past 15 years there has been a near revolution in both microeconomic theory and macroeconomic theory: a comparison of the 'state of the art' at the beginning of this period with the state now shows a significant improvement in the economic theory of behaviour under uncertainty. It would be a churlish person indeed who would deny this.

One feature of the discoveries of recent years (and this may well be a feature that applies to all disciplines) is that the increased light generated by these discoveries has revealed the existence of numerous further problems, hitherto unimagined. In this sense, our understanding has increased. But, as our understanding increases, so does the complexity of our economic models. How far can this process sensibly continue?

14   THE FUTURE?

As this chapter is essentially a personal postscript in conclusion, it would seem appropriate to revert to the first person singular. This, then, may be a rather odd time to admit to a sense of schizophrenia during the writing of this book. But it is true, as perhaps the reader has already noted: I have been constantly pulled two ways. On the one hand, I have profound respect for the apparatus of Neumann–Morgenstern utility (and Bayesian learning): it is a delightfully consistent structure, and has led to numerous important insights – as this book bears witness. On the other hand, however, I am all too often reminded of the amazing sophistication that this apparatus requires of the agents whose behaviour it is describing. I ask myself: do I behave like that? All too often the answer is no.

The problem originates from a fundamental requirement of (current) economic theorising: namely, that economic agents behave in a consistent fashion. This requirement is now so engrained in our thinking that we take it for granted: inconsistencies, particularly intransitivities, create problems – in a sense they inevitably imply *un*economic behaviour. (If an individual prefers A to B, B to C and C to A, then someone else can endlessly make money out of that individual by exchanging him A for A.) If inconsistencies are ruled out, we are almost inevitably led to Neumann–Morgenstern utility theory. Once we have accepted that, the acceptance of Bayesian learning follows almost automatically. The logic is almost inexorable.

This argument ignores the existence of computational cost, however; once the existence of this is admitted, we may be able to avoid being led down this logical cul de sac. At the same time, we could drop the insistence on *global* consistency: instead we could adopt the simpler requirement that, if *choice* is *costless*, then choices must be transitive. When choice is costly, that is, when the actual *process* of decision-making imposes *costs* on the decision-maker, the meaning of 'optimal choice' is no longer clear: one is led into an infinitely regressing argument. (To decide is costly; therefore one needs to decide whether it is worth deciding. But to decide whether to decide is costly; therefore one needs to decide whether it is worth deciding whether it is worth deciding. And so on . . . without limit.)

This line of thought leads me to the conclusion that Neumann–Morgenstern utility theory is eminently suitable for simple decision problems – that is, those in which the computational and other decision costs are essentially ignorable – but for more complex problems, it is more realistic to suppose that the decision-maker adopts some simple 'rules of thumb'. Of course, if the decision-maker meets the same problem repeatedly, he may eventually adapt his behaviour so that it approaches the true optimal. (In this case the decision costs are being spread over many decisions.) But this is a problem with 'rules of thumb' – they may *not* converge to the optimal as the decision cost sinks to zero, nor as the number of experiences of that decision increases. (Indeed, this is a problem with the 'rule of thumb' described in Section 6.5.) How one gets round this I am not sure.

A possibility is one I suggested at the end of Chapter 9. There I put forward the idea that when faced with a complex environment, the decision-maker proceeds in two stages: first, he simplifies the complex environment to a much simpler abstraction; second, he then behaves optimally with respect to the abstraction. Thus, while overall the decision-making process may look like a 'rule of thumb', Neumann–Morgenstern utility theory in fact plays a crucial rôle. If this two-stage process is a true description of actual decision-making, the interesting questions that remain to be answered relate to the first stage: how is the simplification made? Does it change as the individual learns? And crucially: does the optimal rule with respect to the changing abstraction converge to the truly optimal rule?

As the contents of this book clearly show, recent years have witnessed a significant increase in the complexity of the problems supposedly solved by the economic agents. This is particularly so in the branch of economics devoted to the investigation of disequilibrium. We may expect this process to continue in the future.

Consider the present 'state of the art' in macroeconomics. The current preoccupation is with equilibrium states relative to the 'rules of the game': in these one requires that agents' decisions are consistent in the sense that each agent is choosing optimally given the decisions of all the other agents. Presumably, the next surge of analysis will be occupied with equilibrium *adjustment processes* (relative to the 'rules of the game'). In this, one will require that *adjustment* decisions of agents are consistent in the sense that each agent is *adjusting* optimally given the *adjustment* decisions of all the other agents. But just imagine the informational requirements: these are severe enough in the present (quantity-constrained or conjectural) equilibrium analysis, but they will be an order of magnitude more severe in the future equilibrium adjustment analysis. It is surely unrealistic to impose such informational requirements on actual human beings and expect them to continue to behave as optimisers.

The problem, as we have already argued, is that optimality and equilibrium go hand-in-hand. Under conventional methodology, if we require our agents to behave optimally, then we are restricted (at the market or economy level) to analysing equilibrium: whether it be equilibrium states, equilibrium adjustment processes, equilibrium adjustment of adjustment processes, or whatever. True disequilibrium analysis requires us to abandon optimality.

To my mind, this appears to indicate what we should be doing next. Rather than extend indefinitely optimality analysis to increasingly complex environments, we should be modelling true disequilibrium through the use of *reasonable* 'rules of thumb'. I stress the word 'reasonable', as I believe actual behaviour is generally reasonable: people do not go around using stupid 'rules of thumb' – certainly not for very long! Naturally, I would like to say what 'reasonable' means, and how one models 'reasonable' behaviour; unfortunately, my thoughts along these lines are insufficiently well-developed to commit to print.

One inevitable implication of reasonable (rather than optimal) behaviour is that it is necessarily random: the predictions of optimal theory are essentially deterministic; those of reasonable theory will be stochastic. This seems to accord more closely with actual behaviour. Moreover, when it comes to the econometric testing of the predictions the 'disturbance' (or stochastic) term will arise naturally out of the theory, rather than being tacked on at the end (as is usually the case with optimal theory).

At the present time there are increasing signs that more and more of the profession are reasoning along these lines: 'evolutionary' models and simulation methods are becoming respectable once again; 'behaviouralists' are crawling out of the woodwork. Ironically, it is the sophisticated state of optimality theory (as described in this book) which has led to this growing awareness. But the profession is not moving *away* from optimality through ignorance; rather it is moing *on* from optimality through knowledge. The future looks promising ... and exciting.

NOTES

CHAPTER 1   INTRODUCTION

1. A partial survey can be found in Hey (1979a).

2. All agents were asked to express their demands and supplies
    conditional on being able to buy or sell *any amount* they
    wished at the prevailing price. But out of equilibrium that
    condition cannot be satisfied.

CHAPTER 3   UTILITY THEORY

1. The following derivation assumes $R \neq 0$. If $R = 0$, then rather
    trivially it follows that $U(x) = a + bx$, and the individual is
    risk-neutral.

2. Unless $R = 1$ in which case $U(x) = a + b \ln x$.

3. Preference here is not *strict* preference; in other words,
    preference includes indifference.

4. For mathematical purists, we should remark that our proof
    has assumed that all utility functions are twice-differentiable,
    while the one in (3.22) clearly is not. It can be considered,
    however, as the limit of a sequence of utility functions which
    are twice differentiable; the proof works, though it is somewhat
    messier.

CHAPTER 4   OPTIMISATION IN PASSIVE SITUATIONS

1. In contrast, in an adaptive situation the individual can learn,
    and in an active situation the individual can control the number
    of realisations of certain random variables.

2. An example familiar from elementary microtheory is that of the perfectly competitive firm: the optimal choice of inputs $Y_1, \ldots, Y_n$ for output price X can be found in two stages. First, the optimal output Y given X is found; second, the optimal values of $Y_1, \ldots, Y_n$ given Y are found.

3. But note that (4.7) being true *everywhere*, although *sufficient* for (4.11), is not *necessary*.

4. This statement, and our discussion, assumes *strict* concavity (and convexity); analogous results hold for *weak* concavity (and convexity).

5. Note that a mean-preserving *introduction* in risk and a Sandmo increase in risk are both special cases of a Rothschild–Stiglitz *increase* in risk; thus the sufficient conditions derived in Section 4.2 remain sufficient.

6. A parallel argument shows that Y^* increases if the individual is risk loving and displays increasing absolute risk aversion.

7. At the end of these T periods the individual is assumed to die, or, at least, lose interest in the problem under discussion.

8. Equation (4.46) is found by setting to zero the derivative, with respect to Y, of the term in curly brackets in (4.45); it is assumed that an interior solution exists.

9. The following assumes that the probability distribution of the date of death is *independent* of the choice of Ys by the individual and the realisations of the Xs; if, on the contrary there was dependence, the solution would be much more difficult. In many interesting problems (such as cigarette-smoking), however, dependence does exist.

CHAPTER 5   OPTIMISATION IN ACTIVE SITUATIONS

1. In statistics, the term 'stopping problems' is also commonly used.

2. In some early search models, and most notably the seminal work of Stigler (1961, 1962), a predetermined sample size strategy was assumed; in this strategy the searcher decides, in advance of search, the number of observations he will make. Clearly this is a suboptimal strategy under our assumptions. See

Hey (1979a, pp. 83–7) for details and further discussion and references.

3. Clearly, from the structure of the problem, if it is not worth searching once more it cannot be worth searching twice more, or three times more, or....

4. A fuller discussion of the distinction between stationary and non-stationary problems will be found later in the chapter.

5. Alternatively (5.6) may be derived from the following expression for V_x

$$V_x = A + AF(x) + A[F(x)]^2 + A[F(x)]^3 + \ldots$$

where

$$A = -c + \int_x^\infty t \, dF(t).$$

If 'success' means 'an observation greater than x', then the first term represents success on the first search, the second term success on the second search, and so on.

6. $F(x^*)$ must be less than 1 since c is positive.

7. Strictly speaking, 'the' should read 'an': it is a matter of indifference whether the equality in (5.23) holds or not. Thus there are several optimal sets, though they all give the same expected net reward.

8. A formal proof of the optimality of this informally-derived solution can be found in Hey (1979b).

9. Note that in the formulation of this section, the reward on stopping is $U(x)$ *per period* for an infinite lifetime; this reward stream has discounted value $U(x)/(1-\rho)$.

10. Assuming that $U(x)[1-F(x)]$ approaches zero as x approaches infinity.

11. The inequality may be replaced by an equality in some rather odd degenerate cases with which we shall not be concerned.

CHAPTER 6 OPTIMISATION IN ADAPTIVE SITUATIONS

1. We implicitly assume that information is costly; if it were free, there would be no economic problem to discuss.

2. The form appropriate for a univariate discrete random variable is almost identical in structure to (6.6).

3. From (6.10) and (6.11) it is immediately seen that the denominator of (6.12) is simply $e(w)$.

4. Note that if a variable Y is normally distributed with mean μ and variance σ^2 its pdf is given by

$$(1/\sqrt{2\pi\sigma^2}) \exp\{-(y-\mu)^2/2\sigma^2\} \qquad -\infty < y < \infty.$$

5. If X is $N(\mu, \sigma^2)$ then $E[\exp(tX)] = \exp[\mu t + \tfrac{1}{2}\sigma^2 t^2]$; see any standard statistics text, for example, Mood, Graybill and Boes (1974).

6. The variance of W is $1/p$ plus $1/r$.

7. It can be shown by straightforward integration that, if X is $N(\mu, 1/r)$ then

$$E[\exp(-tX^2/2)] = \sqrt{r/(t+r)} \exp[-tr\mu^2/2(t+r)].$$

8. For details, see Degroot (1970), p. 160.

CHAPTER 7 HOUSEHOLDS

1. Without (we hope) risk of confusion, we will use V_1 and V_X interchangeably to refer to the partial derivative of $V(X, Y)$ with respect to its first argument; we will use whichever notation results in the simpler expression.

2. Two alternative interpretations of this distribution are possible: in the first, the distribution is taken to be the distribution of prices across firms; in the second, the distribution is taken to be the subjective assessment of the price of each and every firm. Since the theory we are about to develop requires the distribution to remain constant as search proceeds, the first interpretation requires that sampling is done with replacement or that the number of firms is infinite; no such problem arises with the second interpretation. We favour the second.

3. Note that we have assumed that the individual will always buy exactly one unit of the good irrespective of the purchase price and of the amount expended on search; we will have something to say about this feature in due course.

4. 'On-the-job' search will be considered briefly later.

5. This result can be derived using the methods discussed in Section 4.2. A risk-lover will also increase x^*, but whether by less or more than the shift in the distribution cannot be unambiguously determined.

6. We assume that individuals die between periods and not within them (very considerate of them!).

7. Indeed, there are certain infamous instances where the candidate, if offered the job, will get his interview expenses only if he accepts the offer. This kind of situation adds new dimensions to the search problem – not the least of which is the implication that there are other aspects of the job about which the interviewee is uncertain.

CHAPTER 8   FIRMS

1. By default, therefore, we omit applications which are highly tedious mathematically, and which yield conclusions only under extremely restrictive conclusions. Surveys of the theory of the firm under uncertainty can be found in Ahsan and Ullah (1978), Hey (1979a), Lippman and McCall (1978) and Newbery (1978).

2. In addition to physical inventory (on the supply side), there may also be metaphysical *goodwill* (on the demand side) constituting a linking factor between successive time periods. As we have noted earlier (Hey, 1979a, pp. 165–6 and 230–1), however, most writers neglect this factor. Some preliminary exploration of goodwill can be found in Hey (1981a).

3. Additionally, from note 6 of Chapter 4, it follows that a risk-loving firm which displays increasing absolute risk aversion will react by increasing output.

4. Under plausible assumptions, given any output choice, there exists a unique number of workers (and hence output per

worker) that maximises the objective function of the firm, and vice versa.

5. Compare (8.11) and (8.1), but remember the differing definitions of the variables Y and Z.

6. The second-order conditions hold only if the firm is risk averse.

7. Implicit in our assumptions is the consequence that it will always be optimal for the retailer to satisfy demand if he can.

8. An alternative (but less elegant) proof is given in Hey (1979a), pp. 160–1; there equation (22.4) is our (8.25).

9. Further details can be found in Zabel (1967, 1971).

10. Assuming (for $C'' > 0$) that $C'(0) < x^*$; if this is not the case, optimal production is zero, and the problem degenerates to the no-production case.

11. There are no inventories in Krouse and Senchak's model; thus Z is identically zero. Their model can be generalised to include stocks.

CHAPTER 9 OTHER ECONOMIC AGENTS

1. Note that X measures the number of units of the exporter's currency per unit of the importer's currency; thus an increase in X is a devaluation as far as the importer is concerned.

2. Since the 'X' in the second situation is the reciprocal of the 'X' in the first situation, the result that $E(1/X) > 1/EX$ is useful in deriving this conclusion.

3. Readers unfamiliar with the properties of Poisson processes might consult, for example, Feller (1968).

4. Borch gives the following example: let $x = (\sigma_1\mu_2 - \sigma_2\mu_1)/(\sigma_1 - \sigma_2)$, $p = (\mu_1 - \mu_2)^2/[(\mu_1 - \mu_2)^2 + (\sigma_1 - \sigma_2)^2]$, $y_1 = \mu_1 + \sigma_1(\sigma_1 - \sigma_2)/(\mu_1 - \mu_2)$ and $y_2 = \mu_2 + \sigma_2(\sigma_1 - \sigma_2)/(\mu_1 - \mu_2)$. Then (x, p, y_i) has mean μ_i and standard deviation σ_i ($i = 1, 2$). By the assumption of *préférence absolue* (μ_1, σ_1) and (μ_2, σ_2) can lie on the same indifference curve only if $y_1 = y_2$. But, as elementary algebra shows, this implies $(\mu_1 - \mu_2)^2 + (\sigma_1 - \sigma_2)^2 = 0$, or that $\mu_1 = \mu_2$ and $\sigma_1 = \sigma_2$.

5. Interestingly, the paper makes heavy and early use of the idea of reservation values (cf. Chapter 5) as the representation of the outcome of a behavioural or satisficing mode of behaviour; ironically, the appendix shows how such reservation values are determined *using an optimising framework.*

6. Beginners to Shackle could well start with his recent book, Shackle (1979), and continue from there. Reference could also be made to Loasby (1976) and Wiseman (1980) who share many ideas with Shackle.

7. If $P(A) = p$, then the indifference condition implies $pu^* + (1-p)\,0 = 1$.

CHAPTER 10   MARKETS

1. The world of theory contains a further 'possibility': the famous Walrasian Auctioneer. A description of how this fictitious being is supposed to behave is given in Hey (1979a, pp. 175–7).

2. A variable is said to have a degenerate distribution if it is a constant; conversely, a non-degenerate distribution has at least two values with non-zero probability (density).

3. For example, the Phillips curve.

4. Unless a 'behavioural' model is being constructed. On this, see later.

5. Though it is debatable whether this is an optimal strategy on the part of sellers. Unless considerations of goodwill are being invoked (which is rather strange in a time-independent model), it is not clear why supply should exceed the output at which price and marginal cost are equal. Of course, if marginal cost is constant, there is no problem.

6. Or, in other words, no equilibrium exists. See the discussion on the paper by Salop and Stiglitz (1977) above.

7. Compare Section 9.4 above.

CHAPTER 11   GENERAL EQUILIBRIUM AND DISEQUILIBRIUM

1. Or disutility if the 'good' is a bad. For expositional reasons we will assume throughout this chapter that every good is indeed a good.

2. We should perhaps point out that, in view of the budget constraint $\mathbf{X} . \mathbf{Y}^* = 0$, at least one element of the vector $\mathbf{Y}^*$ is necessarily negative and at least one element is positive (unless all are zero); moreover, if an element is negative the individual wishes to be a seller of that good, while if an element is positive the individual wishes to be a buyer of that good.

3. See Hey (1979a, Chapter 27) for a more extended discussion.

4. Compare this with the relative neglect of theorising about why particular trading processes exist (compared with theorising about the pattern of trade *given* a particular trading process), as discussed in Section 10.2.

5. There is one possible confusion that we ought to clear up at the outset. The 'quantity rationing' in the title of this section refers to the markets which exist at a particular time. Rather trivially, if a market for a certain good does not exist, then, as no trade in that good can take place, quantities are indeed constrained in that market. Strictly speaking, then, this section relates to situations in which either quantities are unrestricted or quantities are restricted to be zero; however, all individuals are presumed to know which situation prevails. Thus *no quantity uncertainty exists* (in currently existing markets).

6. An alternative interpretation is to consider J as being sufficiently large to include all goods available at some time period, and let $\bar{Y}_j^{it} = 0$ for all i indicate that good j is not available in period t.

7. Two features should be noted: first, that money does not directly enter into this function; second, that there is no bequest motive.

8. Except for a problem which arises only in our highly simplified model: strictly speaking, since all agents die in period T, there are no demanders of money in period T; thus the price of money in T must be zero. (Indeed this argument suggests that the price of money will be zero in every period.) This oddity disappears if we move to an infinite horizon world, however, or one in which generations overlap.

9. Of course, if one or more of the $\mathbf{X}^T$, $\bar{\mathbf{Y}}^T$ and $\bar{Z}_T$ are known with certainty, then the distribution is degenerate in that (or those) dimensions.

10. To tie up with our standard practice, these optimal values should have an asterisk superscript. So as to achieve uniformity with Chapter 4 we omit the superscript.

11. There is a potential problem with forward trading. Since no money changes hands until the future period, there is, in principle, scope for individuals to enter into agreements which they subsequently find they cannot honour. In the real world, this could lead to bankruptcy (which is why, in many forward markets there is either a limit to the amount of the commit-ment, or a restriction on who can trade in that market). In the world of theory, the possibility of bankruptcy has, until very recently, largely been ignored.

12. If $\mathbf{Y} = \mathbf{Y}(\mathbf{Y}^*)$, where $\mathbf{Y}(\,.\,)$ was known by the individual, then the utility-maximising $\mathbf{Y}^*$ would maximise $U(\mathbf{Y}(\mathbf{Y}^*) + \bar{\mathbf{Y}})$ subject to $\mathbf{X} \cdot \mathbf{Y} = 0$.

13. We should stress that such behaviour is not necessarily direction-less or totally erratic. A useful analogy is to a random variable (with a given distribution).

14. Readers unfamiliar with the theory of Markov processes could consult Feller (1968) or Cox and Miller (1965).

CHAPTER 12 MACROECONOMICS

1. One possible reason is that the price-vector prevailing is not the market-clearing vector.

2. We will amplify this point below.

3. Of course, decreasing returns to the factor labour might make this operation unprofitable.

4. Of course, it may be that economists are following a wild-goose chase by attempting to formulate a micro theory first and then building macro theory on the microfoundations; after all, no physicist would attempt to predict the behaviour of an individual atom of a gas, though he could predict with great

accuracy the behaviour of the gas as a whole. The analogy is thought-provoking, but not, we feel, complete.

5. A certain amount of schizophrenia is in evidence, however: for questions relating to disequilibrium phenomena in simple economies, models of the type discussed here are used; for questions concerning wider issues (particularly those relating to open economies) more traditional *IS–LM*-based models are still being employed. In view of the complexity of even the simplest of the 'new' models, this division is hardly surprising.

6. This implies that the household does not consider it advantageous to indulge in commodity speculation; this, in turn, implies some restrictions on the various expectations about future prices.

7. The model as formulated does not include taxes. Their incorporation would not affect the structure of the model, though it would increase the notational complexity.

8. Which implies that the firm always has sufficient of the good (production plus inventories) to satisfy government demand.

9. This issue is also explored in Muellbauer and Portes (1978), wherein a more detailed discussion of the derivation of (12.3) can also be found (pp. 796–8).

10. Readers should satisfy themselves that the contour map must have the general properties illustrated before proceeding. (Consider a fixed L and examine what happens to total expected lifetime utility as C increases from zero: initially utility rises but after a point the decreased utility of future consumption (working through M) more than offsets the increased utility of present consumption. A similar argument applies for increases in L with a fixed C.)

11. Muellbauer and Portes (1978) give a full description of the derivation of (12.10) on p. 802 and in an Appendix. Further motivation for (12.10) can be found in our Chapter 8, particularly Section 8.2.

12. This may be a suitable stage to point out that, under the 'rules of the game', neither the intersection of $\bar{C}^s$ and $\bar{C}^d$ nor the intersection of $\bar{L}^s$ and $\bar{L}^d$ can constitute equilibria – since these would imply that both sides of the same market were being simultaneously constrained.

13. A continuous-time version is also possible, though the economic rationale for such a construct is not altogether clear.

14. A cynical aside may be appropriate at this stage: while economic theorists imbue the economic agents in their models with almost super-human skills of comprehension and calculation, they themselves often need things reduced to a two-dimensional diagram before they find them understandable!

CHAPTER 13   THE PAST AND THE PRESENT

1. Of course, we can always fall back on the old favourite – the 'as if' argument. But there are problems with this, as we have already noted.

2. Section 6.5 provides an illustration of such a 'rule of thumb'.

3. Possibly that reflects a prevalence for firms to take large sets of decisions at widely separated points of time and for households to take small numbers of decisions close together?

REFERENCES

Ahsan, S. M. and Ullah, A. (1978) 'Recent developments in the theory of the firm under uncertainty: A brief survey' (mimeo).

Akerlof, G. A. (1970) 'The market for "Lemons": Quality uncertainty and the market mechanism', *Quarterly Journal of Economics* **84** (3), August, 488-500.

Albright, S. C. (1977) 'A Bayesian approach to a generalised house selling problem', *Management Science* **24** (4), December, 432-40.

Allais, M. and Hagen, O. (1979) *Expected Utility Hypotheses and the Allais Paradox. Contemporary Discussions of Decisions under Uncertainty with Allais' Rejoinder*, Reidel, Dordrecht.

Allingham, M. G. and Sandmo, A. (1972) 'Income tax evasion: A theoretical analysis', *Journal of Public Economics* **1**, 323-38.

Amihud, Y. (1976) *Bidding and Auctioning for Procurement and Allocation*, New York University Press.

Apostol, T. M. (1951) *Mathematical Analysis*, Addison-Wesley, Reading, Mass.

Arrow, K. J. (1971) *Essays in the Theory of Risk Bearing*, Markham, Chicago.

Arrow, K. J. and Hahn, F. H. (1971) *General Competitive Analysis*, Oliver and Boyd, Edinburgh.

Arzac, E. R. (1976) 'Profits and safety in the theory of the firm under price uncertainty', *International Economic Review* **17** (1), February, 163-71.

Azariadis, C. (1975) 'Implicit contracts and underemployment equilibria', *Journal of Political Economy* **83** (6), December, 1183-202.

Baily, M. N. (1974) 'Wages and employment under uncertain demand', *Review of Economic Studies* **41**, 37-50.

Baily, M. N. (1977) 'On the theory of layoffs and unemployment', *Econometrica* **45** (5), July, 1043-63.

Baldwin, C. Y. and Meyer, R. F. (1979) 'Liquidity preference under uncertainty', *Journal of Financial Economics* **7** (4), December, 347-74.

Baron, D. P. (1976) 'Fluctuating exchange rates and the pricing of exports', *Economic Inquiry* **14** (3), September, 425-38.

Barro, R. J. and Grossman, H. I. (1971) 'A general disequilibrium model of income and employment', *American Economic Review* **61** (1), March, 82-93.

Barro, R. J. and Grossman, H. I. (1976) *Money, Employment and Inflation*, Cambridge University Press.

Bayes, T. (1763) 'Essay towards solving a problem in the doctrine of chances', *Philosophical Transactions of the Royal Society* **53**, 307-418.

Benassy, J.-P. (1975) 'Neokeynesian disequilibrium theory in a monetary economy', *Review of Economic Studies* **42** (4), October, 503–24.

Bigman, D. and Leite, S. P. (1978) 'Welfare and trade effects of exchange rate uncertainty', *Southern Economic Journal* **45** (2), October, 534–42.

Böhm, V. (1976) 'Disequilibrium dynamics in a simple macroeconomic model', CORE discussion paper 7628.

Borch, K. (1969) 'A note on uncertainty and indifference curves', *Review of Economic Studies* **36**, 1–4.

Bradfield, J. (1979) 'A formal dynamic model of market making', *Journal of Financial and Quantitative Analysis* **14** (2), June, 275–91,

Bradfield, J. and Zabel, E. (1978) 'Price-making in a competitive market', *Economics Letters* **1**, 19–22.

Braverman, A. (1980) 'Consumer search and alternative market equilibria', *Review of Economic Studies* **47** (3), April, 487–502.

Burdett, K. (1978) 'A theory of employee job search and quit rates', *American Economic Review* **68** (1), March, 212–20.

Burdett, K. and Mortensen, D. T. (1978) 'Labor supply under uncertainty', *Research in Labor Economics* **2**, 109–57.

Bush, R. R. and Mosteller, F. (1955) *Stochastic Models for Learning*, Wiley, New York.

Butters, G. R. (1977) 'Equilibrium distributions of sales and advertising prices', *Review of Economic Studies* **44** (3), October, 465–92.

Carlton, D. W. (1978) 'Market behaviour with demand uncertainty and price inflexibility', *American Economic Review* **68** (4), September, 571–87.

Cigno, A. (1979) 'Search and consumer surplus: A generalisation', *Bulletin of Economic Research* **31** (2), November, 98–9.

Clower, R. W. (1965) 'The Keynesian counter-revolution: A theoretical appraisal', in F. H. Hahn and F. Brechling (eds) *Theory of Interest Rates* IEA Series, Macmillan, London, 103–25.

Cook, P. J. and Graham, D. A. (1977) 'The demand for insurance and protection: The case of irreplaceable commodities', *Quarterly Journal of Economics* **61** (1), February, 143–56.

Cox, D. R. and Miller, H. D. (1965) *The Theory of Stochastic Processes*, Methuen, London.

Cross, J. G. (1973) 'A stochastic learning model of economic behaviour', *Quarterly Journal of Economics* **87** (2), May, 239–66.

Cyert, R. M. and Degroot, M. H. (1971) 'Interfirm learning and the kinked demand curve', *Journal of Economic Theory* **3** (3), September, 272–87.

Cyert, R. M., Degroot, M. H. and Holt, C. A. (1978) 'Sequential investment decisions with Bayesian learning', *Management Science* **24** (7), March, 712–18.

Day, R. H., Aigner, D. J. and Smith, K. R. (1971) 'Safety margins and profit maximization in the theory of the firm', *Journal of Political Economy* **79**, 1293–301.

Degroot, M. H. (1970) *Optimal Statistical Decisions*, McGraw-Hill, New York.

Diamond, P. A. and Stiglitz, J. E. (1974) 'Increases in risk and in risk aversion', *Journal of Economic Theory* **8** (3), July, 337–60.

Dixit, A, (1976) 'Public finance in a temporary Keynesian equilibrium', *Journal of Economic Theory* **12**, 242-58.

Dixit, A. (1978) 'The balance of trade in a model of temporary equilibrium with rationing', *Review of Economic Studies* **45** (3), 393-404.

Drazen, A. (1980) 'Recent developments in macroeconomic disequilibrium theory', *Econometrica* **48** (2), March, 283-306.

Drèze, J. (1975) 'Existence of an equilibrium under price rigidity and quantity rationing', *International Economic Review* **16**, 301-20.

Ehrlich, I. and Becker, G. S. (1972) 'Market insurance, self-insurance and self-protection', *Journal of Political Economy* **80**, 623-48.

Engelbrecht-Wiggans, R. (1980) 'Auctions and bidding models: A survey', *Management Science* **26** (2), February, 119-42.

Epstein, L. G. (1978) 'Production flexibility and the behaviour of the competitive firm under price uncertainty', *Review of Economic Studies* **45** (2), June, 251-61.

Epstein, L. G. and Tanny, S. M. (1980) 'Increasing generalized correlation: A definition and some economic consequences', *Canadian Journal of Economics* **13** (1), February, 16-34.

Feder, G., Just, R. E. and Schmitz, A. (1980) 'Futures markets and the theory of the firm under price uncertainty', *Quarterly Journal of Economics* **94** (2), March, 317-28.

Feldstein, M. S. (1976) 'Temporary layoffs in the theory of unemployment', *Journal of Political Economy* **84**, 937-57.

Feller, W. (1968) *An Introduction to Probability Theory and its Applications* 3rd edn, Vol. 1, Wiley, New York.

Fisher, F. M. (1976) 'The stability of general equilibrium: results and problems' in M. J. Artis and A. R. Nobay (eds) *Essays in Economic Analysis*, Cambridge University Press.

Fisher, F. M. (1981) 'Stability, disequilibrium awareness, and the perception of new opportunities', *Econometrica* **49**, March, 279-318.

Gale, D. M. (1978) 'Economies with trading uncertainty', University of Cambridge, Economic Theory Discussion Paper No. 5.

Gittins, J. C. (1979) 'Bandit processes and dynamic allocation indices', *Journal of the Royal Statistical Society* Series B **41** (2), 148-77.

Goodhart, C. A. E. (1975) *Money, Information and Uncertainty*, Macmillan, London.

Gordon, D. F. (1974) 'A neoclassical theory of Keynesian unemployment', *Economic Inquiry* **12** (4), December, 431-59.

Grandmont, J.-M. (1977a) 'Temporary general equilibrium theory', *Econometrica* **45** (3), April, 535-72.

Grandmont, J.-M. (1977b) 'The logic of the fix-price method', *Scandinavian Journal of Economics* **79** (2), 169-86.

Green, J. R. (1980) 'On the theory of effective demand', *Economic Journal* **90** (358), June, 341-53.

Green, J. R. and Majumdar, M. (1975) 'The nature of stochastic equilibrium', *Econometrica* **43**, 647-61.

Grossman, H. I. (1977) 'Risk shifting and reliability in labor markets', *Scandinavian Journal of Economics* **79** (2), 187–209.

Hahn, F. H. (1977) 'Exercises in conjectural equilibria', *Scandinavian Journal of Economics* **79** (2), 210–26.

Hahn, F. H. (1978) 'On non-Walrasian equilibria', *Review of Economic Studies* **45**, 1–7.

Hanoch, G. (1977) 'Risk aversion and consumer preferences', *Econometrica* **45** (2), March, 413–26.

Hey, J. D. (1979a) *Uncertainty in Microeconomics*, Martin Robertson, Oxford.

Hey, J. D. (1979b) 'A simple generalised stopping rule', *Economics Letters* **2** (2), July, 115–20.

Hey, J. D. (1979c) 'A note on consumer search and consumer surplus', *Bulletin of Economic Research* **31** (1), May, 61–6.

Hey, J. D. (1980) 'Measuring risk and measuring risk aversion' in D. A. Currie and W. Peters (eds) *Contemporary Economic Analysis*, Vol. 2, Croom-Helm, London.

Hey, J. D. (1981a) 'Goodwill – investment in the intangible' in D. A. Currie *et al* (eds) *Microeconomic Analysis,* Croom-Helm, London.

Hey, J. D. (1981b) 'A unified theory of the behaviour of the profit-maximising, labour-managed and joint-stock firms operating under uncertainty', *Economic Journal* **91** (362), June, forthcoming.

Hey, J. D. and Mavromaras, K. G. (1981/2) 'The effect of unemployment insurance on the riskiness of occupational choice', *Journal of Public Economics,* forthcoming.

Hey, J. D. and McKenna, C. J. (1979) 'To move or not to move?' *Economica* **46** (182), May, 175–85.

Hey, J. D. and McKenna, C. J. (1981) 'Consumer search with uncertain product quality', *Journal of Political Economy* **89** (1), February, 54–66.

Hirshleifer, J. and Riley, J. G. (1979) 'The analysis of uncertainty and information: An expository survey', *Journal of Economic Literature* **17** (4), December, 1375–421.

Holthausen, D. M. (1979) 'Hedging and the competitive firm under price uncertainty', *American Economic Review* **69** (5), December, 989–95.

Honkapohja, S. and Ito, T. (1979) 'A stochastic approach to disequilibrium macroeconomics', NBER Technical Working Paper No. 1, September.

Huang, C. C., Kira, D. and Vertinsky, I. (1978) 'Stochastic dominance for multi-attribute utility functions', *Review of Economic Studies* **45** (3), October, 611–15.

Huang, C. C., Vertinsky, I. and Ziemba, W. T. (1978) 'On multiperiod stochastic dominance', *Journal of Financial and Quantitative Analysis* **13** (1), March, 1–13.

Ishii, Y. (1977) 'On the theory of the competitive firm under price uncertainty: Note', *American Economic Review* **67** (4), September, 768–9.

Kahneman, D. and Tversky, A. (1979) 'Prospect theory: An analysis of decision under risk', *Econometrica* **47** (2), March, 263–91.

Karni, E. (1979) 'On multivariate risk aversion', *Econometrica* **47** (6), November, 1391–401.

Karni, E. and Schwartz, A. (1977) 'Search theory: The case of search with uncertain recall', *Journal of Economic Theory* **16** (1), October, 38-52.

Keynes, J. M. (1936) *The General Theory of Employment, Interest and Money*, Macmillan, London.

Kihlstrom, R. E. (1974) 'A Bayesian model of demand for information about product quality', *International Economic Review* **15** (1), February, 99-118.

Kihlstrom, R. E and Mirman, L. J. (1974) 'Risk aversion with many commodities', *Journal of Economic Theory* **8** (3), July, 361-88.

Kohn, M. G. and Shavell, S. (1974) 'The Theory of Search', *Journal of Economic Theory* **9** (2), October, 93-123.

Kolm, S.-C. (1973) 'A note on optimum tax evasion', *Journal of Public Economics* **2**, 265-70.

Kraus, M. (1979) 'A comparative statics theorem for choice under risk', *Journal of Economic Theory* **21** (3), December, 510-17.

Kreps, D. M. and Porteus, E. L. (1978) 'Temporal resolution of uncertainty and dynamic choice theory', *Econometrica* **46** (1), January, 185-200.

Kreps, D. M. and Porteus, E. L. (1979a) 'Dynamic choice theory and dynamic programming', *Econometrica* **47** (1), January, 91-100.

Kreps, D. M and Porteus, E. L. (1979b) 'Temporal von Neumann-Morgenstern and induced preferences', *Journal of Economic Theory* **20** (1), February, 81-109.

Krouse, C. G. and Senchack, A. J. (1977) 'Probing for information as a behaviour of the firm under demand uncertainty', *Journal of Economics and Business* **29** (3), 163-70.

Lambert, P. J. and Hey, J. D. (1979) 'Attitudes to risk', *Economics Letters* **2** (3), August, 215-18.

Landsberger, M. and Peled, D. (1977) 'Duration of offers, price structure and the gain from search', *Journal of Economic Theory* **16** (1), October, 17-37.

Leijonhufvud, A. (1968) *On Keynesian Economics and the Economics of Keynes*, Oxford University Press.

Leland, H. E. (1979) 'Quacks, lemons and licensing: A theory of minimum quality standards', *Journal of Political Economy* **87** (6), 1328-46.

Levhari, D., Paroush, J. and Peleg, B. (1975) 'Efficiency analysis for multivariate distributions', *Review of Economic Studies* **42**, 87-91.

Levhari, D. and Srinivasan, T. N. (1969) 'Optimal savings under uncertainty', *Review of Economic Studies* **36**, 153-64.

Levy, H. (1973) 'Stochastic dominance, efficiency criteria and efficient portfolios: The multi-period case', *American Economic Review* **63**, 986-94.

Levy, H. and Paroush, J. (1974a) 'Toward multivariate efficiency criteria', *Journal of Economic Theory* **7**, 129-42.

Levy, H. and Paroush, J. (1974b) 'Multi-period stochastic dominance', *Management Science* **21**, 428-35.

Levy, H. and Sarnat, M. (1972) 'Safety-first: An expected utility principle', *Journal of Financial and Quantitative Analysis* **7**, June, 1829-34.

Levy, H. and Sarnat, M. (1977) *Financial Decision Making under Uncertainty*, Academic Press, New York.

Lim, C. (1980) 'The ranking of behavioural modes of the firm facing uncertain demand', *American Economic Review* **70** (1), March, 217-24.

Linnerooth, J. (1979) 'The value of human life: A review of the models', *Economic Inquiry* **17** (1), January, 52-74.

Lippman, S. A. and McCall, J. J. (1976a) 'The economics of job search: A survey. Part I: Optimal job search policies', *Economic Inquiry* **14** (2), June, 155-89.

Lippman, S. A. and McCall, J. J. (1976b) 'The economics of job search: A survey. Part II: Empirical and policy implications of job search', *Economic Inquiry* **14** (3), September, 347-68.

Lippman, S. A. and McCall, J. J. (1978) 'The economics of uncertainty: Selected topics and probabilistic methods', UCLA Western Management Science Institute Working Paper No. 281.

Lippman, S. A. and McCall, J. J. (1980) 'The economics of belated information', *International Economic Review* **21** (2), June.

Loasby, B. J. (1976) *Choice, Complexity and Ignorance*, Cambridge University Press.

Luce, R. D. and Raiffa, H. (1957) *Games and Decisions*, Wiley, New York.

Malinvaud, E. (1977) *The Theory of Unemployment Reconsidered*, Basil Blackwell, Oxford.

Mavromaras, K. G. (1979) 'Insurance and protection of irreplaceable commodities: The case of one's own life', *Economics Letters* **3**, 9-13.

McKenna, C. J. (1979) 'A theory of contractual decisions under uncertainty', University of York, ISER/Department of Economics Discussion Paper No. 27.

McKenna, C. J. (1980) 'Wage offers, layoffs and the firm in an uncertain labour market', *Manchester School* **48** (3), September, 255-64.

Meyer, J. (1975) 'Increasing risk', *Journal of Economic Theory* **11**, 119-32.

Meyer, J. (1977) 'Second degree stochastic dominance with respect to a function', *International Economic Review* **18** (2), June, 477-87.

Mood, A. M., Graybill, F. A. and Boes, D. C. (1974) *Introduction to the Theory of Statistics*, 3rd edn, McGraw-Hill, New York.

Muellbauer, J. and Portes, R. (1978) 'Macroeconomic models with quantity rationing', *Economic Journal* **88** (352), December, 788-821.

Nayak, P. B. (1978) 'Optimal income tax evasion and regressive taxes', *Public Finance/Finances Publiques* **33** (3), 358-66.

Nelson, R. R. and Winter, S. G. (1975) 'Factor price changes and factor substitution in an evolutionary model', *Bell Journal of Economics and Management Science* **6** (1), Autumn, 466-86.

Newbery, D. M. G. (1978) 'The theory of the firm under uncertainty', Section 3 of *An Overview of the Economic Theory of Uncertainty and its Implications for Energy Supply*, Electric Power Research Institute.

Parkin, J. M. and Wu, S. Y. (1972) 'Choice involving unwanted risky events and optimal insurance', *American Economic Review* **62** (5), December, 982-7.

Patinkin, D. (1956) *Money, Interest and Prices*, Harper & Row, New York.

Pissarides, C. A. (1981) 'Contract theory, temporary layoffs and unemployment: A critical assessment', in D. A. Currie *et al* (eds) *Microeconomic Analysis,* Croom-Helm, London.

Pratt, J. W. (1964) 'Risk aversion in the small and in the large', *Econometrica* **32** (1-2), January-April, 122-36.

Pratt, J. W., Wise, D. A. and Zeckhauser, R. (1979) 'Price differences in almost competitive markets', *Quarterly Journal of Economics* **93** (2), May, 189-211.

Pye, R. (1978) 'A formal decision-theoretical approach to flexibility and robustness', *Journal of the Operational Research Society* **29** (3), March, 215-27.

Pyle, D. H. and Turnovsky, S. J. (1970) 'Safety-first and expected utility maximization in mean-standard deviation portfolio analysis', *Review of Economics and Statistics* **52** (1), February, 75-81.

Radner, R. (1975) 'A behavioural model of cost reduction', *Bell Journal of Economics and Management Science* **6** (1), Spring, 196-215.

Radner, R. and Rothschild, M. (1975) 'On the allocation of effort', *Journal of Economic Theory* **10** (3), June, 358-76.

Riley, J. G. (1979a) 'Informational equilibrium', *Econometrica* **47** (2), March, 331-59.

Riley, J. G. (1979b) 'Noncooperative equilibrium and market signalling', *American Economic Review* **69** (2), May, 303-7.

Rosenhead, J., Elton, M. and Gupta, S. K. (1972) 'Robustness and optimality as criteria for strategic decisions', *Operational Research Quarterly* **23** (4), December, 413-31.

Rothschild, M. (1974) 'Searching for the lowest price when the distribution of prices is unknown', *Journal of Political Economy* **82**, 689-711.

Rothschild, M. and Stiglitz, J. E. (1970) 'Increasing risk: 1. A definition', *Journal of Economic Theory* **2**, 225-43.

Rothschild, M. and Stiglitz, J. E. (1971) 'Increasing risk: 2. Its economic consequences', *Journal of Economic Theory* **3**, 66-84.

Rothschild, M. and Stiglitz, J. E. (1976) 'Equilibrium in competitive insurance markets: An essay on the economics of imperfect information', *Quarterly Journal of Economics* **90** (4), November, 629-49.

Roy, A. D. (1952) 'Safety first and the holding of assets', *Econometrica* **20** (3), July, 431-49.

Russell, W. R. and Seo, T. K. (1978) 'Ordering uncertain prospects: The multivariate utility functions case', *Review of Economic Studies* **45** (3), October, 605-10.

Salop, S. C. (1973) 'Systematic job search and unemployment', *Review of Economic Studies* **40** (2), April, 191-201.

Salop, S. C. (1977) 'The noisy monopolist: Imperfect information, price dispersion and price discrimination', *Review of Economic Studies* **44** (3), October, 393-406.

Salop, S. C. and Stiglitz, J. E. (1977) 'Bargains and ripoffs: A model of monopolistically competitive price dispersion', *Review of Economic Studies* **44** (3), October, 493-510.

Sandmo, A. (1970) 'The effect of uncertainty on saving decisions', *Review of Economic Studies* 37, 353-60.

Sandmo, A. (1971) 'On the theory of the competitive firm under price uncertainty', *American Economic Review* 61 (1), March, 65-73.

Satterthwaite, M. A. (1979) 'Consumer information. Equilibrium industry price and the number of sellers', *Bell Journal of Economics and Management Science* 10 (2), Autumn, 483-502.

Selden, L. (1978) 'A new representation of preferences over "certain X uncertain" consumption pairs: The "Ordinal Certainty Equivalent" Hypothesis', *Econometrica* 46 (5), September, 1045-60.

Selden, L. (1979) 'An OCE analysis of the effect of uncertainty on saving under risk preference independence', *Review of Economic Studies* 46 (1), January, 73-82.

Shackle, G. L. S. (1979) *Imagination and the Nature of Choice*, Edinburgh University Press.

Shaked, A. and Sutton, J. (1979) 'The self-regulating profession', (mimeo), London School of Economics.

Shaked, A. and Sutton, J. (1980) 'Imperfect information, perceived quality and the formation of professional groups', (mimeo), London School of Economics.

Shavell, S. (1979) 'On moral hazard and insurance', *Quarterly Journal of Economics* 92 (5), November, 541-62.

Simon, H. A, (1955) 'A behavioral model of rational choice', *Quarterly Journal of Economics* 64 (1), February, 99-118.

Simon, H. A. (1978) 'Rationality as process and as product of thought', *American Economic Review* 68 (2), May, 1-16.

Singh, B. (1973) 'Making honesty the best policy', *Journal of Public Economics* 2, 257-63.

Smallwood, D. E. and Conlisk, J. (1979) 'Product quality in markets where consumers are imperfectly informed', *Quarterly Journal of Economics* 93 (1), February, 1-23.

Spence, M. (1974) *Market Signalling*, Harvard University Press.

Srinivasan, T. N. (1973) 'Tax evasion: A model', *Journal of Public Economics* 2, 339-46.

Stigler, G. J. (1961) 'The economics of information', *Journal of Political Economy* 69, June, 213-25.

Stigler, G. J. (1962) 'Information in the labor market', *Journal of Political Economy* 70 (5), October, 94-105.

Stiglitz, J. E. (1977) 'Monopoly, non-linear pricing and imperfect information: The insurance market', *Review of Economic Studies* 44 (3), October, 407-30.

Sutton, J. (1980a) 'Pricing in the trade cycle: A quasi-competitive model' in D. A. Currie and W. Peters (eds) *Contemporary Economic Analysis*, Vol. 2, Croom-Helm, London.

Sutton, J. (1980b) 'A model of stochastic equilibrium in a quasi-competitive industry', *Review of Economic Studies* 47 (4), July, 705-22.

Svensson, L. E. O. (1980) 'Effective demand and stochastic rationing', *Review of Economic Studies* **47** (2), January, 339–55.

Turnovsky, S. J. (1969) 'A Bayesian approach to the theory of expectations', *Journal of Economic Theory* **1**, 220–7.

Varian, H. R. (1977a) 'The stability of a disequilibrium *IS–LM* model', *Scandinavian Journal of Economics* **79** (2), 260–70.

Varian, H. R. (1977b) 'Non-Walrasian equilibria', *Econometrica* **45**, 573–90.

Venezia, I. and Levy, H. (1980) 'Optimal claims in automobile insurance', *Review of Economic Studies* **47** (3), April, 539–49.

Weintraub, E. R. (1977) 'The microfoundations of macroeconomics: A critical survey', *Journal of Economic Literature* **15** (1), March, 1–23.

Weintraub, E. R. (1979) *Microfoundations: The Compatibility of Microeconomics and Macroeconomics*, Cambridge University Press.

Weiss, L. (1976) 'The desirability of cheating incentives and randomness in the optimal income tax', *Journal of Political Economy* **84**, December, 1343–52.

Weitzman, M. L. (1979) 'Optimal search for the best alternative', *Econometrica* **47** (3), May, 641–54.

Wilde, L. L. (1979) 'An information-theoretic approach to job quits', in S. A. Lippman and J. J. McCall (eds) *Studies in the Economics of Search*, North-Holland, Amsterdam.

Wilde, L. L. (1980) 'On the formal theory of inspection and evaluation in product markets', *Econometrica* **48** (5), July, 1265–80.

Wilde, L. L. and Schwartz, A. (1979) 'Equilibrium comparative shopping', *Review of Economic Studies* **46** (3), July, 543–53.

Wilson, C. A. (1979) 'Equilibrium and adverse selection', *American Economic Review* **69** (2), May, 313–17.

Wilson, R. (1977) 'A bidding model of perfect competition', *Review of Economic Studies* **44** (3), October, 511–18.

Wilson, R. (1979) 'Auctions of shares', *Quarterly Journal of Economics* **92** (5), November, 675–89.

Wiseman, J. (1980) 'Costs and decisions', in D. A. Currie and W. Peters (eds) *Contemporary Economic Analysis*, Vol. 2, Croom-Helm, London.

Yaari, M. E. (1969) 'Some remarks on measures of risk aversion and on their uses', *Journal of Economic Theory* **1**, 315–29.

Zabel, E. (1967) 'A dynamic model of the competitive firm', *International Economic Review* **8** (2), 194–208.

Zabel, E. (1969) 'The competitive firm and price expectations', *International Economic Review* **10** (3), October, 467–78.

Zabel, E. (1971) 'Risk and the competitive firm', *Journal of Economic Theory* **3** (2), June, 109–33.

Zabel, E. (1979) 'Competitive price adjustment without market clearing', University of Rochester, Department of Economics Discussion Paper 79-5.

AUTHOR INDEX

SUBJECT INDEX

(**Bold** page numbers give the most important reference to the item.)